Birding Georgia

Giff Beaton

10/8/02

To David —
It was great to meet you at Kennesaw
and hope this book helps you find some
birds in Georgia!

Giff Beaton

FALCON®

HELENA, MONTANA

A FALCON GUIDE ®

Falcon® Publishing is continually expanding its list of recreational guidebooks. All books include detailed descriptions, accurate maps, and all the information necessary for enjoyable trips. You can order extra copies of this book and get information and prices for other Falcon® guidebooks by writing Falcon, P.O. Box 1718, Helena, MT 59624 or calling toll-free 1-800-582-2665. Also, please ask for a free copy of our current catalog. Visit our website at www.Falcon.com or contact us by e-mail at falcon@falcon.com.

All black-and-white photos by the author unless noted otherwise.
Project Editor: David Lee
Production Editor: Jessica Solberg
Maps by Chris Salcedo
Page composition and charts by Darlene Jatkowski
Book Design by Falcon® Publishing, Inc.

Library of Congress Cataloging-in-Publication Data

Beaton, Giff, 1959-
    Birding Georgia / Giff Beaton.
        p. cm.
    ISBN 1-56044-784-2
    1. Bird watching—Georgia—Guidebooks. 2. Georgia—Guidebooks. I. Title

    QL676.56.G4 B43 2000
    598'.07'234758—dc21

                                                                    99-086293

CAUTION

Outdoor recreational activities are by their very nature potentially hazardous. All participants in such activities must assume the responsibility for their own actions and safety. The information contained in this guidebook cannot replace sound judgment and good decision-making skills, which help reduce risk exposure, nor does the scope of this book allow for disclosure of all the potential hazards and risks involved in such activities.

Learn as much as possible about the outdoor recreational activities in which you participate, prepare for the unexpected, and be cautious. The reward will be a safer and more enjoyable experience.

 Text pages printed on recycled paper.

Dedication

This book is dedicated to the memory of Claudia Wilds, who showed us all how good a birding guide could be. Her wit and grace were a pleasure to be around, and her attention to detail was amazing. One of the true titans of bird identification, she had as much time for beginners as she did for her few peers, and she is sorely missed.

Contents

Coastal Plain Region

Coast Region

Foreword

Georgia is the largest state east of Mississippi, with more than 59,000 square miles. It is 315 miles long by 250 miles wide. Here the Appalachians reach their southern terminus in northernmost Georgia. At the other end of the state are thousands of square miles of live oak forests, sandy beaches, and numerous off-shore islands and salt- and freshwater swamps, undoubtedly the most famous of which is the Okefenokee Swamp.

As Thomas Burleigh points out in his epic 1958 work *Georgia Birds,* the state has a rich historical tradition. Although Georgia was the last of the 13 colonies to be settled, it was the first to be explored, beginning with the expedition of Hernando de Soto in 1540. It also has a long ornithological history. Mark Catesby lived and conducted research near Savannah in the early 1700s. Later most of the famous names of early American ornithology lived in or visited Georgia. This list includes the Bartrams, John Abbot, Alexander Wilson, Thomas Nuttall, John James Audubon, the Le Contes, and William Brewster. This tradition continued through the first half of the 20th century with Arthur H. Howell, Herbert Stoddard, and of course Burleigh.

Since Burleigh's book in 1958, other works on Georgia birds have appeared, including an *Annotated State List* (1986) and *A Birder's Guide to Georgia,* the fifth edition of which was published in 1996. And now we have Giff Beaton's *Birding Georgia.* Giff, a native of Maryland, arrived in Georgia a decade ago and immediately commenced to scour the entire state. He has traveled tens of thousands of miles in preparing this guide, thoroughly checking every route himself, and he has meticulously researched the raw data for the bar graphs. Most notably, he and others established the importance of Kennesaw Mountain as an important stop for our neotropical migrants. Their most important discovery was that the threatened Cerulean Warbler is a fairly common fall migrant here. Largely unknown as a fall migrant elsewhere in eastern North America, more Cerulean Warblers are recorded on Kennesaw Mountain between July and September than probably at all of the other eastern migrant traps combined. Beyond this, their regular and thorough surveys on Kennesaw have finally established the exact timing of our eastern migrants in northern Georgia, which serves as a general indicator for the entire Southeast as well.

I've had the good fortune of birding in Georgia with my good friends Giff Beaton and Bruce Hallett several times over the past decade. Often it was on our way back through Atlanta after Sue Tackett and I had been birding elsewhere in the Southeast. One time we went out and saw the Magnificent Hummingbird in Winder, one of two for Georgia and the only ones from the entire Southeast. Another time we looked at a Broad-tailed Hummingbird near Kennesaw north of Atlanta. Still another visit yielded a LeConte's Sparrow in the Kennesaw Marsh, which I experienced firsthand, sinking in the muck to waist level. Most recently, in

May of 1999, Giff and I birded Kennesaw Mountain, the entire southern border of the state, and then up the coast. We birded many of the spots described in the book. While I wandered off and enjoyed Georgia's birds, I left it to Giff to perform his last, careful double-checks of the directions and mileages given. Although it is hard to pick a favorite place among so many outstanding birding locations, visually I was perhaps most impressed with Harris Neck National Wildlife Refuge, a location near the coast with freshwater swamps, coastal prairie, and enormous live oaks. The heron rookeries, the territorial King Rail, and stunning singing male Painted Buntings will not soon be forgotten.

Birding Georgia is the most important ornithological contribution to Georgia since Burleigh. It will be invaluable for both resident and visiting birders, and will enable one to more fully appreciate Georgia's great natural and ornithological diversity.

Jon L. Dunn

Acknowledgments

No statewide book can be written without lots of help, and *Birding Georgia* is no exception. Many people have been involved in this project from the beginning, and provided help on specific sites, bird distribution, or on the book's general content. Some went along on mapping trips, showed me their best spots or at least how to bird them best, or provided editing help. Several people have graciously tested out these site descriptions for accuracy and ease of use, and provided many helpful tips. For all this help, I would like to thank Brad Bergstrom, Mike Chapman, Kevin Danchisen, Mark Davis, Oscar Dewberry, Harriet DiGioia, Marion Dobbs, Mary Elfner, Dot Freeman, Nancy Gobris, Noel Holcomb, Earl Horn, Pierre Howard, Ty Ivey, Andy Kinsey, Carol Lambert, Chris Loudermilk, Sue Marden, Pat Metz, Mark Oberle, Jim Ozier, Tommy Patterson, Dwight Peake, Georgann Schmalz, Paul Sykes, Karen Theodorou, Sheila Willis, Helena Wood, and Bob and Deb Zaremba. Earl Horn and Helena Wood in particular each test-drove numerous sites and offered many very useful comments. Todd Schneider provided many helpful comments and reviews of text sections, and was a tremendous help with DNR (Department of Natural Resources) resources. I would also like to thank Tim Brown and Leo Dete for flying me around in their planes so I could get aerial photographs of some of the sites. Several artists offered their work for inclusion in this book, and I thank Randy B. Crook and Paul Johnson for their contributions.

A few others were more heavily involved in this project. I would like to thank the following for accompanying me to their favorite spots, and then reviewing not only the location descriptions but frequently whole sections of the manuscript. This list includes some of the top birders in the state, real experts on either their regions or the entire state. For service way beyond the call of duty, I would like to thank Jerry and Marie Amerson, Jeff Sewell, Anne Waters, and Brad Winn. I would also like to thank Jon L. Dunn for reviewing the Status and Distribution Charts chapter, for numerous helpful suggestions throughout the writing of this book, and for his company on several trips in Georgia. Jim Flynn was along on many mapping trips, providing advice, helpful commentary, and entertainment; he also reviewed almost every section of the book, and his suggestions greatly improved it. Bruce Hallett has also been involved in almost every step of this process, visiting sites and reviewing the text, and his thoughtful suggestions and experience helped shape the whole manuscript. Finally, Malcolm Hodges was an invaluable help on almost every segment of this book. His unmatched knowledge of the state, its ecology, and statewide bird distribution, was critical, and I can't possibly repay all the time he spent with me on phone consultations or painstakingly poring over rough draft after rough draft.

I would also like to thank my parents, Connie and Giff Beaton, for encouraging me in this hobby from a young age, and for teaching me how to be accurate and careful while still having fun. Finally, I would like to thank my wife Becky for putting up with all the weird hours that birders keep, for going with me on numerous birding trips, and for unfailingly supporting me during the two and a half years I have been working on this project. I hope the book is both useful and enjoyable!

Cerulean Warbler. RANDY B. CROOK ILLUSTRATION

1. Introduction

Georgia is the largest state east of the Mississippi River, and offers just about any kind of birding you could hope for. The mountains in the northern part of the state have many species in both summer and winter that are at the extreme southern edge of their breeding or wintering range in North America, and the rest of the state has a wide range of interesting species in all seasons, including many sought-after southern specialties like Swallow-tailed Kite, Purple Gallinule, and Swainson's Warbler. Georgia has thousands of acres of both freshwater and saltwater marshes and swamps, as well as several large inland lakes. The coast offers great birding in any season, and access to many coastal and offshore species. Migration offers excellent opportunities to see many other species, both inland and along the coast. The official state list has some 420 species, and an active birder can see about 300 species in almost any year.

In this book you will find concise and complete directions to 52 of the best birding areas in the state, including more than 100 specific locations. These are not the only good areas to bird in Georgia, but are a selection of the best sites chosen with a secondary goal of having locations all across the state that are good all year. Additionally, I have tried to select sites that have great potential for rarities. Just about any species found annually in Georgia can be found at one or more of the sites in this book. I discussed potential sites for this guide with many of the best and most widely traveled birders in Georgia, and the final selection reflects the sites most commonly mentioned and the ones I feel are the most enjoyable and fun to bird. I hope you enjoy birding them as much as I enjoyed writing about them!

One unfortunate part of writing a site guide such as *Birding Georgia* is dealing with the inevitable changes of ownership, development, or other habitat losses. Several of the site descriptions have had to undergo major rewrites due to this type of change. All are current up to January 2000. However, as a way of dealing with future changes in site accessibility or location, I have created a website. The URL is http://www.gos.org/birdinggeorgia.html. Plans for this website include up-to-the-minute details on current conditions for any sites in transition. If you are planning a trip to Georgia, you can simply access this website to see if anything has changed at your target destination. Additionally, you will be able to send me comments if you find site changes not yet posted on the website.

HOW TO USE THIS GUIDE

Georgia is a state blessed with many varied and interesting areas to bird and hundreds of beautiful and fascinating bird species to enjoy. Here are several ways to get maximum enjoyment out of your birding time in Georgia.

The state has been divided into four regions: Mountain, Piedmont, Coastal Plain, and Coast. All the sites and information in the bar graphs are grouped by region. The first several chapters provide general information about how to plan

American White Pelican.

trips in Georgia, describe the various regions within the state, and cover some of the main habitat types. The largest section of the book comprises the site descriptions, with step-by-step detailed instructions for birding all 52 sites. Following are several chapters with more detailed information about each individual species and where and when to find them. Chapter 5 has a graph for each species' exact occurrence in the state by date and region. Chapter 6 has a short discussion of most of the species found in the state, and tips for places to look for them or techniques for finding them.

Each site description follows the same format. Read the entire site description first! After the name of the site and the **County** in which it is located, you will find a listing of the **Habitats** found there. (Details about each type can be found in Chapter 3, Habitats.) Next you will find a listing of **Key birds**—the species that are best found at that particular site, or sought-after ones that you might find there. This is a small fraction of the birds to be found at a given site; many more are listed in the actual site description. The **Best times to bird** section is followed by **The birding** section, which includes a brief description of the site. The bulk of the site description is in the **Directions** section. Here you will find specific directions to the site and tips on how to bird there. Many of the "sites" are actually several good locations near each other. Next is the **General information** section, which contains extra instructions and sometimes other nearby locations. The **Additional help** section gives the **DeLorme Map** quad. The abbreviation "CVB" stands for convention and visitor's bureau.

I measured all mileages using the same vehicle. If your distances differ, try to estimate by how much you are off, and alter the book's mileages accordingly.

Finally, for distances from a variable beginning, such as a wide interstate exit where the difference between arriving from different directions may be several tenths of a mile, all mileages begin at the exact middle of the road you are coming from. This means if you don't cross over the road your mileage will be a little less to the first landmark, and if you do cross over (or under) you need to reset your trip meter at the middle of the starting road.

Georgia has recently renumbered all its interstate exits to reflect mileage. Although this is a necessary and useful step, some of the exits may not yet be renumbered when this book is published. For this reason, and for those who remember the old exit numbers better than the new ones, all interstate exit numbers will have the new number in the text followed by the old one in parentheses. The good news is that now you can estimate distance just by subtracting exit numbers, as in most states.

The information above will get you into any site and contains all you need to bird there efficiently and enjoyably.

If you are interested in really nailing down particular species, the following information will help you use all the different parts of this book effectively. By using different sections in concert with each other, you can enhance your chances of seeing particular species or maximizing the number of species you do see.

The two most common approaches to birding trips are either to pick a site you want to visit or one or more species you hope to see. In the first case, once you have selected a site, you should first read the entire site description. Figure out how to get to the general area by using the large-scale map (see map details in the next chapter). Then, check Chapter 5 for information on seasons in which you can expect to find any particular species. Next, go to Chapter 6 for special details on that species, or tips on how to find it. After noting the **Habitats** section of the site description, go to Chapter 3 for descriptions of each habitat type and what species to look for in each.

If you are starting with a species you want to find, go to Chapter 6 first and see which of the sites listed there you would like to try. Now proceed the same as above. By cross-checking the Status and Distribution Charts chapter and capsule comments in the Species to Look For chapter, you can have a fairly good idea of what you can expect to find, and when. Even more detailed information on this subject can be found in the *Annotated Checklist of Georgia Birds,* published by the Georgia Ornithological Society in 1986. A revision is in the works, but the old one has much useful information. This book is available from the Georgia Ornithological Society at the address listed on the GOS page near the end of *Birding Georgia.*

If you simply want to explore the state, you can start by perusing any of the region maps at the beginning of the four region sections, or the statewide map that precedes the site descriptions. Once you have selected a region, you can find out more about it in Chapter 2, "Climate and Topography." The regional map shows you which sites are in the region; most are best during specific seasons, so you can choose some for each season. This information can be easily found by looking at the **Best times to bird** section at the beginning of each site description.

PLANNING A BIRDING TRIP IN GEORGIA

Georgia is a very large state, and has a vast assortment of choices of birding locations and interesting species. You can find wonderful birding at any season in any part of the state, but those seasons and locations may require different preparations. This section discusses some of your options and offers hints.

When to go. In general, spring and fall offer the greatest variety of species, often in large numbers. Spring is the easiest time to see large numbers of species for two reasons: There are many migrants passing through the state, many of which can only be found in Georgia then; and many of the locally breeding species are busy setting up and maintaining territories, in full song and more conspicuous than at any other time of year. Fall migration brings an equal or greater number of individuals, but many are secretive and more difficult to find. Winter brings waterfowl and other wintering species, such as sparrows, and pleasant temperatures over most of the state. Summer is fairly hot except in the higher mountains, but still offers chances for interesting breeding species (many of which are still singing and defending territories).

What to wear. A few general suggestions: Even though Georgia is fairly temperate, it can be very cold in the mountains in winter and very hot in summer. Many birders find that by wearing several layers they can deal with a wide range of temperatures, a frequent occurrence during a day of birding here. Rain is always a possibility at virtually any time of year, so it always pays to have rain gear. Hats are useful all year long, especially in summer when the sun is strongest. Many birding sites include wet areas such as marshes or flooded pastures, so boots can be helpful.

Equipment to Take
Binoculars
Spotting scope
DeLorme and other maps
Field guide(s); the National Geographic is the best overall guide but take whatever you are familiar with
Clothing for the season and region you will be in
Sunscreen
Insect repellent

Optional items include a camera for bird or scenic shots, a tape recorder for an unfamiliar song or call, or a tape of eastern birds. If you plan to be out in the field all day, a cooler with drinks and snacks is useful.

Maps. All the sites reference the DeLorme *Georgia Atlas & Gazetteer*. This map book is available throughout Georgia at bookstores, service stations, office

Lake Horton and the wetlands below the dam.

supply stores, and any other business that offers maps. You can order one direct from DeLorme at (207) 846-7000 or their website at http://www.delorme.com. Although this atlas does not list all road names or even show all roads, it is an excellent reference and will make traveling around Georgia much easier.

Another excellent and strongly recommended reference is *Georgia on My Mind: Official Travel Guide for the State of Georgia*. This free guidebook lists almost all of the lodging available throughout the state by city, even in the smallest towns, and has contact information for tourist destinations, natural or commercial. It also comes with a general state map. You can order a free copy by phone at (800) 847-4842 or from the website at http://www.gomm.com. It is a great resource, especially for those traveling with nonbirders who need to find alternate nearby destinations.

WMAs and state parks. WMA stands for wildlife management area (a very few are waterfowl management areas, and are noted as such in the text). They are generally good birding, even though most are managed for hunting or fishing. The only problem with birding in WMAs is to make sure you avoid days when hunting is allowed. If there is a local number to call about hunting dates, it is given in the site description. Otherwise, check Appendix A. All state parks have a day use fee of $2, which must be paid upon entry. An annual park pass is available at all parks during business hours for $25; it allows access to all parks. Maps for both types of areas are usually available at the site or from websites listed in Appendix A.

Where to stay. Most sites are near areas with numerous lodging choices, and these are listed in the **General information** section of the site description. In some cases there is no lodging nearby, or limited lodging, and that is also included.

Areas with camping nearby are usually mentioned, depending on the conditions at the facilities. *Georgia on My Mind* lists all nearby options, and supplies phone numbers.

Hazards. Georgia is generally safe. A few precautions follow, but common sense will help you avoid virtually any problem.

Private property. Most of the sites in this book are on public land, including roads you can stray off. If the site description specifically mentions not leaving the public road, or if you are not sure, DO NOT LEAVE THE ROAD! Most private landowners are justifiably upset with trespassing, and some are positively hostile about it. On the other hand, if you see desirable habitat, many landowners are pretty amenable to letting you bird it if you ask first. Not all are friendly (or available for asking), but it's worth a try. It always amazes and disappoints me to see how many birders think they can just bird anywhere they want; that only makes it worse for those of us who respect private property.

Insects. Most of the insects you will encounter are more bothersome than dangerous, but there are a few to beware of. Heading this list is ticks, which can carry the Lyme disease parasite and less well-known diseases. Lyme is potentially very dangerous, and the best way to avoid it is to avoid ticks. Normal precautions include wearing light-colored clothing, tucking long pants into your socks, wearing long-sleeved shirts, and checking yourself for ticks after being in brushy or weedy habitats. Most authorities recommend spraying yourself with insect repellent as well, although this can be tough on sensitive equipment like binoculars and cameras (not to mention sensitive skin). If you choose commerical tick repellents, take care to spray only your clothes and not your skin. If you find embedded ticks, remove them quickly and check with your doctor about symptoms to look for. Most ticks are harmless, even when embedded. Other insects to watch out for are stinging types such as bees and wasps—especially yellow jackets. These small wasps build nests in the ground and if you inadvertently step on one, you may incur the wrath of many members of the nest.

Heading the list of harmless but noxious insects are chiggers. These tiny insects burrow into your skin, usually near the top of your socks or shoes, and set up residence. Within a day or two, a large red welt will grow there from your body's reaction to the interloper, and the welts itch tremendously. Most will go away in a few days, but they are very irritating until they do. The best way to avoid them is to stay away from grass in the summer, especially in fields with livestock. If you keep moving, you are usually safe, but if you sit or lie down in grass you will soon regret it! Once you actually get them, there isn't much you can do about it. A covering of nail polish is supposed to suffocate the chigger under your skin, but this seems to take almost as long as waiting for them to expire on their own. The commercial product Chig-a-rid is a similar treatment, but doesn't seem to work any better. Cortisone cream may provide some relief.

Other irritating biting insects include flies and mosquitoes. The last insect to be wary of is the fire ant, common in many fields and pastures. Watch for the elevated mounds and avoid them, and if you are walking along and feel yourself step on ground that gives way, move away quickly, as it was probably an anthill. Quickly brush off any ants that may have gotten on your shoes or clothing. The bites aren't serious, but you may get several at once.

Snakes. The vast majority of the snakes you will encounter (if any) will be non-venomous and harmless. General snake-avoidance behavior includes watching where you walk and not putting your hands anywhere you haven't looked first. Most snakes, even venomous ones, will flee rather than confront you. Watch especially for cottonmouths below the Fall Line near water and eastern diamondback rattlesnakes near the coast, especially on barrier islands in the bunchgrass or coastal scrub above the beach. A good general rule on these islands is to walk where you can see your feet and avoid pushing through areas of thick underbrush, including stands of palmetto. Do not approach any snake, live or dead. In many years of birding in Georgia, actively looking for snakes, I have seen only a handful of either venomous species and know of no birders who have ever been bitten here.

Bears. Hardly a hazard at all; most birders would consider this an exciting encounter! Black bears do have the ability to inflict damage, though mostly to your camping gear, and especially if you don't take the usual bear precautions with your food. I have seen only one bear in Georgia, and that one was running away from us as fast as its legs would carry it.

THE ETHICS AND ETIQUETTE OF BIRDING

American Birding Association Principles and Code of Ethics
Everyone who enjoys birds and birding must always respect wildlife, its environment, and the rights of others. In any conflict of interest between birds and birders, the welfare of the birds and their environment comes first.

Code of Birding Ethics
1   Promote the welfare of birds and their environment.

1(a) Support the protection of important bird habitat.

1(b) To avoid stressing birds or exposing them to danger, exercise restraint and caution during observation, photography, sound recording, or filming. Limit the use of recordings and other methods of attracting birds, and never use such methods in heavily birded areas, or for attracting any species that is Threatened, Endangered, or of Special Concern, or is rare in your local area. Keep well back from nests and nesting colonies, roosts, display areas, and important feeding sites. In such sensitive areas, if there is a need for extended observation, photography, filming, or recording, try to use a blind or hide, and take advantage of natural cover. Use artificial light sparingly for filming or photography, especially for close-ups.

1(c) Before advertising the presence of a rare bird, evaluate the potential for disturbance to the bird, its surroundings, and other people in the area, and proceed only if access can be controlled, disturbance minimized, and permission has been obtained from private landowners. The sites of rare nesting birds should be divulged only to the proper conservation authorities.

1(d) Stay on roads, trails, and paths where they exist; otherwise, keep habitat disturbance to a minimum.

2 Respect the law and rights of others.

2(a) Do not enter private property without the owner's explicit permission.

2(b) Follow all laws, rules, and regulations governing use of roads and public areas, both at home and abroad.

2(c) Practice common courtesy in contacts with other people. Your exemplary behavior will generate goodwill with birders and nonbirders alike.

3 Ensure that feeders, nest structures, and other artificial bird environments are safe.

3(a) Keep dispensers, water, and food clean and free of decay or disease. It is important to feed birds continually during harsh weather.

3(b) Maintain and clean nest structures regularly.

3(c) If you are attracting birds to an area, ensure the birds are not exposed to predation from cats and other domestic animals, or dangers posed by artificial hazards.

4 Group birding, whether organized or impromptu, requires special care.

Each individual in the group, in addition to the obligations spelled out in Items #1 and #2, has responsibilities as a Group Member.

4(a) Respect the interests, rights, and skills of fellow birders, as well as people participating in other legitimate outdoor activities. Freely share your knowledge and experience, except where code 1(c) applies. Be especially helpful to beginning birders.

4(b) If you witness unethical birding behavior, assess the situation, and intervene if you think it prudent. When interceding, inform the person(s) of the inappropriate action, and attempt, within reason, to have it stopped. If the behavior continues, document it, and notify appropriate individuals or organizations.

Group Leader Responsibilities (amateur and professional trips and tours).

4(c) Be an exemplary ethical role model for the group. Teach through word and example.

Viewing the roosting birds at South Beach with Giff Beaton Sr.

4(d) Keep groups to a size that limits impact on the environment and does not interfere with others using the same area.

4(e) Ensure everyone in the group knows of and practices this code.

4(f) Learn and inform the group of any special circumstances applicable to the areas being visited (e.g., no tape recorders allowed).

4(g) Acknowledge that professional tour companies bear a special responsibility to place the welfare of birds and the benefits of public knowledge ahead of the company's commercial interest. Ideally, leaders should keep track of tour sightings, document unusual occurrences, and submit records to appropriate organizations.

Reprinted by permission of American Birding Association

2. *Climate and Topography of Georgia*

Georgia is blessed with highly diverse birdlife, which follows directly from its diverse topography. There are infinite ways to divide the state into smaller regions, such as by elevation, soil type, geology, climate, and overall habitat. I have used a general division—by overall birdlife—to divide the state into four main regions, which are of course subject to all of the factors mentioned above. These regions correspond to the four main sections of the book: Mountain, Piedmont, Coastal Plain, and Coast. These same regions are used in the Status and Distribution Chart chapter as well.

Of the four, the Mountain region is the most artificial because it is composed of three somewhat different physiographic provinces lumped together because of proximity, elevation, and climate. In the extreme northwest corner of the state is the Cumberland Plateau, a high, flat plateau dominated in Georgia by the Lookout Mountain area (elevations range from 800 to 2,000 feet). Just east and south of here is the Ridge and Valley province, which extends from the Tennessee border south to about Cartersville and east to about US Highway 411. As the name implies, this is an area of alternating narrow ridges and wide valleys, and is the least "mountain-like" area in the Mountain region. It is also the lowest, at 700 to 1,600 feet. Because it gets cold in winter and does have some higher elevations, it fits best with the rest of the Mountain provinces. However, it does have some Piedmont birdlife features. The third province in the Mountain region is the Blue Ridge province, which contains

J. W. Smith Reservoir.

all of Georgia's highest mountains and has the most northern birdlife, including many breeding species found nowhere else in Georgia. Elevations range from 1,600 to 4,700 feet. The Mountain region as a whole is the coldest section in Georgia, with January daily temperatures averaging from 30 to 50 degrees F, and July daily temperatures averaging from 65 to 90 degrees F. This region also gets the most rain in Georgia, especially in the Blue Ridge province.

The Piedmont region is the next region to the south of the Mountain region. It stretches from the Alabama border in the west to the South Carolina border in the east and south to the Fall Line. The origin of some of these terms is pretty illuminating: Piedmont comes from an Italian word meaning "foot of the mountain," which exactly describes the northern edge of this region. Many major East Coast cities are built on the Fall Line, referring to the line of waterfalls and rapids where the rivers pass from the higher elevation of the Piedmont to the lower and flatter Coastal Plain. Not only did these waterfalls and rapids stop early settlers from traveling any farther upstream, they also often provided energy sources for mills and eventually for towns and cities. This line marks the southern boundary of the Piedmont; some of the major Georgia cities on it are Columbus, Macon, and Augusta. The Piedmont has some northern and southern features, but is mostly characterized by rolling topography and larger rivers than the Mountain region. Piedmont elevations are much lower than most of the Mountain region, ranging from 500 to 1,500 feet. Temperatures are intermediate for Georgia, with January averages about 32 to 55 degrees F and summer averages similar to all of Georgia south of the mountains at 70 to 90 degrees F.

South of the Fall Line lies the Coastal Plain region. This encompasses all of the rest of Georgia except for the coast itself. The Coastal Plain is fairly flat, ranging from 70 to 500 feet, and has even larger rivers than the Piedmont with attendant wide areas of floodplain. There are actually two slightly different coastal plains in Georgia: The Atlantic Coastal Plain includes all river basins emptying into the Atlantic, and the Gulf Coastal Plain includes all river basins emptying into the Gulf of Mexico (mostly southwestern Georgia). The Okefenokee basin divides the two, with rivers from it flowing both ways. Winter temperatures average from 35 to 60 degrees F, just slightly warmer than the Piedmont, and July averages about the same as the Piedmont.

The Coast region is easily defined as the immediate coast to about 30 miles inland, and it corresponds to a series of former shoreline areas left behind by falling sea levels. Elevations are from sea level to 70 feet. For site locations in this book, the 30-mile boundary is not absolute; many areas within this distance from the coast actually have Coastal Plain–like features or birds, and so they are placed there rather than here. The Coast is similar in elevation and temperature to the Coastal Plain but is dominated by coastal features such as beaches and islands, and its rivers are tidally influenced. There are also large areas of salt marsh in this region—in fact, one-third of the salt marshes along the Atlantic coast of the United States are in Georgia.

Although it is not a physical region, another distinct area in terms of bird distribution is off the coast, and commonly referred to as pelagic. This includes all adjacent coastal waters out to about 100 miles. This is listed as a category for certain species in the Status and Distribution Charts chapter. Normally the only way to see these species is by boat. Sometimes boats are chartered by birders for this purpose, but not on a regular basis in Georgia. Most of the species birders want to see here are found in the waters of the Gulf Stream, which is typically 65 to 70 miles offshore and takes several hours just to get out to, much less bird in. If you happen to be offshore on a fishing boat, you may see some of these birds. It is easier to see them off the North Carolina coast, where the Gulf Stream is much closer to shore. A regular trip provider there is Brian Patteson at (703) 765-4484, or http://www.patteson.com. Rarely, a powerful hurricane may displace some of these species inland, but they are usually seen there only for the first day or so after the storm.

Migration and weather. Weather and rainfall are a fact of life in Georgia, and are not only important components of all our habitats and regions but can directly affect birding, especially during migration. Some migrants move across the entire state, but most follow one of two routes. Coastal migrants follow the coast north in spring or south in fall. Most inland migrants are trans-Gulf migrants; this group flies across the Gulf of Mexico north in spring, generally departing from the Yucatan Peninsula and landing anywhere from the Texas coast to the middle of the Florida panhandle. They then work their way north or northeast, often following rivers. In fall many of these species fly south along the Appalachian and Blue Ridge Mountains until they run out of mountains, and then travel either overland or down rivers to the Gulf. This is a general description of the two most common routes taken, and there are many exceptions. For instance, some birds fly around the Gulf instead of across it (circum-Gulf migrants), and in many species there is a pronounced shift to the east in fall, when even trans-Gulf migrants may have many individuals flying down the coast.

Weather and/or winds affect many birds during migration. Most weather systems move in from the west, with a few moving up from the Gulf or along the coast. They can have a major effect on migration, especially when large fronts move through a specific area during large-scale migrations. This weather often forces airborne migrants to the ground, and as soon as it passes these birds may be seen in large numbers feeding for the next leg of their journey. Weather systems like this usually provide the best numbers of species and individuals at migrant locations such as Kennesaw Mountain. The northern part of the state receives a lot of precipitation in late winter and early spring, and summer storms provide large amounts of rainfall throughout the state; none of this affects migration much.

An excellent source for further reading on these subjects is *The Atlas of Georgia,* by Hodler and Schretter. This book was printed by the University of Georgia in 1986, and although out of print, it is available at most libraries. Much of the material for this section came from this excellent source.

3. *Habitats*

Habitat types. I have broken down the habitat types found at birding sites into several major categories, keeping in mind both ease of use and accuracy. The list below includes only those habitats that are easy to identify and have significance for birds. Many if not most species can be found in several of these habitats, but some birds are more restricted, and a basic understanding of habitat differences is helpful when trying to find them. A knowledge of plant types is helpful in recognizing habitat types. Readers unfamiliar with any of the terms used in this section should refer to field guides or botany manuals.

Old-growth white pine-hemlock. In Georgia this rare habitat type is found only in the extreme northeast corner of the state. It is at the very southern edge of its range; most of it was logged in the 1800s and early 1900s. White pines have distinctive gray bark and branches growing most of the way down the trunk. If you are as numbers-oriented as most birders, white pine is the only eastern pine with five needles per cluster. Hemlocks have very short, flat needles, and each needle is attached directly to the twig, not in clusters like the pines. This habitat type is much more common farther north and is of interest because of the two northern species that occasionally breed here. These are the Red-breasted Nuthatch and the Golden-crowned Kinglet. Another possible breeder is the Brown Creeper, but this has yet to be documented in Georgia. The only example of this habitat type offered in this book is in the Burrell's Ford area.

Pine forest. This forest type is extremely common in Georgia, thanks in no small part to our healthy forestry industry. In fact, you will constantly be reminded of this through the numerous helpful signs reminding you that "Trees grow jobs." Even though all this vibrant industry actually does help provide numerous good birding areas, when harvest time comes around it can also lead to the rapid disappearance of forests you are used to birding.

Types of pine forest vary widely in Georgia for several reasons, including different pine species, levels of management, and regional differences in soil types or climate. The most common types are loblolly pine plantations in the Piedmont region and slash pine plantations on the Coastal Plain. Longleaf pine once dominated the Coastal Plain and parts of the Piedmont, but has been reduced to a few remnant tracts. The best example of longleaf pine mentioned in this book is at the Okefenokee Swamp–Suwanee Canal Recreation Area.

The typical birdlife found in pine forests varies, but the following species are found in large areas of Georgia. Two of the most sought-after birds for visitors are the Pine Warbler and Brown-headed Nuthatch. Others include Chipping Sparrow and Eastern Wood-Pewee. A special type of pine forest is pine flatwoods. This habitat once covered much of the coastal plain near the immediate coast, but most of it has been converted to young pine plantations. Pine flatwoods habitat consists of large, scattered pines in a flat, wet area similar to a prairie. The only remaining large expanse is at Fort Stewart, a U.S. Army base southwest of Savannah, largely inaccessible. However, this open habitat type is approximated by conditions along large powerline right-of-way areas, such as those at Paulk's Pasture WMA. The key species for birders here is the Henslow's Sparrow. This secretive species rarely occurs and can be very difficult to find even when present, but it winters nowhere else in the state.

Mixed pine/hardwood forest. This forest type is common, and it comes in an even larger variety of shapes and sizes than pine forests. Basically, any forest made up of a significant percentage of pines and hardwoods falls into this category. The typical birds found in this type of forest are extremely variable. Both tanagers are found here, Scarlet farther north and Summer throughout Georgia. Two vireos are also typical, Blue-headed (again in the north) and Yellow-throated throughout the state. A few warblers also prefer this habitat type. Black-throated Green Warblers are found only in the northernmost parts of Georgia (we'll make hemlock an honorary pine for this species), and Black-and-white Warblers are found everywhere above the Fall Line in the mixed pine/hardwood environment. Another warbler that prefers it here is the Yellow-throated Warbler, although once again we will have to appoint a substitute pine species, this time cypress. Along the coast, this warbler is common also in maritime mixed pine/hardwood forest. The coastal form of this forest type is found throughout the barrier islands and along the immediate mainland coast, where the hardwood component is dominated by live oak.

Hardwood forest. This forest type is fairly common in Georgia, with the key feature being the total absence of evergreens of any type. Our three major types of hardwood forest are upland, floodplain, and cypress-tupelo swamp. Upland hardwood forest ranges from dry to moist but is never flooded, whereas both floodplain and cypress-tupelo swamp are either seasonally or constantly flooded. Floodplain hardwood forest and cypress-tupelo swamp forests tend to be broad and cover large expanses in the Coastal Plain, but above the Fall Line they tend to be narrow and confined to river or stream corridors. Birds typically found statewide in upland hardwood forest include the Wood Thrush and Red-eyed Vireo. Upland hardwood forest is more common above the Fall Line, where typical species include Ovenbird and White-breasted Nuthatch. Farther north in the Mountain region the Black-throated Blue Warbler is another typical species. Species found through most of the state in floodplain hardwood forest include Northern Parula, Acadian Flycatcher, Louisiana Waterthrush, and Kentucky Warbler. The Swainson's Warbler is widespread in the Coastal Plain but limited above the Fall Line in this habitat. In the large river floodplain forests of the Coastal Plain, look for Mississippi Kites. In all cypress-tupelo swamps a sought-after species you'll see is Prothonotary Warbler. While cypress is actually a softwood, this habitat type is commonly found adjacent to hardwood floodplain forest and fits best in the hardwood forest category.

Shrubland. This common habitat type comes in many forms and is often transitional. The three most common types are young pine plantations, coastal scrub, and freshwater marsh shrubland. Young pine plantations lose this designation when the trees pass 10 feet in height. Prairie Warblers, Yellow-breasted Chats, and Field Sparrows are typical here. In some areas a few large trees (live or dead) may remain among the young pines; check them for Northern Flickers and Red-headed Woodpeckers. Coastal scrub shrubland is the brushy area found on the edges of many coastal habitats, including marshes, beaches, and forest. A species prized by many visiting birders is the Painted Bunting, which is easily found here. Of the three types of shrubland, coastal scrub is usually the most permanent. Freshwater marsh shrubland is also transitional, depending on local factors that affect water levels. It includes any inland open wet area dominated by shrubs, usually adjacent to or within freshwater marshland. Although this specific habitat doesn't have species unique to it, these are usually very "birdy" areas. Some species are typically found in all three shrubland types, including Common Yellowthroats and Gray Catbirds. Dry oak scrub is another ecologically important shrubland type, but it is of more interest to botanists than birders.

Field. These are generally open areas with low or no plant growth and no woody shrubs or trees. The different types of field are somewhat overlapping, but the following are useful categories. Weedy fields are characterized by broad-leaved herbs such as goldenrod, ragweed, and other wildflowers, and are frequently nothing more than overgrown agricultural fields. They may have a few clumps of shrubs (such as briars) or isolated small trees. Though this may not sound exciting, several interesting species are best found in this habitat, such as Orchard Oriole, Blue Grosbeak, and Indigo Bunting. Another species found here is the Northern Bobwhite, which can be found elsewhere as well. In grassy fields the primary component is some type of grass, ranging from a tall hay field to a closely grazed pasture to a well-manicured sod farm. Grasshopper Sparrows are usually found only in hay fields, but other species found in all grassy field types are Loggerhead Shrike, Eastern Kingbird, Eastern Meadowlark, and Savannah Sparrow. Plowed fields are another transitional habitat. In fact, many other open habitat types may become this type whether you want them to or not! Some birds may be found in plowed fields and short grass fields. Horned Larks and Killdeer, for example, prefer to nest on bare ground but may forage in both. Cattle Egrets are found in both of these types as well, though normally only south of the Fall Line. Plowed fields can be great for shorebirds, especially when they have some standing water, and can also be good for sparrows in winter, especially Vesper Sparrows. Some species are found in all field types, such as Red-tailed Hawk and Eastern Bluebird.

Marshland. Most birders will instantly recognize marshes by their tall, dense, grassy plants growing in water. Typical plants of freshwater marshland include cattails, needlerushes, and various grasses and sedges. It's not important that you be able to identify all these plants (fortunately!), but aside from the aptly named cattail, needlerushes are dense clumps of dark green grass-like plants with sharply pointed tips. Except at the edges, the ground is at least moist if not underwater. A good species to look for here is Sedge Wren. This habitat always seems to have a few good birds around, and it is always worth birding. Freshwater marshes with a few dead trees are also favored areas for Red-headed Woodpeckers. Brackish marsh-land is found where fresh and salt water meet near the mouths of rivers flowing into the ocean. Not surprisingly, this habitat has a mix of freshwater marsh and salt marsh species. Salt marsh is found only in saltwater areas, and is usually dominated by cordgrass. If you don't know what cordgrass is, the next time you try to walk through some in shorts, your bleeding legs will tell you. All of the salt marsh sparrows are found exclusively in this habitat, although Nelson's Sharp-tailed Sparrow may be closer to the shrubland edges. Whole families of some species of birds are best found in marshlands, such as bitterns and rails. Within each family, some species do have clear preferences for fresh water or salt water.

Beach. The two types of beach referred to in this book are very easy to identify. Tidal flats are those areas that the tide floods twice a day, and upper beaches are those areas of bare sand above the high tide line (this area includes the dunes adjacent to the upper beach). Look for all shorebirds on tidal flats, and check the upper beach for Wilson's Plovers, American Oystercatchers, and other nesting shorebirds. Terns and gulls are also partial to tidal flats, and many waders may be found there as well. Reddish Egrets can be found only on shallowly flooded tidal flats.

Water habitats. These areas are loosely grouped together because they include open water. Ocean habitat here includes the Atlantic Ocean; many species of wa-terfowl, such as scoters and Red-breasted Mergansers, are primarily found here and may be seen by scanning from the beach. Northern Gannet is another species found in this way. Some seabirds, collectively known as pelagic species, are only found far offshore in the ocean, except in the most unusual of circumstances, such as when a hurricane has forced them near shore or inland. Examples include storm-petrels, shearwaters, and some terns such as Bridled and Sooty.

Reservoirs are large manmade bodies of water, many of which are called lakes even though they are usually created by dams. These are good places to look for ducks or gulls in winter and are the best places inland to see Common Loons or Horned Grebes. In addition, most Bald Eagle nests in Georgia are on reservoirs, and some have Ospreys nesting or passing through during migration. Ponds are much smaller bodies of water, usually of only a few acres or even smaller. Ponds are good areas for waders, ducks such as Wood Ducks, and Belted Kingfishers. Some reservoirs and ponds have shallow edges that are freshwater mudflats, and are very attractive to shorebirds. These same bodies of water when drained also become mudflats. Especially upstate in late summer and fall, they are excellent areas for waders; look for American Pipits on mudflats. Many managed diked ponds such as at wastewater treatment plants, dredge spoil sites, and fish hatcher-ies have areas of mudflat and are always worth checking.

Lily ponds are small ponds with varying amounts of surface coverage in water lilies or other floating vegetation. These ponds are the only place to find Purple Gallinules, a rare species in Georgia; they are also good for Common Moorhens, Wood Ducks, and Anhingas. Finally, the river habitat includes tidally influenced

The Ogeechee River.

rivers near the coast all the way up to the higher-elevation rivers of the mountains. Bird species again vary widely depending upon the area of the state and the size of river, but they are always worth checking if you can get to a bridge or a boat ramp. Streams and creeks are not included as a separate habitat type because the birds normally found in or near them are usually part of and covered under the larger habitat types along their banks.

4. Georgia's Best Birding Areas

Map Legend

Interstate		City/Town	Dublin _or_ Dublin	
U.S. Highway		Campground		
State/County Road		One-way Road		
Forest Service/ County Road		Picnic Area		
Interstate Highway		Cabin/Building	▪ _or_ ▭	
Paved Road		Elevation	5,281 ft. X	
Gravel Road		Mountain	5,281 ft.	
Unimproved Road		Overlook/ Point of Interest		
Powerline/Gas Line		Observation Platform/Blind		
Birding Site	17	Information/Visitor Center or Ranger Station		
Parking Area	P			
Spring		State Boundary	GEORGIA	
Lake, River/Creek, Pier, Dam, Waterfall		Park/Refuge/Forest Boundary	_or_	
Bridge/Overpass				
Marsh/Wetland		Map Orientation	N	
Boardwalk				
Trail		Scale	0 0.5 1 Miles	
Gate				

18

Map of Regions

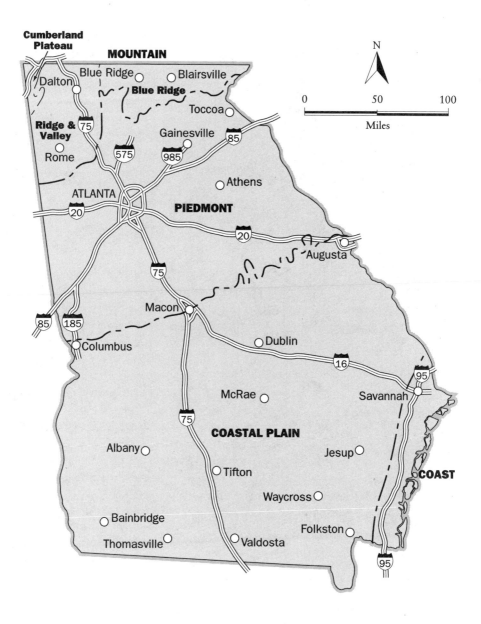

Map of Birding Sites

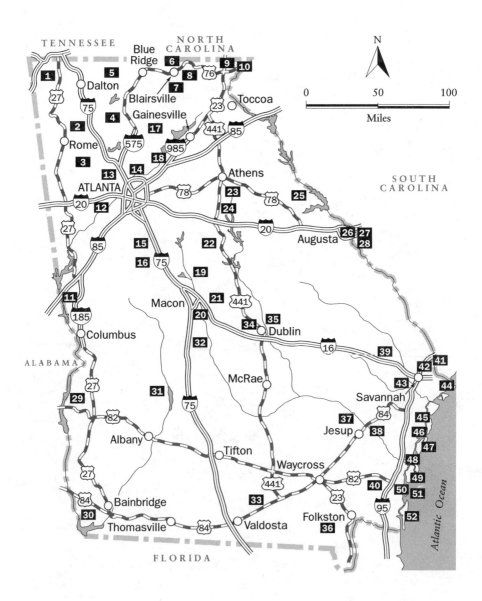

Cloudland Canyon, from the overlook.

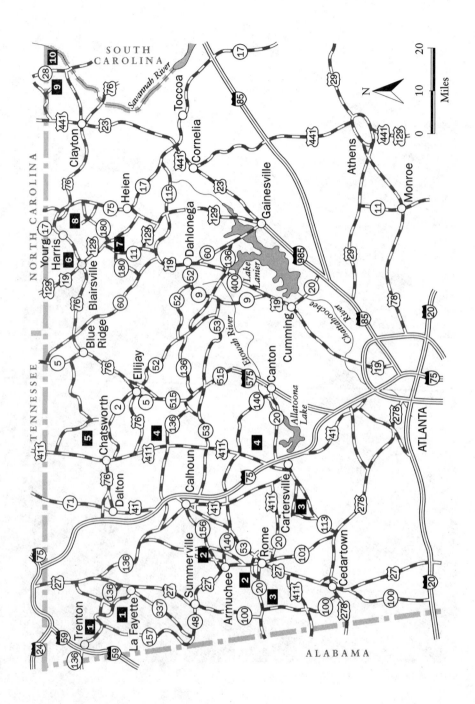

Mountain Region

1 Cumberland Plateau Area

Counties: Walker and Dade.
Habitats: Pine forest, mixed pine/hardwood forest, upland hardwood forest, grassy field, pond.
Key birds: *Crockford–Pigeon Mountain:* Golden Eagle, hawks in general, Red-breasted Nuthatch, sparrows. *Cloudland Canyon:* Worm-eating, Black-throated Green, Yellow-throated, Hooded, and Black-and-white warblers; Louisiana Waterthrush, Ovenbird, Scarlet Tanager, Blue-headed Vireo, Broad-winged Hawk.
Best times to bird: *Crockford–Pigeon Mountain:* October through February. *Cloudland Canyon:* May through September.

The birding: This section highlights several good spots in the extreme northwest corner of Georgia. This area can be accessed from Interstate 75 or from the city of Rome. The Cumberland Plateau extends from northwestern Alabama into southeastern Tennessee and northwestern Georgia. This area of mostly sandstone has been eroded down into flatter terrain very different from the Blue Ridge region of northeast Georgia. The first stop is near Crockford–Pigeon Mountain WMA, a recent Golden Eagle reintroduction site, which in recent years has had successful wild nesting of this species. Some nearby roads go through higher-elevation Virginia pine forests, and there are a few fields and pastures to scan for raptors and other species. Other sections of this WMA offer good land birding and hiking. Cloudland Canyon State Park is a nearby popular camping location that also offers good upper-elevation birding for Georgia, although it is best in summer; the rest of these sites are for winter birding.

Directions: This section starts at the intersection of Georgia Highway 140 and US Highway 27 in Armuchee, Georgia. The quickest access is from Interstate 75. Take Exit 306 (old 128), which is GA 140, west for 15.8 miles to US 27, and turn right (north). If you are coming from the north side of Rome, take US 27 north 7.3 miles from Loop 1 to this intersection. Continue on US 27 for 13.7 miles to GA 48. Along the way, note the sign for James H. "Sloppy" Floyd State Park on the left 11.1 miles northwest of GA 140. This 545-acre park offers two lakes and tent and trailer camping, but is pretty busy in summer. It's worth a short stop if you have extra time on the way back, or are looking for more places to bird than this section offers, but the birding is not as unusual for Georgia as the other locations. The park is very proud of its Eastern Bluebirds, though, and has several nice trails around the lakes. To try it, take Sloppy Floyd Lake Road 1.4 miles to where Marble Spring Road joins from the right. Continue straight ahead for 1.1 miles to the park entrance. The office is on your right between the two lakes, and has maps.

1 Crockford–Pigeon Mountain Wildlife Management Area

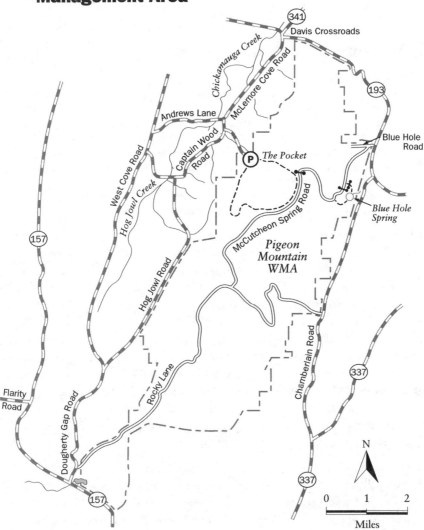

A good landmark for knowing you are near GA 48 is the intersection of GA 100/114 just before GA 48 in the town of Summerville. Keep in mind your last large selection of restaurants or gas for a few hours is in this town. Turn left on GA 48. Your main turn is in 10.9 miles at GA 157, but you can also make a quick stop in the Summerville Fish Hatchery after 3.7 miles on GA 48. Turn left on Fish Hatchery Road; the hatchery is 0.2 mile on your left. During migration there may be shorebirds here if any of the small ponds are drawn down, and there are a few landbirds around the wooded perimeter, but again, this is not a prime site. Check in with hatchery personnel before you bird.

To get to **Crockford–Pigeon Mountain Wildlife Management Area,** turn right on GA 157 (7.2 miles past the hatchery). In 7.4 miles, note the Pleasant Grove Baptist Church on your left. This marks the beginning of the area where the Golden Eagles tend to be found, and you should carefully scan the entire area to your right for soaring birds and any perched raptor. There are also a few small ponds and lots of pastures to scan along the way. This is one of the few spots to find Logger-head Shrikes in north Georgia. In an attempt to reintroduce them into an area where they occurred many years ago, Golden Eagles were released here for 9 years, ending in 1993; they have since nested on their own near here. A total of 111 Golden Eagles were released at a nearby hacking site, but only about 6 to 8 are believed to have stayed in the area. Although very rare in Georgia, Rough-legged Hawks have been found here a couple of times, so it's worth looking for this species in midwinter also. There are lots of Red-shouldered and Red-tailed Hawks and a few American Kestrels here as well.

If you don't see any eagles, you can backtrack about 1 mile on GA 157, or continue 0.6 mile to Dougherty Gap Road. The small marsh on your left at this corner is worth scanning for ducks, and so is the larger lake in the field to your right, although it is usually empty. Turn right on Dougherty Gap Road for 0.3 mile, scanning on both sides, then turn right on Rocky Lane (which is dirt, so be careful of recent rain). Rocky Lane goes through 1.7 miles of pasture until it descends into pine woods in Crockford–Pigeon Mountain Wildlife Management Area. This area should be carefully scanned for eagles. Also check the line of trees above the road and to your left, as the eagles sometimes perch here. These fields along the road are a place to hope for a Lapland Longspur among the Horned Larks that can be found with careful searching, although longspurs have not been found here in recent years. Once you enter the woods, your ability to scan for eagles ends, so if you haven't found any the best plan is to scan all the same spots again. You can bird the woods here, and while this elevation is not particularly birdy in winter, this is a great spot to look for Golden-crowned Kinglet and Red-breasted Nuthatch in winter.

You will have covered most of the eagle area already, but there is more good habitat to explore. Return to Dougherty Gap Road and turn right. Follow this road as it winds down into the Mountain Cove area, but stay on the road at all times as the land here is all private. The road winds downhill through hardwood forest and then pastures (check for blackbird flocks in winter and Grasshopper Sparrows in summer) and reaches Hog Jowl Road in 3.3 miles. If you are still looking for eagles, scan the edges of this large valley for perched or soaring raptors. This is much easier in winter when the trees are leafless. Turn right and follow this road along Hog Jowl Creek for as long as you want, until it ends at Captain Wood Road in 5.4 miles. In summer there are typical low-elevation breeders here including Indigo Buntings and Blue Grosbeaks in open areas and Louisiana Waterthrushes and Acadian Flycatchers along the stream. During spring and fall migration you can usually find a few migrants along the creek as you cross it or its tributaries several times. From here, you can continue to the other side of Crockford-Pigeon Mountain WMA for more lower-elevation forest and winter sparrow habitat, or return to GA 157 for more fields in winter and summer birding in Cloudland Canyon State Park.

To continue, turn right on Captain Wood Road and go 4.6 miles to GA 193 at Davis Crossroads. Note on your right the dirt roads to "the Pocket" and Bluebird Gap, both ways to get back into the WMA if you want to do some hiking or general birding. The Pocket offers easy access to some good birding and wildflowers. Take the entrance road about 1 mile to the parking lot. In addition to a loop trail, there is a wheelchair-accessible 800-foot boardwalk for wildflowers, best in late March and April. The loop trail is about 6 miles long, with interesting rock formations and rare plant types. There is a waterfall about 0.3 mile uphill, and birds to watch for in summer include Acadian Flycatchers, Scarlet Tanagers, Louisiana Waterthrushes, and Wood Thrushes.

Once you get to Davis Crossroads, turn right on GA 193 for 4.3 miles to Blue Hole Road, and turn right. Take the first (almost immediate) left, and follow this dirt road until it splits at 1.3 miles. The fields and pastures along this road are good for sparrows in winter. You can hike up either split for forest birding in any season, although there isn't much here in winter. The left one takes you 0.2 mile to a small parking area at Blue Hole Spring, named for the very blue water. A trail goes from the spring up a steep hill and around to a dirt road, and if you turn right on the road it will lead back to the right split, and you can then return to your vehicle. This loop is about 1 mile. Georgia's largest cave, called Ellison's Cave, is near the top of the dirt road you crossed, about another 0.5 mile uphill from the trail crossing. This trail is very difficult, and the cave requires technical caving skills to enter.

One other option is to continue another 0.8 mile along GA 193 to Chamberlain Road, and turn right. The main entrance to the WMA is 3.4 miles on the right; this dirt entrance road is the other end of Rocky Lane but it is not suitable for a passenger car. Maps are usually available at the check station. You can easily spend hours on this side of the WMA. When you are finished you can either return to the west side the way you came, or exit the area by taking GA 193 into the town of LaFayette and then GA 136 to I-75 at Exit 320 (old 133) south of Dalton.

If you stayed on the west side to continue on Dougherty Gap Road, return to GA 157 and turn right. In 0.7 mile is a small grocery store on your left for snacks or drinks. In 1.5 more miles turn left on Flarity Road. In the first 2 miles there are several pastures and fields worth scanning for larks and (probably in vain!) for longspurs. You will reach the Alabama state line 3.2 miles from GA 157. When you are finished looking, return to GA 157.

At this point you can either return to the original eagle area to scan again, or try **Cloudland Canyon State Park** to the north. This park is the most interesting in summer, even though it has many more visitors then. To go there, turn left on GA 157 for 12.6 miles north to GA 136 and turn left. The entrance to the park is on the right in 3.3 miles. Turn and pay at the entrance station in 0.2 mile, or turn right

1 Cloudland Canyon State Park

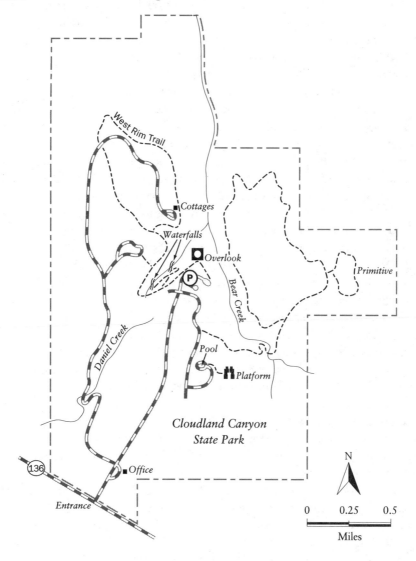

and follow the spur to the park office and pay there. The office has maps and many books on topics including local hikes, geology, and history. The park hours are 7 A.M. to 10 P.M. and the office is open 8 A.M. to 5 P.M. None of the roads in this park have names, so it may be easier to follow these directions by referencing the park map. As you follow the spur road out of the office area, you will reach the main road quickly. From this intersection the easiest choice for noncampers is to turn right (continue straight ahead if you didn't take the office spur). Pass the park gate in 0.8 mile, and turn right to the pool and tennis courts at 1.1 miles. Take this road to a sharp left-hand turn at 0.7 mile and then to the end in another 0.3 mile

27

and park near the brown "Wildlife Watching Area" sign. There should be Eastern Bluebirds around the pool. Walk the short path through the grass and forest to the observation tower, about 0.2 mile. In this open area you will find Yellow-breasted Chats and Field Sparrows, and perhaps swallows flying around the small pond. Go back to the main entrance road, and turn right. Note that if you are planning a long hike, you can visit this small area later in the day.

Almost immediately (0.1 mile), park in the first parking area on your left. The main trails are to the left (follow behind the buildings along the edge of the canyon to the trail signs). The Waterfall Trail takes you down a fairly steep hill for 0.5 mile through a series of switchbacks to Daniel Creek, a lovely spot to do some birding in summer. The West Rim Trail follows the same track until it reaches the creek, and then it climbs the other side to a camping area and another 4 miles of trail. Once you get to the camping area, you have been through the best birding along this trail, and you may want to double back. In summer this area is full of Worm-eating Warblers, with good numbers of Hooded, Yellow-throated, and Black-and-white Warblers as well as Louisiana Waterthrushes and Ovenbirds. There are also a few Black-throated Green Warblers, mostly in areas of mixed forest. In addition, there are many Scarlet Tanagers, Blue-headed and Red-eyed Vireos, Yellow-billed Cuckoos, White-breasted Nuthatches, Chipping Sparrows, and Hairy and Pileated Woodpeckers. There are usually a few Cedar Waxwings around the parking lot. Check for Chimney Swifts and hawks overhead, including Broad-winged and Red-tailed.

After you are finished with the trails, you can walk to the right from your car to the overlook of this entire jaw-dropping canyon, stunning in any season. You can also access the west side of the canyon for more birding without having to hike the whole way over. Go back down the main entrance road to the intersection just on your side of the pay station and office, and turn right. In 0.7 mile you will cross Daniel Creek; check here for Louisiana Waterthrushes and Eastern Phoebes. Continue another 0.8 mile to the tent and trailer camping area. If you are camping here, turn right; there is an easy-access, fairly level trail near the first set of restrooms to the right around the loop. You can use this trail only if you are camping here. Otherwise, continue on the road that crossed the creek 1.5 miles to the end at a small loop, and park in the small area by cottage 15. This is another access to the West Rim Hiking Trail. This loop trail is 4.5 miles long, and some of the best birding is along the canyon rim, near the camping area. If you do this trail from here, follow it to the right. Once you have covered the part of the trail along the canyon rim, it's better (from a birding standpoint) to double back over that section instead of doing the entire loop. Trail maps are also available at the office. This is about the last of your choices in this area.

To check two nearby small lakes in winter, turn right on GA 136 for 0.9 mile, and then turn right again on Sunset Drive. There are two lakes on the right about a half mile down, and there are usually sparrows in the hedgerows along this road. As usual, stay on the public road, as this is all private land. Don't expect a lot of ducks here, but it's worth checking. Back at GA 136, a right turn takes you 5 miles to the city of Trenton and lots of restaurants, hotels, and gas stations. Return to I-75 or Rome the same way you came.

General information: This area is very busy in summer, but almost deserted in winter. If your main goal is to see Golden Eagles, winter is much easier both because there are no leaves on trees and because there are fewer visitors. However, there is great camping and birding in summer at Cloudland Canyon, if you don't mind lots of company. If you are looking for a restaurant in Summerville, a local favorite is Armstrong's BBQ. This restaurant is only 0.5 mile north of Georgia Highway 48 on US Highway 27, on the right. The food is pretty good but not fabulous, but the prices are very low (probably the real reason for its popularity). This area is just south of Chattanooga and all its historical and cultural opportunities. Several other sections in this book are also nearby, including Arrowhead Wildlife Education Center near Armuchee (Site 2) and the Rome sites (parts of Sites 2 and 3). If you do Sloppy Floyd Park last, you can exit the park to the south and run into GA 100 to get to Rome that way (about 2.9 miles to GA 100, and 10.3 miles to GA 20). The Cohutta WMA is just east of here (Site 5). You will have no trouble finding lots to do here in summer!

ADDITIONAL HELP

DeLorme map grid: page 12, F 2/3, E3, C2.
For more information: Georgia Department of Natural Resources; Cloudland Canyon State Park, (706) 657-4050; Dade County Chamber of Commerce, (706) 657-4488.

2 Arrowhead Wildlife Education Center

County: Floyd.
Habitats: Pine forest, mixed pine/hardwood forest, freshwater marsh shrubland, weedy field, pond.
Key birds: Ducks, shorebirds.
Best times to bird: All year.

The birding: Although this former fish hatchery is no longer used for that purpose, the Arrowhead Wildlife Education Center still has the ponds and a couple of nice trails around them. The site is fairly small and can be birded in a couple hours of easy walking on trails along the old dikes. Although there aren't really any key species here, at various seasons this spot attracts many interesting and varied birds and is always worth checking. The ponds are specifically managed for waterfowl and shorebirds, and this prime habitat attracts many good birds in all seasons. Additionally, for winter birders, directions are given to the nearby Garden Lakes, which are excellent for ducks during the winter months. In between the two spots is the large Berry College Wildlife Management Area, with several interesting trails for spring or summer birding.

2 Arrowhead Wildlife Education Center

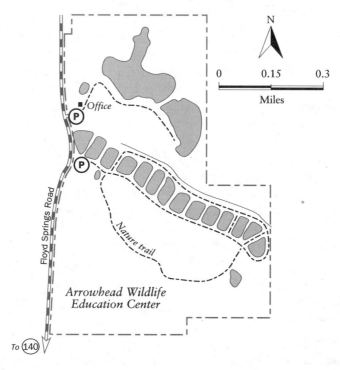

Directions: The quickest access from Interstate 75 is to take Exit 306 (old 128), which is Georgia Highway 140, and head west. In 15 miles, turn right on Floyd Springs Road. Drive 3.9 miles, and turn right into a grass parking area for the ponds at the Arrowhead Wildlife Education Center. A sign at the far end of the parking area directs you to the ponds and trails. Take the trail away from the road, and at your earliest opportunity make a left turn to get down to the dike along the pond edges. Note the wildlife trail that goes off to your right here (about 2 miles long). The ponds generally have more interesting species, but if you have the time you can find upland species along the trail, including the Brown-headed Nuthatch. Once you are down on the dike, just walk all the way around the edges of the ponds, using cross-dikes as necessary to cover whatever areas appeal to you.

You can cover all the ponds by walking straight to the end at the last pond. Then either loop around the far side of the last pond (not usually very well maintained) or take the dike across the front of it to the left, and then walk the dike on the other side of all the same ponds back to your vehicle. In general, some ponds will be dry while others vary from slightly wet to having enough water for ducks. In spring and fall, check the ponds for shorebirds or any other migrants, like rails or Marsh and Sedge Wrens. Look for land migrants in the brush and trees that line most of the dike area, especially the far side along the small creek. In winter, check for ducks when there is water, and for sparrows in all the dry or almost-dry ponds. The ponds are full of Song and Swamp Sparrows then, and

White-throated, Chipping, and Field Sparrows can be found in the drier sections. Keep your eyes open for uncommon species such as Vesper and White-crowned Sparrows as well. In late summer check for herons, mostly Great Blue and Little Blue and Great Egret. Green Herons breed here in summer. This is also a good spot for swallows in spring and summer. Enough rarities have been found that it is always worth checking carefully in all seasons. If you are interested in dragonflies, these ponds are excellent in summer and early fall.

When you are finished with the ponds, there are two larger lakes worth birding. To reach these walk-in lakes, turn right on Floyd Springs Road and take the first right just past the ponds. Park at the office on your left, and walk the road past the closed gate. Check the small pond on the left for Belted Kingfisher or swallows, then turn right at the intersection to scan the two larger lakes. There may be nothing more here than the resident Canada Geese, but they are worth checking if you have time. Return to GA 140 the way you came.

To exit the area, simply go back to I-75 to the left on GA 140. To visit any of the Rome area spots, turn right on GA 140. In 0.8 mile, you will reach US 27; turn left. Drive 7.3 miles to Loop 1, which is also called Redmond Circle. Before this intersection, note Berry College as you pass it (small brown sign on the right to Berry College WMA 4.2 miles south of GA 140). There is a check station along County Road 234 with maps if you want to bird the sprawling campus of Berry College—which can be very rewarding in spring and summer. There are several areas of very different habitat with good birding opportunities. At 6.6 miles on US 27, note the main entrance to Berry College. If you want to bird here, turn in and proceed to the small guardhouse at 0.3 mile. You do not need to check in, but you can get a map of the college to help you find the Mountain Campus. (You need to be out of here by 6 P.M.) Set your odometer to zero and follow the main road and the signs for "Mountain Campus." This will require several turns in quick succession.

After a left turn puts you on a straight road going slightly uphill, watch for overhead powerlines at 0.8 mile and turn right down a small dirt road just past the lines. Park here and walk this trail to an area called Victory Lake. There used to be a lake here, but the limestone under it collapsed, leaving pockets of wet areas instead of a lake. This is a good area for scrub species, and the wet areas may have waders in summer or ducks in winter. Continue uphill on the main road, and at 1.3 miles total (another 0.5 mile) watch for a yellow gate on the right. This trail also takes you into the Victory Lake area. Continue up the hill for 2.4 miles (total 3.7) to an area of buildings, birding along the way if you wish, and turn left at the T intersection. Go 0.1 mile, and ease left to follow the sign for Possum Trot Church. Do not make the hard left—that is the wrong road. This dirt road is about 1.4 miles long; the first 1 mile is through open pasture good for Eastern Kingbirds and Eastern Meadowlarks. At 1 mile the road enters some woods with a small stream, and ends in another 0.4 mile at the church.

After birding here, go back to the beginning of this road, and turn left again to continue uphill. Follow the main road for 0.4 mile as it goes around various buildings of the dairy, and then turn left on the good gravel road to the Old Mill. This road climbs through excellent upland hardwood habitat for 0.5 mile to the Old Mill. The road continues uphill, but it is walk-in or bicycle riding only. If you are up for it, this road forms a 6.5-mile loop called the Snow Loop around the Berry Reservoir, and it has some excellent habitat for species including Black-throated Green and Worm-eating Warblers, Ovenbirds, Wood Thrushes, and Scarlet Tanagers. You can also just go partway if you don't want to do the whole loop. After you have gone 2.1 miles around the loop, there is a trail to the right along a large ridge, which can be outstanding for migrants in spring and fall. You may wish to bird here early and then try the Possum Trot or Victory Lake areas later.

To get to Garden Lakes, turn right on Redmond Circle/Loop 1 when you reach it on US 27. This is 0.7 mile south of Berry College. Drive 2.6 miles; when the main road turns left, continue straight ahead on Garden Lakes Boulevard. The cross-street to mark this intersection is Mathis Street. Continue 0.1 mile on Garden Lakes Boulevard and turn right on Elliott Road. Follow Elliott around to the left for 0.5 mile and scan this first lake. It usually doesn't have much, but may have Gadwalls or American Wigeons in winter. Continue on Elliott another 0.4 mile and turn left again on Shoreline Boulevard. Scan the main lake from whatever spot you can see the flock best. Check carefully, as there have been many rare ducks here over the years, especially during migration in late fall and early spring. Typical species here include Bufflehead, Ruddy and Ring-necked Ducks, American Wigeon, and Lesser Scaup. There may also be grebes here (mostly Pied-billed and a few Horned), and usually at least a few Ring-billed Gulls in winter.

Continue around the lake 0.7 mile back to Garden Lakes Boulevard, and turn left. In 0.6 mile you will be back to Elliott, and in another 0.1 mile is Redmond Circle to US 27. From here you can go back north, or you can take Loop 1 for 7.9 miles to US 411 to head toward I-75 and Atlanta. Turn left on US 411 for 16 miles, then follow US 411 through the turn for another 3 miles. Then take GA 20 to the right directly to I-75 at Exit 290 (old 125).

General information: Services are available at the interstate, and sporadically along all the roads in this section, and in Rome. You can get specific information about Arrowhead Wildlife Education Center at the office there during normal weekday business hours. From Rome you can easily go north to the northwest corner of Georgia, including Crockford–Pigeon Mountain Wildlife Management Area or Cloudland Canyon State Park (Site 1, Cumberland Plateau Area). The Thomas Brothers Grass Farm (Site 3) is also just west of Rome.

ADDITIONAL HELP

DeLorme map grid: page 18, A5; page 18, C4.
For more information: Arrowhead Wildlife Education Center, (706) 295-6041; Greater Rome CVB, (800) 444-1834.

3 Ridge and Valley Sod Farms

Counties: Floyd and Bartow.
Habitats: Grassy field, plowed field, pond, river.
Key birds: Buff-breasted, Upland, Pectoral, and Least Sandpipers; American Golden Plover; Horned Lark; American Pipit; swallows; sparrows.
Best times to bird: Mid-July through September.

The birding: This section consists of two similar sites, Thomas Brothers Grass Farm near Rome and the Atlanta Sod Farm near Cartersville. Both are working sod farms, and require permission to bird from on-site offices. The birding is very simple—merely drive along dirt roads within the sod farm and look for shorebirds and other species of interest working the grassy or dirt areas. A scope is very helpful for distant birds, as you must stay on established roads. There are a few shorebirds in spring; most of the best birding is in fall. In addition to shorebirds, you may find other open area species and also woodland species in areas near the actual farms.

For both areas, finding the birds in all the expanse of grass is usually the hardest part. Except for particularly good areas outlined below, keep the following in mind. Water is always helpful, whether in the form of a small permanent pond, puddles from recent rain, or puddles from one of the large sprinkler systems. Permanently wet ditches may also harbor a few shorebirds. Almost any species of freshwater shorebird can be found at some time or another, so be careful about checking every bird. By far the most numerous shorebirds are likely to be Killdeer and Pectoral Sandpipers. Most of the shorebirds will be found in wet areas like these, except for open-sod birds like Buff-breasted and Upland Sandpipers and American Golden-Plovers. (These three species may also be found near water, at times.)

When viewing large expanses of grass, your eyes tend to unfocus, and it takes real attention to find some of these birds, especially when they are farther from the road. Panning with your scope may be useful. Areas where sod has recently been harvested may be good, and even areas plowed after harvest, especially for Buff-breasted Sandpipers. Check any ponds you find for ducks or waders, as these species also use this habitat. Both of these sod farms are near rivers, used by the farms for water but by birds as migration pathways.

Many other species are found near sod farms. Horned Larks occur year-round at both of these farms, though they can be very tough to find on any given day; in winter American Pipits are regular at both. Swallows love sod farms, which can be good places to see Bank Swallows in late July and August. Just about any of Georgia's swallows can be found here at some time during the year. In open country like this, breeding species of interest include Eastern Kingbird, Orchard Oriole, Blue Grosbeak, and Indigo Bunting. In late fall you may find sparrows, especially Savannah, out along the sod areas. Song Sparrows are common along brushy edges and Swamp Sparrows may be found in wetter brushy areas. Most of the sparrows found in Georgia can be found in small numbers at either of these sites as they pass through on migration.

3 Ridge and Valley Sod Farms

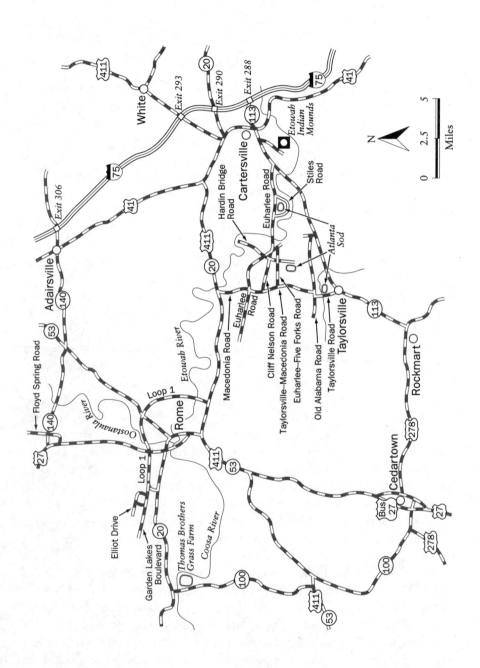

Directions: Both of these farms are northwest of Atlanta and can be accessed from Interstate 75. The larger single area of the two and probably the most consistent for better shorebirds is **Thomas Brothers Grass Farm.** This farm is just west of Rome. From the north side of Rome at the intersection of US Highway 27 and Loop 1 (also called Redmond Circle), go west on Loop 1. Look for Mathis Road on the right in 2.6 miles, and at this point follow Loop 1 as it turns left to go south to Georgia Highway 20. You can also come out from the center of Rome about 2.8 miles to get to this intersection, but there are many traffic lights. From Loop 1 and GA 20, go west (right from Loop 1) on GA 20 for 7.5 miles to GA 100. Turn left, and drive south 1.3 miles to an unnamed dirt road with a "Thomas Bros. Grass" sign, and turn left again. (Also see map, page 34.) Drive 0.4 mile to a large overhead powerline and scan for waders in the wet area on the left, which can be good for sparrows later in the fall, too. Continue another 0.1 mile to the office and check in for permission during the week or on Saturday mornings. On Saturday afternoons and Sundays birders are allowed in anyway, but stay on the established roads and out of the way of all equipment.

There is basically one main road that goes to the left from the office for about 1.4 miles. Slowly drive along here and check out any interesting areas or birds you find. Be sure to scan the small ditch along the right side of the road and the small pond on your left at the end of the road. You may miss birds on the first pass, so keep checking all the likely-looking habitat along here. If there are good birds around, they will probably be mentioned on the RBA (Rare Bird Alert), as this spot gets covered pretty thoroughly.

The **Atlanta Sod Farm** consists of three discrete sections, all west of Cartersville. The following directions will take you in a loop to all three. From I-75, take Exit 288 (old 124). This is both GA 113 and Main Street. Go west toward Cartersville, which is the only way you can go. After you pass by all the stores and restaurants, follow GA 113 through several turns and note Etowah Drive on your left at 2.8 miles (this is at a hard right turn following the turns for GA 113). The Etowah Mounds historical site is 2.4 miles down that road on the left; it is not only interesting from a historical standpoint but has pretty good birding as well. The large grassy areas sometimes have Horned Larks all year and Bobolinks during migration.

Continuing on to the sod farm, follow GA 113 another 2 miles to Euharlee Road (4.8 miles from I-75), and turn right. Go 2.6 miles to Stiles Road, and turn left on this dirt road (note the "Atlanta Sod" sign; the "Stiles Road" sign is easy to miss). Take this loop for 0.8 mile to the office, and get permission inside. During weekends (office is also open Saturday morning), birders are allowed to drive along established roads and walk along established roads where there are closed wire gates. If you aren't sure whether it's an established road, stay off! This section is called Office Farm. A dirt road goes off to the left at the office, and leads to the Etowah River past several areas of sod. Again look over all the areas you can see from the roads, and carefully check puddles or other casual water. After rain these roads can be very muddy, and should be walked, not driven.

One other area to bird in this section of the sod farm is a permanent pond just past the office. Continue on Stiles Road 0.2 mile past the office to a small stone building by the road, and park on the right. Walk along the trail out into the field on the right, and note the pond down in a depression to your right. There are often shorebirds here, and it's always worth a stop. Note also the fields with tall grass in them for Grasshopper Sparrows in summer. When finished here, you can continue on Stiles Road for 0.9 mile back to Euharlee Road. The last section of fields sometimes has Loggerhead Shrikes, tough to find this far north in Georgia.

The second section of Atlanta Sod (Brandon Farm) is usually walk-in only. If you are lucky enough to be here when the gate is down, check in with farm personnel to make sure they don't lock you in when they leave. From your current position at the end of Stiles Road, turn left on Euharlee Road for 2.7 miles to Cliff Nelson Road, and turn left. This turn is 1 mile past the Etowah River, and is the second left. Drive 0.4 mile on Cliff Nelson Road, and turn left on Hardin Bridge Road. Note the intersection at 0.6 mile, which is Euharlee–Five Forks Road, but don't take it. Hardin Bridge Road becomes a dirt road 0.8 mile past that intersection, and in another 0.2 mile you will pass a great-looking swamp on the right; however, there are rarely any birds here. Continue for another 0.7 mile to some large overhead powerlines, and keep your eyes open for Eastern Meadowlarks, Grasshopper Sparrows, and Northern Bobwhites.

Note the cable-gated sod area on your right, and walk in. There are two sod areas, one to your right immediately below the powerlines and one to your left. The area on the left is slightly uphill and hidden by a large hedgerow (which is good for Indigo Buntings and Blue Grosbeaks). The main road in goes away from Hardin Bridge Road for 0.3 mile, and then turns left and forms a 2.3-mile loop back to the entrance. There is a low spot under the powerlines on the right as you come in that is frequently wet; there is also a wet area in the left part, which almost always has some water and is worth scanning.

To get to the third area (Harris Farm), go back on Hardin Bridge Road 1.7 miles to Euharlee–Five Forks Road and turn left. In 1.7 miles, turn left on Taylorsville-Macedonia Road at the five-way intersection. This is the largest road to your left. Go 2.8 miles to a T intersection at Old Alabama Road, and turn right. Turn left in 0.2 mile at the unsigned Taylorsville Road (soon becomes Euharlee Street). At 0.8 mile, just after you cross a creek, turn left at the second dirt road by the "Atlanta Sod" sign into the farm. This road goes back less than 1 mile and is the only road you can drive on. As in the other sections, check in with sod personnel (if you see them). Some of the fields bordering this farm may have been allowed to grow fairly tall, so watch for brushy-habitat birds in them.

When finished here, turn left out of the farm onto Euharlee Street. In 1.2 miles at GA 113, turn left. Go 10.4 miles on GA 113 to get back to your starting point at GA 113 and Euharlee Road.

In summer there is a Cliff Swallow colony under the GA 113 bridge over the Etowah River, 0.3 mile before this intersection. To view them, take the small dirt

American Golden-Plover.

road to the right just past the bridge, and go under the bridge. The Cliff Swallow nests are either on the north side of the bridge (the side facing the railroad track) or underneath the bridge. There are also Barn Swallow nests here.

General information: Both of these areas are working sod farms, and birders are allowed in through the generosity of the owners. Please be courteous to all workers and stay out of the way of any equipment or work vehicles. These dirt roads can be deceptively muddy after rain, which not only could get you stuck but also could churn up their roads, so if in doubt, walk in. For both farms, there are many restaurants, gas stations, and hotels in Rome and Cartersville.

ADDITIONAL HELP

DeLorme map grid: Thomas Brothers Grass Farm; page 18, C3. Atlanta Sod; page 19, E7/8.

For more information: Greater Rome CVB, (800) 444-1834; Cartersville CVB, (800) 733-2280.

4 Pine Log Wildlife Management Area to Carter's Lake

Counties: Bartow, Murray, and Gilmer.
Habitats: Pine forest, mixed pine/hardwood forest, upland hardwood forest, young pine shrubland, freshwater marsh shrubland, grassy field, reservoir, river.
Key birds: Bachman's Sparrow, Blue-winged Warbler, Chuck-will's-widow, Whip-poor-will, Grasshopper Sparrow, Bald Eagle, Cliff and Tree Swallows, Louisiana Waterthrush, Kentucky and Hooded Warblers.
Best times to bird: May through October.

The birding: This section is made up of several sites located along US 411 going north from Cartersville toward Chatsworth. The first is Pine Log WMA, with excellent spring and summer birding for migrants and breeding species in hardwood and mixed forest. The entrance gate is closed except for a short time when you can drive in, but either way the birding can be rewarding. There is another gate with a small area of slightly different habitat where you can see Bachman's Sparrows. The next site is a loop over Johnson Mountain, for roadside birding along grassy fields and a pine plantation. This short loop can be done in about an hour, and gets you close to grass- and scrub-preferring species. The last site is Carter's Lake, with year-round scanning potential and some uncommon breeders as well. There are a few waterfowl here in winter, and also some breeding species in the nearby forest. You probably could hit all these sites in one day, but it would be a long one.

Directions: These sites are arranged from south to north along US 411. Starting from Exit 293 (old 126) on Interstate 75, turn right on US Highway 411. The mileages assume you came from the south on I-75, so if you came from the north add 0.3 mile and turn left on US 411. Turning north on US 411, drive 2.6 miles to the town of White. You will pass Jean's Restaurant on the left as you get into town (2.2 miles from I-75), a change from the fast-food places along I-75. At 2.6 miles, turn right on Stamp Creek Road.

Pine Log WMA is 3.6 miles down Stamp Creek Road, with an entrance on the left. If you want a map, stop at the check-in station on the left just before the entrance. Also there is a small dirt road on the right just past the entrance, which leads down to a small creek; both Kentucky Warblers and Louisiana Waterthrushes breed here. Note: The main gate is open to vehicles only from March 20 to May 15 during turkey season, but you can walk or bicycle in the rest of the year. The turkey hunters tend to vanish into the woods and I have never had a problem birding here during this season. Most of the roads are good gravel roads, with about the first 2 to 3 miles suitable for passenger cars, although they do get worse during periods of heavy logging and/or rain.

Starting at the gate, drive in on Grassy Hollow Road and watch the large field on your right for Blue-winged, Yellow-throated, and Prairie Warblers; Yellow-breasted Chats; Field Sparrows; Blue Grosbeaks; and Indigo Buntings. All breed

4 Pine Log Wildlife Management Area to Carter's Lake

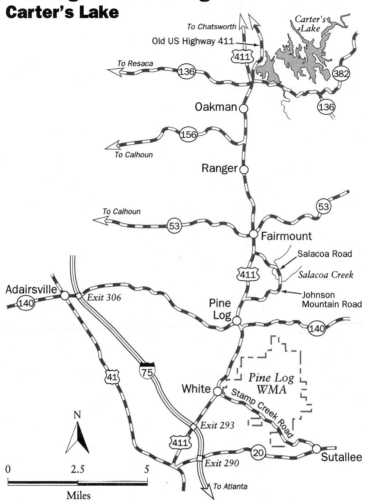

here except the Blue-winged Warbler, but it is pretty regular during migration in late April and early May. You can find these same species in all the open areas in this WMA, and since this area is heavily logged, there are lots of open areas. Other species in open areas are White-eyed Vireo, and both Pine Warbler and Great Crested Flycatcher along the edges. At 0.8 mile from the entrance you will cross Davis Branch; check here for Hooded and Kentucky Warblers. Stamp Creek runs parallel to you on the left, and you may hear Louisiana Waterthrushes, which breed along the length of the stream.

As you drive or walk this road, especially early in the morning, you may find birds anywhere, so keep your eyes and ears open. During peak migration in late April and early May, there can be up to 20 species of warblers along this road. The forested areas have breeding Wood Thrushes, Summer and Scarlet Tanagers,

4 Pine Log Wildlife Management Area

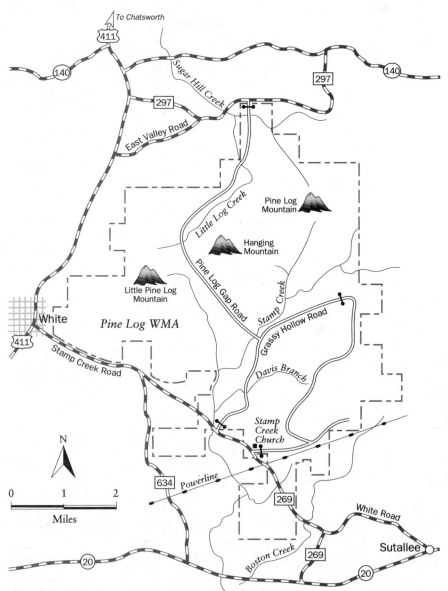

Ovenbirds, and Red-eyed Vireos as well. Look for woodpeckers, including Red-headed and Pileated. Rose-breasted Grosbeaks and Baltimore Orioles may be seen during migration. Black-throated Green Warblers are pretty common during migration, and may breed here at the higher elevations.

Just past Davis Branch is another open area, and both Chuck-will's-widows and Whip-poor-wills breed here. If you can get here before dawn, you will certainly hear them and may see them in your headlights along the road. During daytime, continue

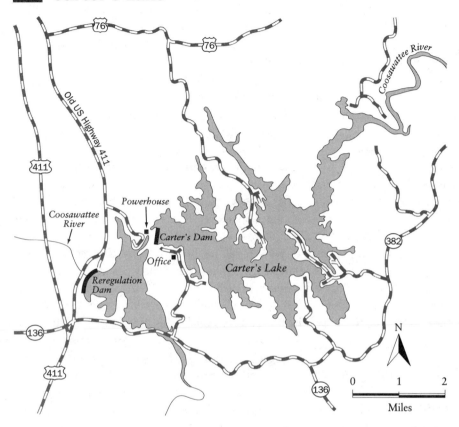

another 0.5 mile to cross another small stream and check for Hooded and Kentucky Warblers again (look for them, as well as Louisiana Waterthrushes and Acadian Fly-catchers, at all stream crossings). In another 0.3 mile (total 1.6 miles) you will reach a turn to the left. This is Pine Log Gap Road. Both ways offer good birding and deterio-rating roads, but staying on Grassy Hollow is best in a car. Continuing ahead, in 0.4 mile (total 2) there is a road to the right that offers the same types of birding as the rest of this area, but in about 0.5 mile the road becomes impassable except to four-wheel-drive vehicles. Continue on Grassy Hollow, birding as you go, for another 0.7 mile to a small spur road on your right. This goes downhill for 0.1 mile to a lovely camping spot in the middle of hardwood forest, good for both birding and camping by another small stream. Grassy Hollow continues for only another 0.2 mile when you reach a locked gate, although you can walk beyond it to another stream crossing. Go back to Pine Log Gap Road when you have finished here.

If you want more birding, cross the concrete bridge over Stamp Creek on Pine Log Gap Road, watching for Louisiana Waterthrush. This road continues almost 7 miles, with good birding all along it, but mostly similar to what you have just done. This road is suitable for high-clearance vehicles only, although four-wheel-drive is usually not necessary. There are several spur trails to walk, such as those at 1.4 miles and 1.7 miles from this intersection, and there are stream crossings at 1.5 and 1.9 miles. At 2.3 miles the road starts to climb to its highest point between Little Pine Log and Hanging Mountains, and increasing dryness results in different wildflowers. This is also the roughest section of road.

As you start down at 3.6 miles, you will cross another stream at 4 miles, and at 4.1 miles is another small spur to the left. This goes 0.1 mile to another good camping spot next to a small pond, also worth birding. At 4.7 miles is another walking trail, and at 5 miles you get to a large field to look for lingering sparrows. After the field you are back in good hardwood forest; there is a stream ford at 5.5 miles. At 6.4 miles you will find a small lake on your right, with an area of open fields on your left, starting at 6.8 miles. This area is good for Wild Turkey. The end of this road is at 7 miles at a locked gate at East Valley Road, but the open fields here do have breeding Grasshopper Sparrows. Return to the entrance the same way you came in, birding any spots you want to try again.

There is another part of the WMA you might want to visit. To get there, turn left on Stamp Creek Road, and drive 0.8 mile. Immediately past the Stamp Creek Baptist Church on your left is another entrance to the WMA, although the sign is hidden until you turn in. This road is not suitable for passenger cars, so park near the entrance. If you have a high-clearance vehicle, this gate is open on the same schedule as the other one. Take this road for 0.6 mile, crossing three small streams, for the same species as the rest of the WMA; watch for the same open-area species also. Turn left at 0.6 mile on a smaller dirt road and go up the hill 0.5 mile to an area where several roads converge. Park in the open area on the left. Walk the "road" (very rough), which is the hardest right turn from the way you came in (a 90-degree turn right).

As this road bends right, start checking the trees on the left. There are still some large scattered pines here, and this area is not only good for Yellow-throated Warblers and the other open-area species, but has had several Bachman's Sparrows in recent summers. Watch for them on higher perches than most sparrows use, and listen for their clear, trilling song. This species is pretty rare this far north in Georgia. This area is also good for Chipping and Field Sparrows. For most of 1999, Red Crossbills were found; watch for them also, although it is not known yet whether they are regular. You can of course also explore any road you wish, but the habitat overall is similar to the other part of the WMA accessed from Pine Log Gap Road. This section is also very good for Chuck-will's-widow and Whip-poor-will. Return to Stamp Creek Road and then to US 411 when finished here.

The **Johnson Mountain Loop** is another 6.9 miles north on US 411 (9.6 miles from I-75). You will pass a gas station at 5.3 miles with Purple Martin houses behind it. The right turn on Johnson Mountain Road is just past a bridge over Pine Log Creek. After 0.5 mile, you will enter a large area of grassy hay fields. Look here for Grasshopper Sparrows, Eastern Bluebirds, Eastern Kingbirds, Blue Grosbeaks, Indigo Buntings, and Eastern Meadowlarks. Listen for the Grasshopper

Sparrow's insect-like buzzy song, and carefully look along the fences along all roads. This land is all private, so do not leave the road.

At 1.3 miles you will start to climb and enter a forest, and at 2.1 miles you will come out into an area planted in pines. This area is full of Prairie Warblers, Yellow-breasted Chats, and Field Sparrows. The Prairie Warblers are very curious and will often fly in to "pishing" noises. This area of pines ends at 2.8 miles, but before then you will see some yellow gates on the left at an old dirt road. During the mid-1990s there were a few Bachman's Sparrows here, but they have not been seen in the past three years. At 2.8 miles you will reenter the forest, coming into more pines and the same species at 3.1 miles, until 4 miles. As you drive downhill, stop at the bridge at 4.2 miles for Wood Thrushes and Louisiana Waterthrushes. There is almost always an Eastern Phoebe nest under this bridge. At 4.4 miles you will reach an unsigned T intersection. Turn left on Salacoa Road.

In 0.9 mile you will cross the stream again, and you can park just beyond the bridge to the right to enjoy this spot. During migration there are often Bobolinks in the field where you are parked, and this bridge usually has an Eastern Phoebe nest. There are plenty of Blue Grosbeaks and Indigo Buntings here as well. Continue 2.3 miles to return to US 411, 3.4 miles north of where you started.

Carter's Lake is another 12.1 miles north (right), which is 25 miles from I-75. Turn right on GA 136 and drive 0.4 mile to Old US 411. Turn left, and drive 0.7 mile to a paved road on the right, which leads 0.2 mile to a small parking area. You will find portable restrooms here. The structure in front of you is the Reregulation Dam; you can climb up the dam over the rocks to scan the lower lake above it. This is not a great place for waterfowl, but there are a few migrant ducks at times. There are frequently Double-crested Cormorants here, and sometimes loons or grebes in winter. Bald Eagles nest at this lake, so always look for them. Cliff Swallows nest on this dam right over the water and usually fly around the area with Barn Swallows.

The Songbird Trail starts from the parking lot and goes about a mile back toward GA 136. It passes through some woods and several marshy areas worth birding in all seasons. This area is full of sparrows in winter. Common Yellowthroats nest here, as do Northern Rough-winged Swallows. Return to US 411, and turn right. In 1.5 miles, after crossing the Coosawatee River, turn right at the "Powerhouse" sign, and drive 0.8 mile to the powerhouse area. This open area is good for Northern Bobwhites and sparrows in winter; check the birdhouses for Eastern Bluebirds and Tree Swallows. This is one of the few places in Georgia where Tree Swallows nest. Scan the lake again, and continue to watch for eagles. When finished, go back to GA 136 and turn left.

After 1.8 miles you will cross Talking Rock Creek, with places to park along the road. This is another Cliff Swallow nesting location, and there are sometimes ducks or waders in the shallow waters. Continue 0.3 mile, and turn left for the resource manager's office and dam. There is a split in the road at 1.8 miles. The right split takes you 0.4 mile to the visitor center, with maps, restrooms, and a great view of the lake. If you wish to explore the upper lake, get one of the Carter's Lake maps here. The left split takes you 1 mile to a parking area below the main dam but above the Reregulation Dam, with a good view of both areas. This is another place to scan for waterfowl in winter or Bald Eagles anytime.

When you are through at Carter's Lake, you can return south on US 411 or go west on GA 136 about 15 miles to I-75. At this point you are about 13 miles south of Chatsworth on US 411, so you can also go north to access the Cohuttas or other spots in northern Georgia from there.

General information: Any of these three areas can be birded by themselves or as part of an all-day trip. If you are continuing north you will be near Site 5, the Cohutta WMA, which includes the Lake Conasauga Songbird Management Area. South of this section are the Atlanta-area sites. There are several small towns along US Highway 411, and most have gas. A few have restaurants, but lodging is available only out at Interstate 75 or up in Chatsworth. The visitor center at Carter's Lake has numerous exhibits about the lake.

ADDITIONAL HELP

DeLorme map grid: Pine Log WMA; page 19, C10. Johnson Mountain; page 19, A/B 10. Carter's Lake; page 13, F/G 10.
For more information: Georgia Department of Natural Resources, Carter's Lake Resource Manager's Office, (706) 334-2248; Chatsworth–Murray County Chamber of Commerce, (706) 695-6060.

5 Cohutta Wildlife Management Area

Counties: Fannin, Gilmer, and Murray.
Habitats: Mixed pine/hardwood forest, upland hardwood forest, beaver pond.
Key birds: Blackburnian, Chestnut-sided, Black-throated Blue, Black-throated Green, and Hooded Warblers; Ovenbird; Eastern Wood-Pewee; Scarlet Tanager; Blue-headed Vireo; Dark-eyed Junco.
Best times to bird: May through September.

The birding: The Cohutta WMA is a huge area of forest in north Georgia, of more than 95,000 acres. This site covers only a small area along good gravel roads in the southern part of the WMA, but the whole area is worth exploring for those with the time and curiosity. The Lake Conasauga Songbird Trail area is great summer birding for Georgia mountain specialties, and nearby Betty Gap and the surrounding area is the best place in Georgia to hope for Red Crossbills in winter, although this is a real long shot. Good Forest Service roads take you to both sites, and the birding can be easy along the road, or more strenuous on hikes.

Directions: This vast area can be accessed in many ways, but the primary one for these specific sites is from the town of Chatsworth, just east of Dalton in the

Cohutta Wildlife Management Area

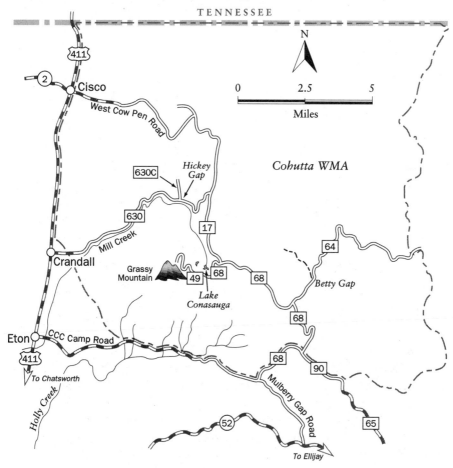

TENNESSEE

Cohutta WMA

Hickey Gap

Grassy Mountain

Lake Conasauga

Betty Gap

Mulberry Gap Road

To Chatsworth

To Ellijay

northwest corner of the state. Go north on US Highway 411 4.2 miles to Eton. Look for CCC Camp Road on your right, and turn right. Follow this paved road for 6 miles until it changes to a good gravel road; note the Purple Martin houses along the right side. Although this section is set up to bird the higher elevations, feel free to stop anywhere along the road to bird. As you get into the better forest and climb, watch for Ruffed Grouse along the road, although these birds are rarely seen. The stream you are driving along has breeding Louisiana Waterthrushes. At 10 miles from US 411 you reach Mulberry Gap Road; turn left at the sign for Lake Conasauga on Forest Road 68. Follow this road 2.4 miles to another intersection, and turn left again to stay on FR 68. There is another sign for the lake here. Climb the turning road for 3.3 miles to the intersection with FR 64, again stopping anywhere you wish to bird. Turn left to stay on FR 68.

You are now approaching the lake, and the birding is good anywhere along here. Open areas along FR 68 have Chestnut-sided Warblers and Indigo Buntings.

5 Lake Conasauga Songbird Management Area

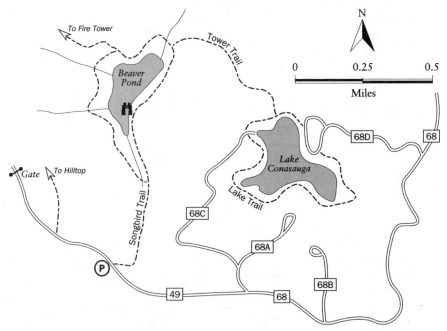

The more wooded areas have Wood Thrushes, Red-eyed and Blue-headed Vireos, Eastern Wood-Pewees, Ovenbirds, and Hooded Warblers. Worm-eating Warblers breed here as well, but in small numbers. Bird along FR 68 for 3.9 miles to FR 17 on the right. This is an alternate route out. Continuing on FR 68, you will see several camping areas for Lake Conasauga. The first is Camping Loop A, on your right in 0.4 mile, followed by Camping Loop B another 0.7 mile farther. These areas are worth birding if you have extra time after you try the Songbird Trail. In another 0.1 mile FR 68 continues straight to a picnic area by Lake Conasauga, 0.3 mile ahead; the only left turn leads down to a boat ramp another 0.6 mile. Both spots are worth checking if you have time later, but for now turn left on FR 49. Park in the small parking area at 0.3 mile on your left. Though this is signed as a fee area, the fee is specifically for campers; there is no fee for hikers or birders. You will be using the Songbird Management Area Trail across FR 49. There are restrooms here.

The trail runs around a beaver pond, through managed coniferous and hard-woods, for about a mile. Go past the restrooms and follow the trail signs. Look and listen carefully throughout, for the best birding is along here. In the conifers be especially alert for Blackburnian and Black-throated Green Warblers, and watch in woods for Black-throated Blue Warblers anywhere along this trail. Dark-eyed Juncos breed here, as do Cedar Waxwings and Hairy Woodpeckers. Black-and-white and Hooded Warbler are also found in this area. Check the wet areas of forest for Acadian Flycatchers. When you have birded the trail area, you can either go back to some of the spots you passed on the way up, try another area, or exit the way you came. If you prefer to exit to the east toward Ellijay, with its shops and restaurants, turn left at Mulberry Gap Road on your way out and follow it onto GA 52 about 5 miles into town.

There is another small area worth walking to from your car if you have time. Continue on FR 49 on foot from where you are parked (away from the lake), and in about 0.2 mile there will be a dirt Forest Service road to the right. It leads to a small hilltop that has recently been burned in an attempt to provide appropriate habitat for the Golden-winged Warbler. Though it has not been found here as of fall 1999, it is worth looking for. There are lots of Chestnut-sided Warblers and Dark-eyed Juncos in here as well.

In winter, you can also try for Red Crossbills, but you won't have most of the other species mentioned so far. The crossbills are very difficult to find, and are seen on only a fraction of trips birders make here. If they have been seen recently, that news will certainly be on the RBA. As a matter of fact you won't find much of anything up here in winter! Dark-eyed Juncos will still be around, and you have a slightly better chance for Ruffed Grouse along any of the Forest Service roads, along with some of the more common permanent residents.

One area that has been slightly better over recent years for Red Crossbills is found by going to where FR 68 nears the top of the climbing portion and FR 64 goes to the right (as you go up the hill). In winter take this road 1.4 miles to Betty Gap. This area has had as many reports of this rare species as any other, both in the conifers along FR 64 and along the trail. It can be very cold up here in winter, and the road may be icy, but this is as good a place as any to search for this elusive species. You can also continue along FR 64 another 2.2 miles to the Mountaintown

Mountaintown Overlook along Forest Road 64.

Overlook, a nice wooden overlook with benches to watch from. If it is windy, as it often is in winter, this is usually a waste of time. To search another area for cross-bills, take the FR 17 exit described above from Lake Conasauga. The first intersection is FR 630. The trail to the right at this intersection (FR 630C) has had cross-bills, and after you turn left on FR 630 the trail to your right at Hickey Gap has also had them. Both of these last two spots are super long shots. You can follow FR 630 down to US 411 at the town of Crandall when you are finished.

General information: The camping areas at Lake Conasauga are nice but pretty heavily used in summer. Lodging is also available in Chatsworth, Dalton, or Ellijay, along with restaurants and other services. To explore other parts of this WMA, you should get a map, either from the Georgia Department of Natural Resources, or from the local check station, which are on both ends of the WMA. The easiest check station to get to is on the west side on East Cow Pen Road about 2.5 miles east of US Highway 411 from the town of Cisco (Cow Pen Road is opposite Georgia Highway 2 at US 411). If you come up here in winter, it can be very cold and the roads may not be in very good shape, so exercise caution. This area is also near several other sites in this book, from Cumberland Plateau in the west (Site 1), Pine Log WMA to Carter's Lake to the south (Site 4), and Brasstown Bald (Site 8) or Neel's Gap to Lake Winfield Scott (Site 7) to the east.

ADDITIONAL HELP

DeLorme map grid: page 13, C9/10; page 14, D1 and C1.
For more information: Chattahoochee National Forest, Cohutta Ranger District, (706) 695-6736; Chatsworth–Murray County Chamber of Commerce, (706) 695-6060; Dalton–Whitfield County CVB, (800) 331-3258.

6 Ivy Log Gap

Counties: Towns and Union.
Habitats: Mixed pine/hardwood forest, upland hardwood forest.
Key birds: Cerulean, Blackburnian, Chestnut-sided Warblers; Scarlet Tanager; Kentucky Warbler; American Redstart; Ovenbird.
Best times to bird: May and June.

The birding: Ivy Log Gap Road is a good condition dirt Forest Service road running through excellent upland hardwood habitat in north Georgia. You can see most of the higher-elevation breeding species that occur in the state here, with the added bonus of Cerulean Warblers. Though nesting has not been confirmed, there are usually a few birds along this road that certainly act like they are on territory! The road is wide enough to stop on easily, and you can bird at your own pace. Early morning is, of course, best because that's when most of the singing is going on. In early May you may see migrants as well as the local breeders.

6 Ivy Log Gap

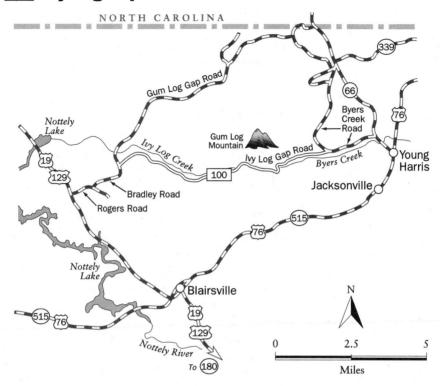

Gum Log Gap Road

339

66

Byers Creek Road

76

Nottely Lake

Ivy Log Creek

Gum Log Mountain

Ivy Log Gap Road

Byers Creek

Young Harris

19

129

100

Jacksonville

Bradley Road

Rogers Road

515

76

Nottely Lake

Blairsville

N

19

515 76

129

0   2.5   5

Nottely River

To 180

Miles

Directions: This loop starts in the town of Young Harris, which is at the intersection of US Highway 76, Georgia Highway 2, and GA 66. Note that US 76 and APD Highway 515 are the same—and that the road is also called the Appalachian Highway. It is in the Chattahoochee National Forest about 8.6 miles east of Blairsville on US 76. From Young Harris, go north on GA 66 0.7 mile and turn left on Byers Creek Road. In 1.7 miles you will see Ivy Log Gap Road (Forest Road 100) on your left. Turn left, and set your odometer to zero. Some species can be found all along this road, at almost all elevations; start looking for them now. These include Hooded and Black-and-white warblers, Ovenbird, Eastern Wood-Pewee, Wood Thrush, Yellow-throated Vireo, and Indigo Bunting. There are also a few Worm-eating Warblers, but they are widely scattered. Additional species are found only in this beginning lower stretch of Ivy Log Gap Road, such as Common Yellowthroat, American Redstart, and Kentucky Warbler. The best way to find any of these is to listen for their songs and then hunt for the source. Even if you don't know all the songs, you can learn them while you are birding along, as you find the singers. The easiest way to do this is to drive slowly until you see or hear something, and then stop and walk or look for as long as you want. The road becomes dirt at 0.8 mile and then starts climbing.

At 2.6 miles, you will reach an angled T intersection as you leave Towns County and enter Union County. Follow the road to the left. Look for a thinning in the forest as you reach a formerly clearcut area on both sides. This area has lots of Chestnut-sided Warblers and a few Yellow-breasted Chats. As you continue to climb, look and listen for the higher-elevation species, such as Blackburnian and Black-throated Green Warblers, Blue-headed Vireo, and Scarlet Tanager. The best areas historically for Ceruleans have been between 3.5 miles and 6 miles. Keep in mind that both Ceruleans and Blackburnians are canopy species, rarely found close to the ground, so you need to be looking and listening up. Areas with good forest on the downhill side of the road may be easier on your neck, but the birds don't always cooperate in this manner! At this point you are at maximum elevation for the road, around 3,000 feet. Continue to bird the entire road until it ends at 9.6 miles.

At this point you have reached Bradley Road, which is paved. Turn left and go 0.5 mile, then turn right on Rogers Road for 0.7 mile. You now have a choice to make. To your right on US 129/19 in 3.7 miles is the Ivy Log Creek arm of Nottely Lake. If the lake is down, there is an area of mudflat near this bridge that has shorebirds during migration. The lake is not usually down to this degree, but it's close enough to check. You may also find waders here under the same conditions, and it's worth looking for waterfowl in winter even though they are rare here in the mountains. If you don't wish to try this, turn left on US 129/19 for 2.7 miles and you will be back in Blairsville at US 76/GA 2.

One other quick place to stop is the ranger station near here along US 76/GA 2. Turn right on US 76 and in 1.5 miles look for it on the right. There are exhibits here, and they sell maps and books also. The tall pine trees around the building always have a few Yellow-throated Warblers.

General information: This area is usually cool early in the morning, but can be pretty warm by midday. Make sure you take enough water or other fluids, as it may take several hours to bird this wonderful road. There are plenty of gas stations, restaurants, and lodging in both Blairsville and Young Harris, but not much in between, and nothing on Ivy Log Gap Road.

ADDITIONAL HELP

DeLorme map grid: page 15, B7, and B8.
For more information: Chattahoochee National Forest, Brasstown Ranger District, (706) 745-6928; Towns County Chamber of Commerce, (706) 896-4966; Blairsville–Union County Chamber of Commerce, (706) 745-5789.

7 Neel's Gap to Lake Winfield Scott

County: Union.

Habitats: Pine forest, mixed pine/hardwood forest, upland hardwood forest, lake.

Key birds: Canada, Blackburnian, Black-throated Blue, Black-throated Green, and Chestnut-sided Warblers; American Redstart; Veery; Scarlet Tanager; Rose-breasted Grosbeak; Blue-headed Vireo; Acadian Flycatcher.

Best times to bird: May through September.

The birding: This section is made up of several small sites all close together. Any of them can be birded alone or as part of a loop, although some offer only a small enclosed area and others are near very long trails for hikers. This area is also near Brasstown Bald (Site 8). Basically this route takes you along good paved roads to spots where you can either stop along the road to bird or start a morning hike. Several of them offer slightly different sets of birds, so you might want to read the whole section first to choose what interests you most. In addition to breeding species, look for migrants during late spring or early fall.

Directions: Drive south from Blairsville on US Highway 129 for 7.9 miles to Georgia Highway 180 East, the road to Brasstown Bald. Continue on US 129 another 4.8 miles to Byron Herbert Reece Park on your right, and park here. This is where the birding starts, by accessing the Appalachian Trail. Note: If you want detailed hiking information, drive another 0.5 mile south on US 129 to the Walasi-Yi Center, which has supplies, maps, and information about area trails, including the

Female Black-throated Green Warbler.

7 Neel's Gap to Lake Winfield Scott
8 Brasstown Bald

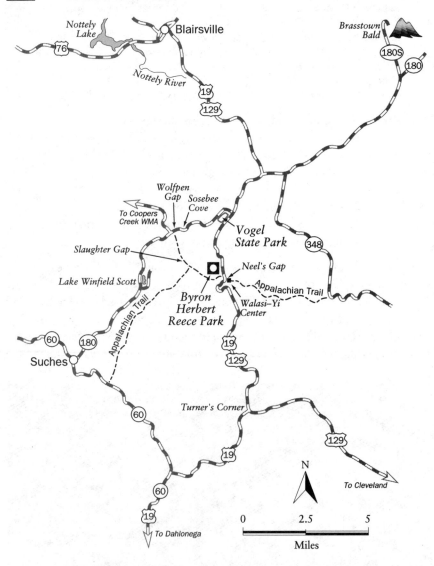

Appalachian Trail. You cannot park at the center to bird, so return to Reece Park when you have the information you need. At Reece Park, walk up the spur trail to the Appalachian Trail, about 0.4 mile. From here you can hike as long or as little as you wish, and there are lots of great birds to see!

Typical sought-after birds of the higher elevations in Georgia include all of the birds listed in the Key Birds section above except Veery and American Redstart. This first section is especially good for Blackburnian Warblers. Other birds to look for are Chestnut-sided, Hooded, Yellow-throated, and Black-and-white Warblers;

Blue-headed and Red-eyed Vireos, Wood Thrushes; Dark-eyed Juncos; Broad-winged Hawks; and Eastern Wood-Pewees. Up higher you can also look for Veeries, Common Ravens, and Canada Warblers. A few of the latter are on this trail approaching Blood Mountain, about 2 miles. When you are finished hiking, return to your car and turn left on US 129 to go north.

In 2.2 miles you will reach Vogel State Park, which has camping and some trails. It is heavily used in summer. Look for Acadian Flycatchers around the campground. Unless you are staying here, continue on US 129 for 0.3 mile and turn left on GA 180 West. This road has much less traffic than US 129 and is easier to bird along. In 2.9 miles from US 129 you will reach Sosebee Cove, with a small parking area on the right. Pull in here for a good short stop, with a couple of small loop trails. One of the benefits of stopping here is that you are on the side of a hill, and species that tend to stay up high in trees will be at eye level for you. Look for the same species as before.

When you are ready, continue on GA 180 for 0.3 mile to Wolfpen Gap and park in the pullout. An entrance to Cooper's Creek Wildlife Management Area is on your right, and offers decent general mountain birding through a series of dirt roads that are usually in pretty good shape. Across GA 180 where you are parked is the beginning of the Duncan Ridge Trail. This trail goes 1.9 miles up a moderate grade to Slaughter Gap, and is blazed blue and yellow because two trails pass here. This trail gets few hikers and has the same species as the other areas. It also gets high enough in the last 0.8 mile to have Canada Warblers. When finished here, continue on GA 180 West.

Another 3.4 miles will take you to Lake Winfield Scott Recreation Area. Turn in to the left, and go 0.2 mile to the $2 fee station. You can either park here or continue 0.6 mile to the camping area and a short 0.3-mile loop around the campground. Bird around the cleared area at the pay station and then walk toward the lake. This is about the most reliable area in Georgia for breeding American Redstarts, but you may have to walk around for a while before you find one. In addition to redstarts, most of the other species from the other spots can also be found here, although in lower numbers, and the walking is generally easier because this spot is mostly level. This is another good spot for Veeries. This is the last stop on this route, so you can return to any spot you want more time in, or depart the area.

General information: Several of these spots offer camping, though in summer many are pretty crowded. There are cabins along US Highway 129, and more conventional lodging in Blairsville, or farther south in Cleveland or Dahlonega. Most restaurants are also where the towns are, but there are many good spots for a picnic lunch. Except for one gas station/general store on US 129 between Georgia Highway 180 East and West, gas is available only in the towns. The Walasi-Yi Center offers detailed hiking information and maps for those who want to get farther away from the roads and people. Brasstown Bald (Site 8) is about 20 minutes away.

ADDITIONAL HELP

DeLorme map grid: page 15, D7, E7.
For more information: Vogel State Park, (706) 745-2628; Chattahoochee National Forest, Brasstown Ranger District, (706) 745-6928; Walasi-Yi Center, (706) 745-6095; Blairsville–Union County Chamber of Commerce, (706) 745-5789.

8 Brasstown Bald

See map on page 52

Counties: Union and Towns.
Habitats: Pine forest, mixed pine/hardwood forest, upland hardwood forest.
Key birds: Common Raven, Ruffed Grouse, Veery, Rose-breasted Grosbeak, Canada and Black-throated Blue Warblers, Scarlet Tanager, Winter Wren.
Best times to bird: May through September.

The birding: Brasstown Bald is the tallest mountain in Georgia at 4,784 feet. Several species that breed only at the highest elevations in the state can be found here pretty easily, and the views are spectacular. This is really the only spot in Georgia to drive into Canada Warbler and Common Raven habitat, but nonbirders can also drive here easily, so the drawback to accessibility is crowds. The entrance road has good general birding along the shoulders as you climb up the mountain, and there are several good trails from the large parking lot, including short ones for birding and long hiking trails. There is a very interesting USDA Forest Service visitor center with exhibits and a platform for scanning. The Neel's Gap to Lake Winfield Scott area (Site 7) is nearby for additional mountain birding.

Directions: From Blairsville, drive south on US Highway 129 for 7.9 miles to Georgia Highway 180. You may also approach from the south by following US 129 north from Cleveland for about 22 miles, or GA 60 from Dahlonega north for about 12 miles to US 129 and then another 12 miles north to GA 180 East. However you get to US 129 and GA 180 East, take GA 180 East for 7.2 miles to GA 180 Spur, the road to Brasstown Bald. The parking lot is 2.5 miles ahead, and there are several pullouts on the way up to stop and bird. The best one is 1.3 miles from GA 180. Look for Wild Turkeys along the road. When you reach the parking lot, pay the $2 fee, and park.

One option is to cruise around the edge of the parking lot and look for birds along the edge. Scan for Common Ravens anytime, and check out any large black birds to make sure they are not crows, which also occur here. Listen for the raven's loud croaking. This is really the best spot in Georgia for these large corvids, so if this is one of your main goals, scan continuously and stay out in the open where you can see them if they fly over. There may also be a few Turkey Vultures soaring, and Broad-winged Hawks breed here. You should find Dark-eyed Juncos and Chestnut-sided Warblers around the edges, along with Indigo Buntings and Eastern

Wood-Pewees. Just slightly into the woods are Blue-headed Vireos, Black-throated Blue and Hooded Warblers, Ovenbirds, Scarlet Tanagers, and Rose-breasted Grosbeaks. Canada Warblers breed throughout this area, but aren't usually out in the open, though you may get lucky. Listen for the ethereal spiraling song of the Veery, and keep your eyes open for this shy thrush. Both Barn and Northern Rough-winged Swallows breed here and are usually flying around the parking lot. There are picnic tables scattered around the edge for a place to stop and rest or just take in the scenery. When you are ready to head up to the visitor center, go back to the entrance end of the parking lot.

There is a shuttle to the top that you can purchase a ride on, but you will bypass most of the birding unless you walk. Some of the trails are steep, so go slowly if you feel tired. As you walk along the short trail to the visitor center (about 0.5 mile), look for the same species listed above. When you come to a small dirt trail cutting across the paved one you are on, turn right. This is Wagon Train Road. This is the best place to look for Ruffed Grouse and Canada Warblers, so proceed slowly and quietly. In about 0.5 mile the trail widens out and becomes rockier; this is where Winter Wrens have nested in recent years. This is the only place in Georgia this species reliably nests, although there are only a couple of pairs. When you have gone as far as you like, return to the paved trail and continue up the mountain. At the top you can check out the exhibits in the Visitor Center (which also has restrooms) or go outside and scan for ravens and hawks from the observation deck.

General information: You can access several long trails from this parking lot; probably the two most interesting for birders are the Arkaqua and Jack's Knob trails. You can find Canada Warblers on both of these. More hiking information is available at the Walasi-Yi Center, on US Highway 129 just south of Georgia Highway 180. The Appalachian Trail is near here also; see Site 7 for it and other nearby birding spots. There are a few opportunities for lodging along US 129, but almost all the gas stations and restaurants are in Blairsville or south in Dahlonega or Cleveland.

ADDITIONAL HELP

DeLorme map grid: page 15, C9.
For more information: Chattahoochee National Forest, Brasstown Ranger District, (706) 745-6928; Walasi-Yi Center, (706) 745-6095; Blairsville–Union County Chamber of Commerce, (706) 745-5789.

9 Rabun Bald

County: Rabun.
Habitats: Mixed pine/hardwood forest, upland hardwood forest.
Key birds: Common Raven, Canada and Black-throated Blue Warblers, Scarlet Tanager, Veery, Rose-breasted Grosbeak, Ruffed Grouse. Nearby: Least and Willow Flycatchers.
Best times to bird: May through September.

The birding: Rabun Bald is the second-highest mountain in Georgia at 4,696 feet, but it has the best view. The summit can be reached by walking about 2 miles up a good Forest Service trail with a moderate grade and plenty of places to stop and bird along the way. There are rarely other people here, which adds to the beauty of this short hike. Nearby are spots to search for both Least and Willow Flycatchers.

Directions: Rabun Bald is best when hiked early in the morning. Drive north from Clayton on US Highway 23/441 through Dillard. Turn right on Georgia Highway 246 1.1 miles north of Dillard (measured from the Dillard House). In 3.7 miles this road becomes North Carolina Highway 106 as you cross into North Carolina. Continue another 3.1 miles (total 6.8 miles) to Hale Ridge Road and turn right. On your right is the region's only ski area, Ski Scaly. You will cross back into Georgia in 1.9 miles; meanwhile, all along this stretch of road, listen for Least Flycatchers. It may be worth pulling onto a couple of the side roads to listen. This small flycatcher is at the extreme southern limit of its breeding range here, and the couple of pairs that breed annually move nest sites along this road each year. In another 0.1 mile, Hale Ridge Road goes left, so stay to the right on the main road, which becomes Bald Mountain Road. As you wind around the curves, listen for Chestnut-sided Warblers, which often call from cutover areas.

When you are 1.3 miles from the fork (3.3 miles from NC 106), turn left on Kelsey Mountain Road; this is just as you start down a hill. Drive 0.2 mile and park near the "Rabun Bald Four-Wheel-Drive (4WD) Only" sign, making sure you don't block any of the driveways. Though you can theoretically drive partway up the mountain, the road is virtually impassable even for high-clearance vehicles, and you will miss many of the birds. Incidentally, when you are finished you can simply continue on Bald Mountain Road another 2.9 miles and you will be back at NC 106. This will take you past the entrance to a golf and residential community called Sky Valley. In some years, a pair of nesting Least Flycatchers is found in here; when this happens, directions will be on the RBA.

At this point you are just under 4,000 feet, and you should start hearing Ovenbirds and Black-throated Green and Black-and-white Warblers. Look and listen for Scarlet Tanagers, Veeries, and the many Dark-eyed Juncos as well. Try to pick the thinner song of the Blue-headed Vireo out from the more numerous Red-eyed Vireos. Take the wide trail to the right past the sign. The first 1.1 miles is a wide Forest Service road through open hardwood forest. Most of the key species are closer to the top, but you may have good birds anywhere along this road. There

9 Rabun Bald
10 Burrell's Ford

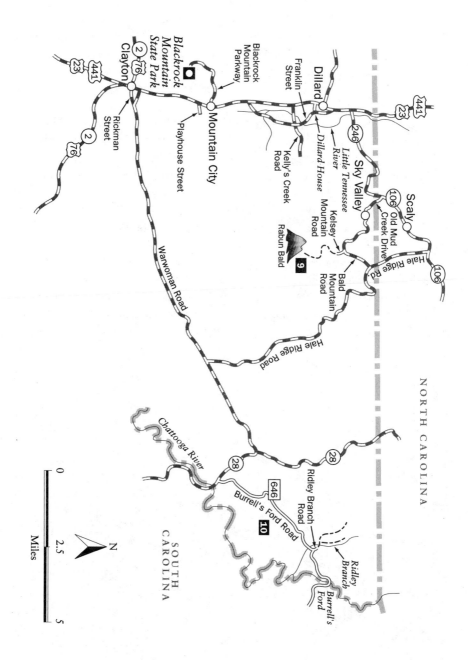

are a few Ruffed Grouse along this road, and some lucky birders have seen them, although this is the exception. Winter Wrens have been seen here in summer but not reliably, and should be reported to the RBA if found. The next landmark is an opening in the trail at the end of the "road," which is at about 4,500 feet. You should start seeing Rose-breasted Grosbeaks, and you might see or hear Common Ravens from here to the summit. The trail becomes much narrower from here to the summit, which is about 0.5 mile. This is the area to look for Canada Warblers. There are several pairs along this trail, though they may not always be easy to see. Your best strategy is to work slowly and listen for the song or sharp "chip" of this secretive species.

There is a nice observation tower at the summit, with a commanding 360-degree view of north Georgia and several adjoining states. This is a great place to bring a picnic lunch and simply enjoy the view or continue searching for ravens. Broad-winged Hawks breed here, and may be soaring along with Turkey Vultures. In fall this is a good hawk-watch station the day after a strong cold front. You may also find small flocks of migrating warblers along the trail in fall. Enjoy the downhill hike when you are finished, and you may find birds you missed on the way up.

Back in Dillard is a fairly reliable spot for Willow Flycatchers. This is one of only a handful of breeding pairs in Georgia, and the only one on public land. Return to Dillard, and turn left into the Dillard House, 1.1 miles south of GA 246 on US 23/441. Turn right at the T in 0.2 mile, which is Franklin Street, and drive downhill 0.8 mile toward the Little Tennessee River. The flycatchers usually nest at the bridge, so

The Little Tennessee River.

park in the pullout beyond the bridge and listen for the *"witz-bew"* song. This site receives a lot of pressure, so please do not use tapes.

There are other species to enjoy while you are waiting, such as the numerous swallows and birds along the river. Yellow Warblers sometimes breed here as well. If you don't find any Willow Flycatchers, continue 0.3 mile past the bridge to Kelly's Creek Road. Check the scrubby area across the intersection on the left, if you can hear above the Indigo Buntings. The last spot to check is the other river crossing, 0.3 mile to your right on Kelly's Creek. In winter scan the Franklin Street sewage pond back at the last intersection for ducks, usually scaups or Wood Ducks. To get to the sewage pond, turn left on Kelly's Creek, instead of right; it is immediately on your left. When you are finished, take Kelly's Creek Road back out to US 23/441, 0.3 mile past the Little Tennessee River.

General information: This area is full of restaurants, gas stations, and lodging in summer, but many businesses close in winter. Blackrock State Park is 2.8 miles south of Kelly's Creek Road on US Highway 23/441, and has both good general summer birding as well as camping, though it is heavily used in summer. Take Blackrock Mountain Parkway up the hill to the park. Another winter spot is just 0.4 mile south on US 23/441; turn left on Play House Street at the sign for Mountain City RV Park, and drive 0.3 mile to Cox Lake Road, then turn right. In 0.2 mile you can scan this small lake for ducks. The Mountain Region of Georgia does not get many ducks in general, but this spot usually has at least a few during the winter months. Another nearby summer site is Burrell's Ford (Site 10).

ADDITIONAL HELP

DeLorme map grid: page 16, A3/4.
For more information: Rabun County CVB, (706) 782-4812; USDA Forest Service, Tallulah Ranger District, (706) 782-3320; Blackrock Mountain State Park, (706) 746-2141.

10 Burrell's Ford

See map on page 57

> **County:** Rabun.
> **Habitats:** Old-growth hemlock–white pine forest, mixed pine/hardwood forest, freshwater marsh scrubland.
> **Key birds:** Red-breasted Nuthatch, Golden-crowned Kinglet, Swainson's Warbler, Whip-poor-will, Worm-eating Warbler, Ovenbird, Louisiana Waterthrush.
> **Best times to bird:** All year, but breeding species are best May through September.

The birding: The area near the Chattooga River along Burrell's Ford Road is not only beautiful but offers some of the only remaining old-growth hemlock–white pine forest in Georgia. Both Red-breasted Nuthatches and Golden-crowned Kinglets have been found here in summer and are probably breeding in very small numbers; this is a good place to look for both species in winter. In summer this nice gravel road road offers looks at many of Georgia's mountain-breeding warblers. There is camping here as well.

Directions: Start in the town of Clayton, on US Highway 441. This is your last chance for food or gas. In the center of town, where US 76 and Georgia Highway 2 come in from the west, take Rickman Street to the east toward South Carolina. This is slightly north of where US 76 heads east from Clayton—don't take that by mistake. On Rickman, proceed 0.5 mile to a stop sign and turn right on Warwoman Road. Drive 13.2 miles to GA 28, and turn right. In 1.7 miles, on the left is Forest Road 646 (Burrell's Ford Road). Before going up that road, continue on GA 28 another 0.4 mile to a small pullout on the left, just before the Chattooga River and South Carolina. The small marsh here is worth birding for a few minutes in any season. Look for warblers in spring and fall, and sparrows in winter. There are almost always Dark-eyed Juncos by the hordes in winter. Go back to FR 646, and turn right.

You are starting at about 1,800 feet. There is good birding all along this road in summer; it is 16.8 miles to the river again. The old-growth forest is mostly within the last half mile. To bird the road, drive until you see an interesting spot or hear something, which won't take long. You may also want to just walk along and return for your vehicle. At night you may be deafened by the Whip-poor-wills all along this road. An especially nice area is 5.2 miles down the road, where a small stream comes in from the left. This is Ridley Branch Road, though there is no sign. You can't drive this road, but it offers good hiking as well as good birding.

There is a fork down this road just after the stream ford, and both sides are good hiking. There is also an area used by many campers but it is not an official campground. The right fork offers a nice fairly strenuous hike uphill into more good habitat, but don't try it unless you are in excellent shape. The area along this road near FR 646 is fairly cool, easy walking, and has all the local warblers in summer, including the Swainson's Warbler and Louisiana Waterthrush, which have very similar songs. Listen for the waterthrush's extra ending. Hooded Warblers are plentiful here, as are Northern Parulas, and there are a few Worm-eating and Black-throated Green Warblers as well. Listen for Yellow-throated Warblers in areas of pine.

Back on FR 646, in another 0.4 mile you will reach maximum elevation of 2,500 feet for this road. From here the good birding continues down a gentle slope toward the river. The last half mile before the Chattooga is the best old-growth forest, and this is an excellent place to look for Red-breasted Nuthatches in any season. Listen for the toy horn sound of this curious nuthatch. Golden-crowned Kinglets are found throughout this area in winter, and this is the same area to look for them in summer. There are very few of either of these two species here in summer, but both are worth looking for and should be reported to the RBA when found. The river is worth stopping at just because it is so beautiful. There is more old-growth forest on the South Carolina side, as well as an official campground. You have now dropped to about 2,100 feet elevation. As with most summer birding, early morning is best. As a last note, Red Crossbills have been reported here but are extremely rare, and you would be incredibly fortunate to find any. Please report them if you do!

General information: This area offers many recreational opportunities, especially in summer. Rabun Bald (Site 9) is nearby, and so are the flycatcher spots. There are lots of brochures at the welcome center on US Highway 441 just north of Rickman Street for activities such as river rafting on the Chattooga, and there are loads of hotels, motels, and more rustic things such as bed and breakfasts and cabin rentals. For nonbirding companions, there are many antique stores close by, many general hikes, and waterfalls. Be aware that this area can be very busy in summer, and you would be wise to make plans for lodging early.

ADDITIONAL HELP

DeLorme map grid: page 16, A5, B5.
For more information: Rabun County CVB, (706) 782-4812; USDA Forest Service, Tallulah Ranger District, (706) 782-3320.

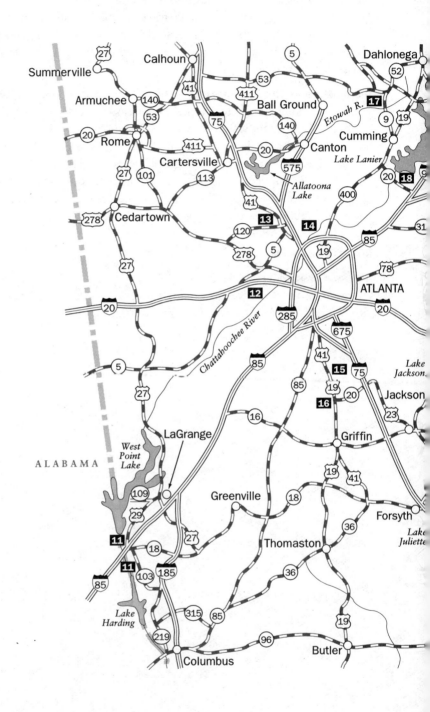

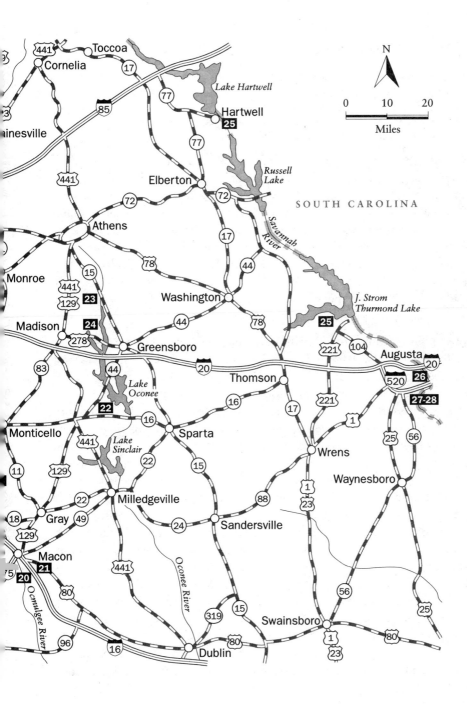

Piedmont Region

11 West Point Dam and Nearby Spots

Counties: Harris and Troup.
Habitats: Pine forest, mixed pine/hardwood forest, weedy fields, freshwater marshland, reservoir.
Key birds: Common Loon, Horned Grebe, gulls, ducks, Wild Turkey.
Best times to bird: October through March.

The birding: This section will cover West Point Lake Dam and the Blanton Creek Wildlife Management Area. Whereas the entire lake can be good birding, this section concentrates on the dam area for waterfowl, which is one of the best areas for these migrants in Georgia. The dam is also good in winter for gulls, and has hosted several rarities over the past few years. Blanton Creek WMA is not far downstream on the Chattahoochee River, and has a good marsh area for dabbling ducks as well as some good general land-birding in forests and fields. The two dams to the south on the Chattahoochee River (Lake Harding and Goat Rock) are currently off-limits to birding, but directions are included in the hope that these areas will once again become accessible.

Directions: This section starts from the north, but could easily be birded in reverse order. To begin at **West Point Lake,** exit Interstate 85 at Exit 2 (old 1). Go west toward the Alabama border on Georgia Highway 18, 1.4 miles to the town of West Point, which is the best spot for food or gas along this route. Turn right on US Highway 29/GA 14 for 3.3 miles to Resource Management Drive and turn left. There is a large sign for West Point Lake here. At 1.6 miles on this road, the resource manager's office is on your right; it has exhibits, maps, restrooms, and information; you can pick up a map to bird other areas of the lake. The woods around the office usually have a few landbirds present; check the feeders in back. Continue toward the dam, which begins in 0.3 mile. You have several choices here. You can park in the small lot on your right before the dam and scan all of the area above the dam. Or you can drive completely across the dam, take the first left (0.9 mile from the parking lot), and turn left again in 0.2 mile to reach a parking area and overlook, below the spillway. Both areas are good.

Below the dam is a good spot to look for gulls. Most will be Ring-billed, with a few Herring and sometimes Bonaparte's as well. This lake can be good in late fall and early winter for Forster's Tern. Although seeing them is unlikely, keep your eyes open for any other species of gull as well. Above the dam, scan for any waterfowl. Common Loons are usually seen in winter, along with Horned Grebes in deep water and Pied-billed Grebes around the shoreline. During duck migration especially, almost any duck species can be found, so scan carefully. This can be as good a lake as any in migration for scoters, and it has been good in recent years for

11 West Point Dam and Nearby Spots

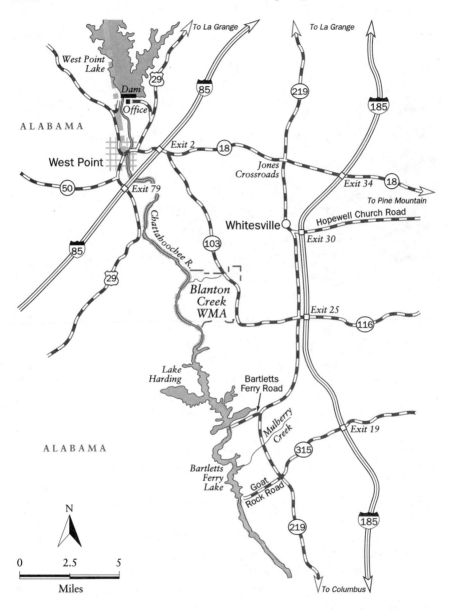

Common Goldeneyes in midwinter. Most of Georgia's rarer ducks have been seen here at one time or another. If the dam is not generating, many of the gulls and terns as well as Double-crested Cormorants will be loafing above it. There are some pretty good pine forests around the dam area to look for landbirds too.

When ready, take the road continuing from the small parking lot above the dam on a 0.5-mile loop that offers more lake to scan and takes you back to the

The Mark Prevatt Marsh at Blanton Creek Wildlife Management Area.

main road. Turn left to return to US 29/GA 14. Return to I-85, but continue under the interstate for 0.4 mile to GA 103, and turn right.

The first entrance to **Blanton Creek WMA** is 7.3 miles on the right. This dirt road is usually in good shape, but be careful if it has rained recently. The best duck spot is Mark Prevatt Memorial Marsh (no hunting allowed), but there are some great weedy fields for sparrows and mixed woods for landbirds along the way, so bird your way along this road for 1.7 miles. At a T intersection, turn right and park immediately at the sign. Walk down the left-hand road 0.2 mile toward an open area and a bright green sign. To get to the marsh, walk down the hill below this sign. Unfortunately, the way this spot is designed, you are walking down a graveled hill directly toward the water, and the ducks know you are coming long before you can actually see most of them. Consequently, this may be an excellent opportunity for you to practice your "ducks in flight" identification skills! You may try walking slowly down the hill, scanning along the way, or walking along the edge of the trail to avoid most of the gravel. Once at the bottom you can scan both sides for ducks—usually dabbling ducks, due to the shallowness of the area. Wood Ducks are permanent residents, and in the past several years, this has been a good spot for wintering wild Mallards and American Black Ducks. The mixed pine/hardwood forest around the marsh offers good birding as well. Some years a few Rusty Blackbirds winter here.

To leave, retrace your route back to GA 103. Turn right on GA 103 and drive east 6.5 miles to GA 219. Note the WMA check station is 0.5 mile past where you rejoin GA 103A; it is not usually manned. At GA 219 continue straight ahead to I-185 at Exit 25 (old 11) to exit the area.

Although new fences have eliminated the birding at the two smaller dams downstream, here are directions to them in the hope that they will become accessible in the future. The first is Lake Harding Dam. Turn right on GA 219 from GA 103, and at 6 miles note Bartlett's Ferry Road on the right. There is a gas station and convenience store at this corner. Bartlett's Ferry dead-ends in 1.7 miles at a large fence, with no current lake access even though there is a huge dam. There used to be access to the water, but now you can only look from behind the fence, so it is not worth trying to bird.

The last dam is Goat Rock Dam, the smallest of the three, also currently closed. Continue 3.7 miles on GA 219 to Goat Rock Road, where there is another gas station and a restaurant with some of the finest home-made barbecue sandwiches you will ever find. The atmosphere isn't much, and be careful about ordering the hot sauce, as it is not for amateurs. Turn right; the dam is 2.4 miles down Goat Rock Road. The road dead-ends at another new fence; from behind it, you can't see a thing. Return to GA 219 the way you came. From here the easiest route back to an interstate is across GA 219 on GA 315 for 4.3 miles to I-185 at Exit 19 (old 10).

General information: Until recently, there was access to both Lake Harding and Goat Rock Dams, obvious from the well-worn trails visible on the other side of the new (and very large) fence. Birders are hopeful that someday access will be restored to these areas, for they have good birding potential, especially Lake Harding.

ADDITIONAL HELP

DeLorme map grid: page 24, E2/F2; page 32, H1.
For more information: West Point Resource Management Office, (706) 645-2937. Georgia Department of Natural Resources.

12 Sweetwater Creek State Park

County: Douglas.
Habitats: Mixed pine/hardwood forest, upland hardwood forest, reservoir.
Key birds: Ducks, especially divers such as Ruddy Duck, passerines in migration.
Best times to bird: October through March for ducks; April, May, and August through October for passerine migrants.

The birding: The lake at Sweetwater Creek is large and fairly deep; it attracts more divers than most shallower lakes and usually has at least several duck species all winter. Good viewing access is available for almost the entire lake. There are several nice walking trails along Sweetwater Creek itself, good for viewing migrants during spring and fall.

Directions: Follow Interstate 20 to Exit 44 (old 12), which is called Thornton Road and is also Georgia Highway 6. Turn south on Thornton (left if you came

12 Sweetwater Creek State Park

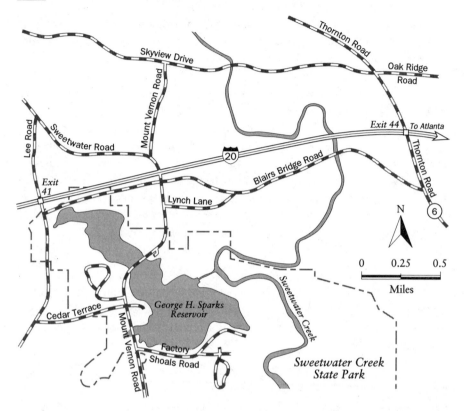

from Atlanta) for 0.4 mile, and turn right on Blairs Bridge Road. There are several car dealers on this corner. Drive 2.1 miles to a four-way stop, and turn left on Mount Vernon Road. In 0.5 mile you will see a sign for Sweetwater Creek State Park, followed by a small parking lot on the left. You can scan part of the lake from here, but the best spots are farther along. You will cross part of the lake just past here, and almost all of the ducks at this spot will be in the main lake to your left. The first left (1 mile from the stop) is Cedar Terrace Road; turn left into the boat ramp and office area. You have to pay the daily state park fee of $2 to use this park, and you may pay either at any of the small fee boxes in the parking lots, or at the office.

While at the boat ramp, scan all of the lake. This is the best place to view the deeper parts of the lake. Ruddy Ducks, Lesser Scaups, and Buffleheads are very reliable here, and rarely you may find other divers such as Canvasbacks, Redheads, and Common Goldeneyes. Horned Grebes and Common Loons are sometimes found in migration, and Red-throated Loons are almost annually reported here, even though obviously rare. Almost every species of duck and a few gulls and terns are seen every year. There is a flock of American Coots and Mallards of dubious lineage that frequents the ramp area, and if you see a child approaching

12 Sweetwater Creek State Park

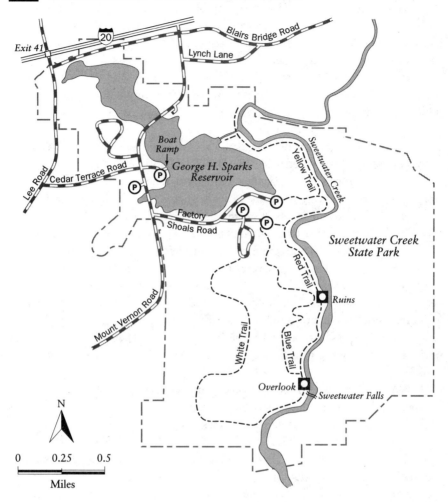

with a piece of bread I would advise hiding quickly, lest you be trampled in the ensuing melee. Sometimes the wild ducks start consorting with this gaggle, which usually includes a tame Mute Swan, and can offer unusually good viewing.

When you have scanned enough, return to Mount Vernon Road and turn left. In 0.1 mile, a covered picnic area on the right offers mature pines to look for Golden-crowned Kinglets and Brown-headed Nuthatches. A short trail leads from the tables to a small dock offering views of another shallow corner of the lake. Pied-billed Grebes are usually found here, and it is a good place to check for Hooded Mergansers. Continuing along Mount Vernon Road, cross the lake again, then turn left on Factory Shoals Road. This road is only 0.3 mile from the boat ramp parking lot.

As soon as you turn onto Factory Shoals Road, pull into one of the many picnic table areas on your left and walk down to the water. This part of the lake is hidden from the ramp area, and this is the only way to check it. Along this road is a good area to look for migrants during spring and fall. In 0.4 mile, Factory Shoals Road forks. The left fork dead-ends in another 0.4 mile, where you can scan the last small corner of the lake. Also, a gated and paved road goes off into the woods. Hermit Thrushes are always present in winter, and the more common sparrow species frequent the forest edge.

Just into the woods, a dirt road leads off to the right and begins the yellow trail. This good path runs down to Sweetwater Creek; turn left and walk along it until you reach a large bridge. A left turn before the bridge will take you along a smaller creek all the way to the bottom of the dam. This entire walk is good for wintering passerines such as Blue-headed Vireos, Winter Wrens, and both Golden-crowned and Ruby-crowned Kinglets. During migration any area along either stream is good for migrating warblers and vireos. When you reach the dam, you can either go back the way you came or walk up to the top of the dam and follow a fisherman's trail to the left back to the parking lot. This trail can be good for checking the lake near the dam, but it is not in very good shape.

When finished, go back to the fork and turn left. In 0.3 mile this road ends in a small parking lot. There are several trails to choose from here. The red trail, from the bottom of the parking lot, goes down along Sweetwater Creek and is very good for migrants. The first 0.6 mile, until you get to the mill ruins, is easy walking. From there the trail follows the stream and is a little more difficult over rocks. This trail ends in another 0.5 mile at an overlook. The rocky stream is very pretty and seems out of place in the South, but even when the birding is slow, the walk is very pleasant.

If you go all the way to the overlook, you may take either of two trails back. The blue trail, marked by blue paint at frequent intervals, is about 1.5 easy miles back to the parking lot. The white trail, marked by white paint, is a more difficult and longer trail at about 3 miles and also ends near the parking lot. Just after you leave the creek the trail passes by a pond, which may have ducks but is rarely checked. Both trails meander through hardwood forest with typical Piedmont bird species. You can also walk back the way you came. You have now birded the entire park, and if you have been here long you may want to check the lake on your way out for new arrivals.

General information: The mill ruins along the red trail are what's left of a textile mill that operated here from 1849 to 1864. This still-imposing five-story structure was taller than any building in Atlanta in 1860. Information about the factory and other historical points is available at the office, open from 8 A.M. to 5 P.M. The park itself is open from 7 A.M. to 10 P.M. daily.

ADDITIONAL HELP

DeLorme map grid: page 25, B10.
For more information: Sweetwater Creek State Conservation Park, (770) 732-5871; Georgia Department of Natural Resources.

13 Kennesaw Mountain National Battlefield Park

County: Cobb.

Habitats: Mixed pine/hardwood forest, upland hardwood forest, floodplain hardwood forest, freshwater marsh shrubland, grassy field, freshwater marshland.

Key birds: *Mountain:* Raptor and landbird migrants. *Forest Trails:* Hooded and Kentucky Warblers, Wood Thrush, Summer Tanager. *Marsh:* Red-headed Woodpecker, Sedge Wren, Brown Creeper, Lincoln's Sparrow.

Best times to bird: *Mountain:* April, May, August to October. *Forest Trails:* May through August. *Marsh:* October through April.

The birding: Kennesaw Mountain offers the best inland migration birding for warblers, vireos, and other landbirds in Georgia, if not the Southeast. Warbler counts of more than 20 species in a morning are not uncommon during peak migration, and this is one of the best spots in the East to see a migrant Cerulean Warbler. Hawk migration is scattered, but over a season ten or more raptor species can be seen, including all the falcons. It is very easy to bird here: Just walk up a paved road for 1.5 miles to the summit, and you may find birds anywhere along the road; the road gets a little steep in places. The mountain is also heavily birded, which means that there is a good database being built of migration records and that there are usually other birders here during migration. The park also has several other lower-elevation trails with interesting breeding species. Near the mountain is a 10-acre freshwater marsh with a small but reliable population of Sedge Wrens in winter and some good hardwood forest to check for Brown Creepers.

Directions: Kennesaw Mountain National Battlefield Park is just northwest of Atlanta. Take Interstate 75 to Exit 269 (old 116), which is Barrett Parkway. Go west (follow the signs) 2.1 miles to Old Route 41, and turn left at the light. Go 1.3 miles, passing the park entrance sign, and turn right on Stilesboro Road. Immediately turn left into the visitor center parking lot, and park. Note that this gate is opened at irregular hours, usually around 7 A.M., but if it's not open you can park along Old Route 41 in the designated areas and walk in. From here you have a couple of options. The best way to see as many birds as possible is to walk up and then back down the mountain. During the week you may drive up the mountain and bird from there (however, the only parking is near the top). You will miss many birds along the way, but this is certainly an easier way for those who cannot walk far. You can't drive up on weekends but there is a shuttle bus that will take you up or down on the half-hour, starting at 9:30 A.M. It does not stop along the way. This can be frustrating, when you zip past birders obviously enjoying a good bird along the way! A donation of a dollar is suggested for the bus. If you do ride up, pick up the directions wherever you park or get off. The visitor center has restrooms, but they are not unlocked until 8:30 A.M. The center also has historical books, a show, maps of the park, and bird checklists.

13 Kennesaw Mountain National Battlefield Park

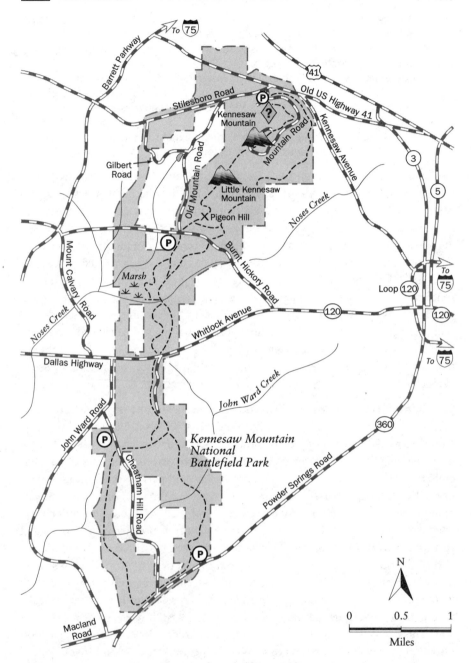

There are several basic strategies to keep in mind anywhere on the mountain. During migration many warblers, vireos, and so forth will travel together in small feeding flocks, so if you find a couple of birds anywhere, look for others traveling with them. Chickadees and titmice are very vocal and often travel with these flocks, so pay attention to them, too. Some of the flocks consist of 50 to 60 warblers, and it is at once thrilling and frustrating to have this huge flock wash over you as you try to see as much as you can and realize you are missing most of them! Edges of open areas or fields tend to concentrate birds, so check them carefully. On cool mornings look for trees getting sunlight, as the birds will be in them first. Fast-moving weather systems with rain can bring a lot of migrants down (if they pass through here at night, which is when most of these birds fly), so being here the next morning can be very rewarding, even if the wet weather is lingering a bit. If you miss the first morning after some weather like this, the birds brought down by rain will trickle out over a period of days, so it's worth trying a day or two later. Finally, on windy days you will find more birds on the side out of the wind, so keep walking around the mountain until you find calmer conditions. If you find something really rare, please call the RBA, and leave a checklist at the visitor center.

It's always worth making a loop around the parking lot before you go up, especially very early in spring or later in fall. At the lower part of the parking lot is a picnic area and a trail running parallel to Stilesboro Road. This area is very good for thrushes, especially in fall when they tend to linger a few days among the dogwood trees. There are also several trees, especially a large sourgum (also called black gum), along the edge of the parking lot (near the steps to the picnic area) that get lots of thrushes, tanagers, and vireos. You can also walk the edge of the small field away from the entrance. As you start up the road, there is a small paved road to the right that leads to the maintenance area. Walk this road to the fence, checking the trees on both sides. This area is especially good in early spring. Walk back to the mountain road and head right.

The gate is not opened for cars until about 8 A.M., but you can walk the road anytime. Just past the gate is a dirt trail to the right, which goes all the way to the summit. Although you can generally see more thrushes in the forest interior on this trail, you generally see fewer of everything else. However, it's worth going in about 100 feet, as warblers will sometimes be in the scrubby trees near the start of this trail. Any area of forest like this is worth checking for Ovenbirds. If there is water in the drainage culvert, look for birds drinking. The very few waterthrush records from the mountain are mostly from here. Return to the road and turn right again. The small area of tangles behind the visitor center is worth a look, and the drain area at the bottom of the culvert may have water. Check the field on your left for sparrows early in April, and for nesting bluebirds anytime. You may also see a few swallows over this field, mostly Barn or Rough-winged. Check the edge of the field for migrants early and late in the year.

As you get back into forest, this is the least productive part of the road, so you can move through here fairly quickly. About 0.4 mile up the road is a trail across the road. The trail to the right connects with the trail from behind the visitor center to go up the mountain, and is called the Cape May Trail by local birders. Sometimes in spring it is worth just walking the first 100 feet of it to check the scrubby area on the right. The downhill part of the trail stays in forest and winds up on Burnt Hickory Road, with minimal migrant opportunities. Continuing up the hill just past the trail is an area of tall dead trees on the left. Look here for flycatchers, but don't count on them. You will soon notice a slightly more open area on the right and a steep drop on the left, called the Quarry. The area on the right can be good for birds that stay close to the ground, like Canada and Hooded Warblers. The pine trees near here will usually produce at least a singing Pine Warbler; the few Yellow-throated Warbler sightings here are usually in pines as well. The Black-and-white Warbler is one of the warblers that breed here, and you may hear or see them anywhere along here, or higher up.

Just past this point on the road you will notice a small yellow stake on the right, marking a drain. These stakes have been numbered so birders can use them to give directions. The area between stake 1 and stake 3 has good scrub on the uphill side of the road. At stake 3 there is an open area just off the road on the downhill side, and you can often see and hear birds working the edge of it. Prairie Warblers are frequently heard here in spring. Just before stake 4 is a vine tangle on the left, which is always worth checking—it's another good spot for Canada and Worm-eating Warblers. Between stake 5 and stake 8 is the creatively named First Big Open Area, which is excellent for scrub-preferring species like Blue- and Golden-winged Warblers, and it is always worth checking. Indigo Buntings breed here, and you can often see tanagers or Rose-breasted Grosbeaks. The uphill side is slightly better because you can see it better, but don't neglect the downhill side. From this point on it's worth scanning the sky for raptors, Chimney Swifts, or swallows. Both Cooper's and Sharp-shinned Hawks are seen during migration from here on up to the summit.

The rest of the mountain is great habitat for migrants, and because you never know when or where you will find a flock, just check it all. Continuing up, just past stake 9 is a rocky outcrop on the right with more scrub, and just a little farther is a bend to the right with your first view of Little Kennesaw Mountain off to the left. This small opening is worth scanning for warblers and vireos and just for enjoying the view. The hillside on the left around stake 10 is fairly steep, so you get a great chance to see treetop species like Cerulean and Blackburnian Warblers at eye level. The uphill side is not as good, of course, but don't ignore it. At the end of this stretch you will reach another open area on the left and another trail across the road. This is the trail to Little Kennesaw and beyond to Burnt Hickory Road. It's called the Saddle Trail, and is worth walking if you have time. It is a little more difficult to bird since it is more closed in (not to mention steeper), but this trail goes by several open areas along the hillsides, which you can get out to on short

Looking down into the Snag Area.

spur trails, and can be very productive. The bottom of the saddle can be good for Ovenbirds and Canada Warblers.

The dirt trail going up Kennesaw at this point goes to the summit, and is very steep. This section of the road is the best place to scan for raptors or other fly-by migrants. There are even a very few records of Double-crested Cormorants, and both Common and Red-throated Loons, mostly from this vantage point. A few local birders conduct nocturnal thrush counts from here (with park permission) and have recorded amazing numbers of these vocal migrants at night. The area of scrub at the top of the Saddle Trail is very good for migrants, and is the best spot on Kennesaw to look for Orange-crowned Warblers, especially in mid-April.

As you continue around the corner on the road, the area on your left is good birding the rest of the way, especially the open areas near stakes 12 and 15. The open area centered around stake 13 is called the Snag Area; on both sides of the road it's one of the best spots on the whole mountain for migrants. The uphill side almost always has something in it, and can be full of birds at times. With all the exposed perches, this can be a good area for flycatchers. The downhill side is very similar to the area near stake 10, and is worth looking over. If you were to pick just one area to concentrate on, you might as well pick from the Saddle Trail to here. Continue up to the upper parking lot, and carefully work all sides of the lot. Especially work the area from the trail up from the bottom near the bench, to the stairs up to the summit. The trail near the bench is the end of the trail from behind the visitor center—the uphill side of the Cape May Trail.

Time for more choices. The dirt trail that goes past the gate runs along the backside of the hill, and can be worth working slowly. Another option is to climb the stairs and take the paved trail to the summit. Both choices are good, but the trail up to the top gets you into more habitat and more open areas. Do both if you have time. In either case, check the area at the base of the stairs carefully, because it can be very good. The small row of brush along the stairs and first portion of the trail above should be checked carefully for shy species such as Kentucky and Canada Warblers. Walk the path up to the top, and take the fork to the right. This brings you out into the upper part of the Snag Area, which is always good. It's worth spending a few minutes here scanning both the sky above you and the scrub before you. In addition to the "winged" warblers, this area is good for Palm, Magnolia, and Prairie Warblers, as well as Common Yellowthroats. The mountain doesn't get many Yellow-breasted Chat records, but they are usually here, if anywhere. In fall this mountain is used as a staging site by Chimney Swifts. Some days their numbers build into the hundreds, and they may be swooping around just barely above your head. This is another good area to watch for migrant raptors or swallows. All of Georgia's swallows have been seen here, although in low numbers.

When you are finished on top, another option is to continue on the trail across the summit and back down to the saddle area, but this trail is quite steep. Keep in mind that you may run into as many or more flocks and birds on the way down as on the way up, so keep working at it. The action does slow down quite a bit by around 11 A.M., so if you had lots of birds on the way up and took a while, it may be slow going down. In general, the bar graphs in Chapter 6 for landbird migrants in the Piedmont were based on data from Kennesaw; check them for specific dates and species to hope for. This is not true for water-loving species like Swainson's and Prothonotary Warblers, and both waterthrushes. All have been seen here, but in very low numbers. The mountain has had many of the rarer migrants, such as Olive-sided Flycatchers, Black-billed Cuckoos, Warbling and Philadelphia Vireos, and Connecticut Warblers, and is one of the best places to hope for them, even though they are reliable nowhere. The only exception is the Philadelphia Vireo, which is seen regularly in September.

There are several other parts of the park worth birding for various species. For summertime birding, three trails offer fairly easy hikes and go through similar floodplain stream areas. The species of interest are Wood Thrush, Hooded and Kentucky Warblers, and Summer and sometimes Scarlet Tanagers. The trail to the marsh I will treat last, even though it is the best. The other two are portions of the Cheatham Hill Trail.

To get to the Cheatham Hill Trail, you have two choices. Turn left out of the parking lot onto Stilesboro Road, and drive 0.5 mile to Old Mountain Road. Turn left, and go 1.4 miles to a T intersection at Burnt Hickory Road, and turn left. In 1.2 miles you will reach Whitlock Avenue. Turn right. In 1.6 miles, turn left on John Ward Road. In 0.6 mile, turn left on Cheatham Hill Road and turn into the small parking lot on the right in 0.2 mile. This trail runs slightly downhill for about 0.8 mile to John Ward Creek. It goes through a pine forest where you might find Pine Warblers and Brown-headed Nuthatches. At the steepest part of the downhill, just before the creek, there is a dirt trail to the right. This trail follows the stream through good floodplain forest until it dead-ends at a subdivision in about 0.4 mile. In addition to the floodplain species mentioned above, Acadian Flycatchers have bred here.

Back on the main trail you will soon reach a boardwalk through the woods; it goes by a small swampy area and then crosses the creek where you'll find a wet field good for Common Yellowthroats and Eastern Kingbirds. This trail creates a large loop and eventually returns to the lot where you parked, but the loop is about 5.3 miles long and has stretches that aren't very birdy. If you want to try the entire trail, you should get a map from the visitor center.

To easily access another good section, continue down Cheatham Hill Road another 1.7 miles to Powder Springs Road. Turn left and look for a small gate on the left in only 0.3 mile. This is part of the same loop, but you can park here and walk to the right about 1.1 miles to another crossing of John Ward Creek, worth looking for the same floodplain species. This section of trail also goes through more pine forest. From here, you can return the way you came, or if you want to leave the area, continue northeast on Powder Springs Road (the way you had been coming from John Ward Road) for 3.7 miles to the South Marietta 120 Loop. Turn right and you will reach I-75 in 2.8 miles.

The Kennesaw Marsh has similar species to the trails above, but has more possibilities for migrants and is a great place to bird in late fall or winter. The marsh area and the field it is in may be very wet, so wear appropriate footwear. To get here, turn left out of the lot at the visitor center on Stilesboro Road for 0.5 mile and then turn left on Old Mountain Road. When it dead-ends in 1.4 miles at Burnt Hickory Road, park along Burnt Hickory in the spaces provided. Walk down the good dirt trail away from Old Mountain Road. At the bottom of the first small hill is an open area of scrub, good for migrants in spring and fall including (but rarely) waterthrushes in the small creek. Hooded and Kentucky Warblers breed here. In winter, this area is good for sparrows and other landbirds, such as Ruby-crowned Kinglets.

As you climb the hill away from here, at the top (about 0.3 mile from Burnt Hickory Road) there is a trail off to the right. This is an alternate route to the marsh, which in late fall and winter is fairly reliable for Brown Creepers. To find these elusive birds, walk carefully along the trail to an area of large, mostly hardwood trees, and check out the trunks carefully. If you have good ears, listen for the single, thin *"seee"* call. The best area is about 100 yards down this trail, but the whole trail is worth investigating. It winds around a bit, and where it has a short, steep downhill section (about 0.6 mile), look for a small trail to the right at the bottom of the hill. Pick up the directions at the end of the next paragraph.

If continuing on the main trail, go another 0.4 mile to a larger stream, Noses Creek. Check the field on your right on the way, including the scrub area out in the middle. At the stream, turn right *before* the bridge and follow the small trail along the side of the creek. When the trail turns slightly away from the creek, scan the scrubby area on your left as you walk because it can be good for migrants. Where the trail makes a sharp uphill turn to the right (only about 100 to 200 yards), look for a small trail that goes straight ahead along the creek. There is a large downed tree right here, which the trail goes around.

From either direction, take this small trail. The park does not maintain it, and it may be somewhat overgrown, but follow it only 100 feet or so into a large overgrown field. The area you just passed through has breeding Hooded and Kentucky Warblers in summer. The field is excellent for sparrows in fall and winter. The brushy areas along the edge are good for White-throated Sparrows, and Song and Swamp Sparrows in the more open parts. In late October and early November, this area has produced several Lincoln's Sparrow records, which makes it as reliable as any for this elusive and rare species. Lincoln's has only been found on days when there are lots of sparrows in this field, indicating a push of migrants. The field may also be overgrown; what passes for a "path" is made by horseback riders who come through. Sometimes they don't ride often and the weeds really take over.

This is also a good area for wrens. House Wrens can be found along the edges of the field in winter and Winter Wrens can be anywhere along the creek or near the field. In fall it is not uncommon to see several Winter Wrens per day. Also, this marsh has one of the northernmost inland wintering populations of Sedge Wrens in Georgia. Though there will be only 10 to 12 birds per winter, if you learn their *"jib-jib"* two-noted call you can usually find one out in the wetter area. Common Yellowthroats breed here, and are rare in winter. This juncus marsh looks perfect for migrant Least Bitterns or wintering American Bitterns but none have been found . . . yet! There are a few Sora rails in migration, but they are very difficult to hear, much less see. In late summer, there may be a few herons, including Little Blue Heron and Great Egret. Great Blue and Green Herons breed here but there are only a couple and they are not reliable on any given day. In summer, White-eyed Vireos, Gray Catbirds, and Indigo Buntings breed here. At the very bottom of this field, by the thickest part of marsh, look over to an area of dead trees. Watch for perched raptors and look for the many woodpeckers that frequent this area, including the Red-headed, which nests here. In any season, this is a great place to just come and bird.

General information: Park hours are dawn until dusk, and the visitor center is open from 8:30 A.M. to 5 P.M. Kennesaw Mountain is also a great place for history lovers. There is a movie at the visitor center, along with a large Civil War bookstore and informative handouts. Maps are available for trails and historical sites in the park. Food, gas, and lodging are in plentiful and ever-increasing supply along Barrett Parkway, which also includes a large shopping mall. This area is just northwest of Atlanta, a popular destination in its own right. Numerous other sites in this book are found near here as well.

ADDITIONAL HELP

DeLorme map grid: page 20, G1.
For more information: Kennesaw Mountain National Battlefield Park, (770) 427-4686; Cobb County CVB, (800) 451-3480.

14 Chattahoochee River National Recreation Area

Counties: Cobb and Fulton.
Habitats: Mixed pine/hardwood forest, floodplain hardwood forest, freshwater marsh shrubland, weedy field, grassy field, river.
Key birds: Migrants, including raptors, waterbirds, and landbirds.
Best times to bird: For migrants: April, May, August through October.

The birding: The Chattahoochee River National Recreation Area (CRNRA) is a series of sections along the Chattahoochee River near Atlanta that have been set aside for all kinds of recreation. It just so happens that nearly all of the sections are great for birding. Though you may have to share space with joggers, bike riders, pets, and who knows what else, some parts are much less heavily used and offer good birding, right near metro Atlanta. Since all rivers in Georgia are used as migration pathways, and this is one of the larger ones, both spring and fall migration can be spectacular. The units covered here are Vickery Creek, Gold Branch, Johnson Ferry North and South, Cochran Shoals, and Paces Mill/West Palisades. Also included is the Chattahoochee Nature Center, a private nonprofit facility in the middle of these other areas. Just about anywhere you can get down along the river can be good birding, but these units are a combination of the best from both an accessibility and habitat standpoint.

All units offer good trails, access right on the river, and good parking areas. Particular highlights for each area are covered, but the following is true for all of these areas. During migration, the earlier you can go in the morning, the better. The first few hours of daylight are much better for migrants as they feed to replenish their energy stores before the next leg of their journey. This is tempered in very early spring and late fall when mornings can be chilly; under these circumstances the first rays of the sun are necessary to get things moving. For migrants, listen and watch for mixed feeding flocks, often moving along the immediate banks of the river, but also sometimes in nearby fields. These flocks may contain local residents such as chickadees and titmice as well, so investigate any birds you find. In more heavily used areas such as Cochran Shoals, you may have to get away from the crowds to find bird activity, especially on the first sunny spring days when it seems the entire city turns out. In winter, birding early is not so critical. There is a $2 fee to park in any of these areas, using the pay boxes provided at all the parking lots. An annual pass is available for $20.

The river is second only to Kennesaw Mountain for migrants, and it gets a few the mountain does not. Best examples of these are wet-habitat warblers such as

14 Chattahoochee River National Recreation Area

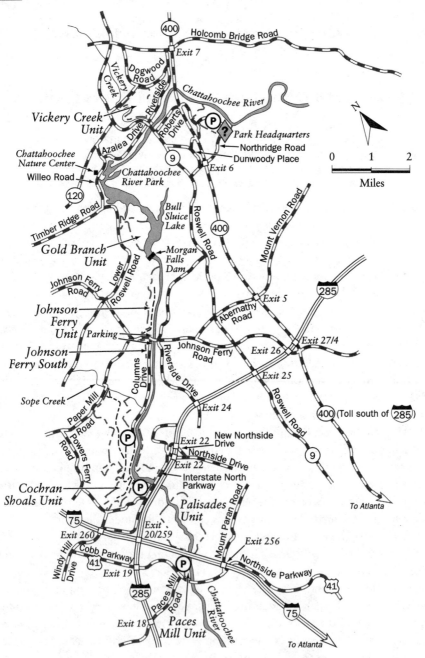

Prothonotary and Common Yellowthroat, which breed here, and both water-thrushes, Louisiana and Northern, which are common migrants. The river is also better than Kennesaw Mountain for Yellow Warblers, which can be common in migration. Raptors and waterfowl also use the river during their migration, so keep your eyes open for them as well. Just about all of the hardwood floodplain breeding species occur along the river, so even after migration in summer there are interesting birds to find—if you don't mind the summertime heat. Early is best in summer. In the many areas of mature pines, both Brown-headed Nuthatches and Pine Warblers are common. Of course, there are so many mature trees in various stages of growing or dying that there are loads of woodpeckers along the river. All of Georgia's woodpeckers except Red-cockaded are found here. Many of these areas also have open fields or scrub for other species like Indigo Bunting, Gray Catbird, and Yellow-breasted Chat.

Directions: These different areas are listed from north to south along the river, but you can start and stop at any point. The first area is the **Vickery Creek Unit.** Take Georgia Highway 400 just north of Interstate 285 to Exit 7B, Holcomb Bridge Road (also GA 140). Go west on Holcomb Bridge Road for 0.3 mile to the second light, and turn left on Dogwood Road. Stay on Dogwood as other roads join; in 1 mile it becomes Riverside Road. At 1.9 miles turn right into a small concrete entrance road at the brown park sign and proceed into the parking lot. Look at the trail sign to get oriented, and then find a trail right along the creek for almost a mile of good hardwood floodplain forest. In addition to the typical breeding species, this hike is good for migrants. In your car, return to Riverside Road and turn right. You will cross Atlanta/Roswell Road immediately; your road becomes Azalea Drive. The next 1.6 miles or so are part of the Chattahoochee River Park in Fulton County. There aren't many trails, but you can check the river at 0.7 mile from Roswell Road on the left for waterfowl in winter.

Continue on Azalea Drive another 0.9 mile to Willeo Road, and turn left. The large oxbow lake on your left can be good for dabbling ducks in winter, but the only places to view it are a couple of pullouts on the left starting at 0.2 mile from this turn. If you want to do this, go down another 0.4 mile (0.6 from the turn) and turn around, then come back so you can pull off in the right direction. Scan this lake for ducks any time in winter, or for shorebirds when the water level is down during migration.

When finished, continue in the original direction 0.4 mile from here to the **Chattahoochee Nature Center** on the right. Drive up the hill to the parking area and store. The hours here are 9 A.M. to 5 P.M. Monday through Saturday, and 12 to 5 P.M. on Sunday. They are open every day except New Year's, Thanksgiving, and Christmas. Admission is $5 for adults, $3 for seniors and children. The birding is great all year long, with several ponds, trails, and a river boardwalk trail along the Chattahoochee. There is a well-stocked nature store and a hands-on interpretive center for curious minds (and hands). The center also has guided walks and other programs. You can easily spend all day here, but when you are ready to move on, return to Willeo Road and turn right. You will again note parts of Bull Sluice Lake on your left, and there is a small pullout on the left at 0.6 mile if you want to scan. Otherwise continue another 0.2 mile (0.8 from the nature center) to Timber Ridge/Lower Roswell Road, and turn left onto Lower Roswell Road.

The entrance to the **Gold Branch Unit** is on the left in another 0.6 mile; turn in and drive into the parking lot on the right. Again there are several trails, so check the trail map sign. The easiest way to the river is down the hill to the yellow trail, but there are several miles of other interesting trails through good hardwood forest to keep you busy. To continue, go back to Lower Roswell Road and turn left. In 2.2 miles you will reach Johnson Ferry Road; turn left. Go downhill 1.6 miles to Columns Drive, and choose from the following options.

The **Johnson Ferry North Unit** is on your left; turn in to the parking lot. A large field bordered by woods lies along the river, and there are more trails here. A short one follows a tributary inland and another one is along the river. The open areas here and at the South Unit are good for swallows. On the opposite side of Johnson Ferry is the **Johnson Ferry South Unit.** Turn onto Columns Drive, and choose from the following two areas. The first turn-in, Area 1, is 0.1 mile on the left. Park here to access the river, or walk across the large open field to bird around a nice emergent-scrub marsh. There aren't any trails into this marsh, and the only other way to bird it is along Columns Drive, but this isn't recommended except perhaps early in the morning when there is no traffic. This marsh is great for sparrows in winter, especially Swamp Sparrows. The drier areas are also full of sparrows, including a few Fox Sparrows in the areas with some small saplings mixed into the brush. This is also a great area for House and Winter Wrens in winter, and in migration you may find a flycatcher using the tall dead trees, if you are lucky. Area 2 is another 0.4 mile along Columns Drive on the left, with another parking lot. There is a trail along the river that connects both areas, good in winter for sparrows and in migration. The brushy areas around this parking lot are also very good in winter or summer.

The next area, the **Cochran Shoals Unit,** has access at both ends of a long loop trail. The east end is accessed from Columns Drive, another 1.9 miles from Area 2. Birding here is discussed in the next paragraph. To exit this area, take Columns Drive back to Johnson Ferry Road and turn right. As soon as you cross the river, you can go right on Riverside Drive to I-285, but this can have lots of traffic. Continue on Johnson Ferry for 1.1 miles from Columns Drive, and turn left on Abernathy Road. In 2 miles you will reach GA 400 again at Exits 5A and 5B.

To go directly to the main access point for the Cochran Shoals Unit, from I-285 take Exit 22 (old 15), which is New Northside Drive, Northside Drive, and Powers Ferry Road. From the east, turn right on New Northside Drive for 0.2 mile to the traffic light and go straight across onto Interstate Parkway North.

14 Chattahoochee River National Recreation Area: Cochran Shoals and Sope Creek Units

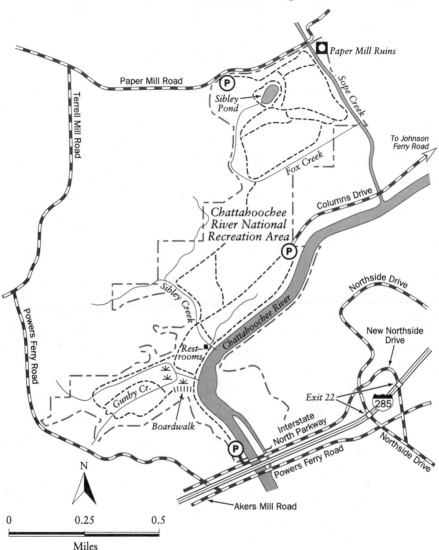

From the west, turn left on Northside Drive to cross I-285 and turn left at the first light for Interstate Parkway North (0.1 mile). Once on Interstate Parkway North from Exit 22, drive 0.8 mile to the Cochran Shoals entrance *just* after you cross the river, and turn right into the parking lot. You will pass another entrance just before this to the Powers Island Unit, but Cochran Shoals is better. This can be a very busy place, but the birding can be spectacular and it's worth putting up with all the joggers, bikers, and walkers. You may get a few funny looks, but that's the way it goes.

You have several choices here, all of them good. Check the trail map before you start to make sure you know where you are going. The main trail along the river is just under 1 mile to the Columns Drive end, and then you can return along the river again or take the other part of the loop back. Leaving from this end at Interstate North, walk the main trail along the river. A spur trail to the left about 0.3 mile in has a boardwalk through a marshy area and a loop trail along Gunby Creek, excellent birding in any season. Continue along the main trail to an intersection, where the trail to the left is the back part of the loop. Even if you choose to stay along the river both ways, you should walk up this spur to the left a 100 yards to the other end of the marshy area. Great for migrants or sparrows in winter, it is always worth checking. There are lots of dead trees to attract woodpeckers, including Red-headed, and there are usually lots of swallows, including Purple Martins in season.

You can view wet areas on both sides of the trail, and as it bends right to parallel the river there is another small dirt trail off to the left that goes behind the large wetland area. You can often see Wood Ducks in any of these wetland areas. Return to the main trail, and continue along the river. You will next reach a large field, with restrooms and water along the trail. The field isn't much good unless the grass is allowed to grow, which it usually isn't, but the edges can be great for migrants or any landbirds in winter. From here, the main trail follows the river, with good habitat on both sides of the river to the end of the trail and back again. Take your time, and check the trees alongside the trail, the sky overhead, and the river itself. You can easily spend several hours here, especially during migration. If you ever get finished, return to your car and exit the way you came.

The other area to cover is the **Paces Mill/West Palisades Units** (refer back to map, page 80). Get on I-75 just south of I-285, and take Exit 256 (old 108) for Mount Paran Road. Go just slightly west (0.1 mile) to US 41, Northside Parkway, and turn right. As soon as you cross the Chattahoochee River in 1.1 miles, turn left at the sign for the Paces Mill Unit. Follow this curving road 0.4 mile as it comes back under US 41 to the parking lot. This is a busy unit in summer with boaters, but check out the trail map sign again and park in the back part of the lot. There are restrooms and a concession stand open in summer only. Another trail follows the west bank of the river under I-75 and connects with the West Palisades Unit and its trail system. The total length of trail along the riverbank is about 1.3 miles, and the birding for migrants is as good here as at Cochran Shoals, with just a fraction of the foot traffic. There isn't as much wetland habitat for breeders, though, and this unit is not as good in winter. You can exit onto US 41 either north or south when finished.

General information: A map of this entire recreation area is available from the National Park Service. It will show you areas not covered in this book. Virtually any of these sections can be great birding, so try them all! The most popular area with birders has been the Cochran Shoals Unit; the Atlanta Audubon Society offers field trips at 7:30 A.M. every Saturday during migration. Rafting and canoeing are also very popular in summer, and can be arranged at the Johnson Ferry North or Paces Mill Units. Since this area goes right through metro Atlanta, there are restaurants, gas, and lodging near just about every unit.

ADDITIONAL HELP

DeLorme map grid: page 20, H2, G3.
For more information: Chattahoochee River National Recreation Area, (770) 399-8070; Chattahoochee Nature Center, (770) 992-2055; Atlanta CVB, (800) 285-2682; Atlanta Audubon Society, (770) 955-4111.

15 E. L. Huie Land Application Facility and Newman Wetlands Center

County: Clayton.
Habitats: Ponds with mudflats, pine forest, floodplain hardwood forest.
Key birds: Ducks and shorebirds at E. L. Huie; Prothonotary Warbler, Louisiana Waterthrush, and Winter Wren at Newman Wetlands Center.
Best times to bird: All year.

The birding: The **E. L. Huie Land Application Facility** is a 4,000-acre wastewater treatment site about 20 miles south of downtown Atlanta, and is a must-visit location for nearly the entire year. Featuring a series of ponds that can be great in migration for shorebirds and equally good for ducks in winter, as well as a board-walk trail and several other birdable areas, E. L. Huie has also built up an impressive list of rarities over the years. There are five ponds, four roughly square ones of more or less equal size (although one currently has a buildup of dirt replacing some of the water), and a much larger one on the south end of the complex called, appropriately enough, the South Pond.

Because these holding ponds are part of the wastewater treatment process and not specifically managed for bird habitat, the range in depth at any given time from full to bone dry. Fortunately, there is usually at least one that has low enough water or puddles to provide good shorebird habitat in spring and fall. In winter most of the ponds remain full and house a good population of duck species. The area is fairly small (a drive around all five ponds is only about 1.5 miles) and there is a road system along the dikes that allows birders to drive all the way around each of the five ponds. The next most significant section to bird in this area is the nearby Newman Wetlands Center, a new area of swampy woods with a very nice 0.5-mile combination boardwalk and trail, and an interpretive nature center with nature and water-cycle exhibits.

Directions: From the north, take Interstate 75 south to Exit 235 (old 77), which is US Highways 19 and 41, and is also called Tara Boulevard. At the end of this exit is a traffic light at Upper Riverdale Road. Go straight through this light on Tara

15 E. L. Huie Land Application Facility and Newman Wetlands Center

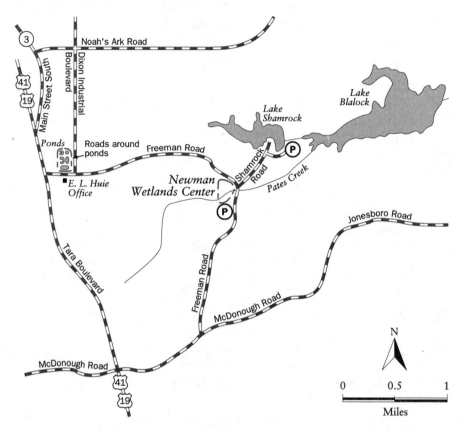

Boulevard for 7.9 miles to Freeman Road and turn left. This turn creeps up on you, but when the multilane, multibusiness road becomes a less-developed two-lane each way, you are getting close. The last light before Freeman Road is Mundy's Mill Road; then you pass under a large set of high-tension wires. Freeman Road is 0.6 mile from these wires. Another landmark is the new water authority building on the corner, which is a huge modern-looking structure with lots of glass. There are no other buildings like it near there. Go down Freeman for 0.2 mile, passing the E. L.Huie Land Application Facility office building on your right, and turn left on Dixon Industrial Boulevard. By this time you should have noticed the dikes on your left behind a chain-link fence, so turn left into the pond area shortly after joining Dixon.

To get here from the south, take Exit 221 (old 71) off I-75. This is Jonesboro Road. Turn left, and drive 6.3 miles to Freeman Road. Note: At 5.3 miles you leave Henry County and move into Clayton County, and Jonesboro Road magically becomes McDonough Road. Turn right on Freeman Road, and drive 3.3 miles to Dixon Industrial Boulevard. Turn right and then left into the pond area.

15 E. L. Huie Land Application Facility and Newman Wetlands Center
16 Atlanta South Lakes Loop

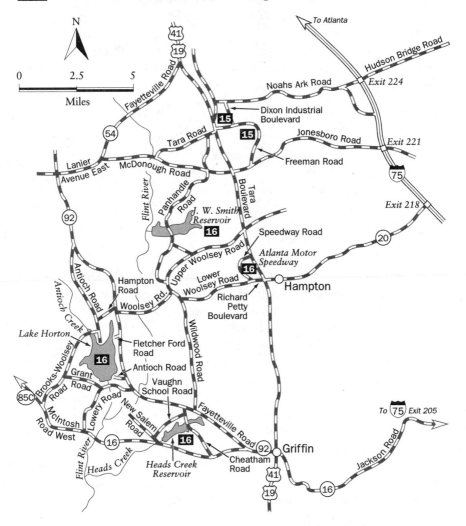

Once at the pond area, carefully drive around the dikes while checking out the birds. Give way to all Water Authority vehicles, and stay on the roads. The pond area is open from 7 A.M. to around 4 P.M. daily (closing time varies). These are dirt roads, so they can be slippery in wet weather, but they are generally driveable in any vehicle. There are Purple Martin houses and bluebird boxes around the ponds, and they are usually used in season. A pair of Tree Swallows has also nested the past several years. During spring and fall, when water conditions are right, you can frequently see 10 or 12 species of shorebirds in very little time. Killdeer are always present. Among sandpipers, Greater and Lesser Yellowlegs, Solitary, Spotted,

Semipalmated, Least, and Pectoral are all fairly common in spring and fall. While the common times for each of the various species differ, all of April and May in spring, and mid-July through September in fall are the best. Western and Baird's Sandpipers are rare in fall, and White-rumped Sandpipers are uncommon in May. Common Snipe live up to their name in winter, and are very common around the edges of the ponds. Most of the really rare shorebirds that have been seen in the Atlanta area have been seen here, including all three species of phalarope, Red, Red-necked, and Wilson's, so it pays to be very careful when picking your way through the shorebirds. Gulls and terns are pretty uncommon, but some Bonaparte's Gulls are seen in spring and a few Black Terns in fall (mostly August).

In winter the spotlight turns to ducks. The first ducks actually start arriving in fall with the Blue-winged Teal in late August; there are ducks in this area until the last blue-wings leave in late April or May (although the blue-wings are only migrants and aren't present in winter). Most of the other species that occur come through as migrants in spring and fall, with some here all winter. Canada Geese and Mallards are permanent residents and impossible to miss, and Wood Ducks are permanent residents also, but not always right on the ponds. The Snow Goose is a quite rare and sometimes maddeningly inconsistent winter visitor, and both Ross's and Greater White-fronted Geese have been seen, although only a few times. The most common ducks in winter are Ring-necked, Lesser Scaup, Bufflehead, and Ruddy. There are usually Northern Shovelers as well, and a few Pied-billed Grebes and Double-crested Cormorants.

Uncommon in migration but rare in winter are Green-winged Teals, Gadwalls, and American Wigeons. Hooded Mergansers are fairly common in winter, and Red-breasted Mergansers are rare late fall or spring migrants. Northern Pintails, Canvasbacks, and Redheads are all highly sought after in the South and will usually be reported a couple of times a year, but they don't show up at any consistent time or stay for any consistent length of time. Occasionally a Greater Scaup will be found among the Lessers, but only a couple of times a season. Although not a duck, there are usually a few American Coots in winter. As in the case of shorebirds, almost all of the species of duck that have ever been seen inland in Georgia have been here at one time or another, so look for them all carefully.

Whereas shorebirds and ducks are the greatest draw to E. L. Huie, many other birds can be found here also. The ponds are great places to see swallows in season, and although Bank Swallow is always rare in Atlanta, this is one of the best spots to hope for one in spring and fall migration. Savannah Sparrows and American Pipits can usually be found in small numbers in winter around the ponds or on the dikes, and in late summer the buildup of waterbirds can be impressive (mostly Great Egrets, Great Blue Herons, and a few Little Blue Herons). Late fall brings large flocks of European Starlings, Brown-headed Cowbirds, and a few blackbirds

E. L. Huie Land Application Facility ponds.

to the dikes (mostly Red-winged, but sometimes a few Rusty and rarely a Brewer's). Since this is a pretty open area, it pays to watch overhead for raptors.

When you are through here, head over to the **Newman Wetlands Center.** Turn right out of the ponds on Dixon again to Freeman Road. Scan the powerline right-of-way in front of you for Wild Turkeys, which can sometimes be seen feeding along the edges of the clearing, and listen for Northern Bobwhites, which call near here. Turn left on Freeman Road, and drive 2 miles to Newman Wetlands Center, which is on the right. The small creek you cross over just before the center's entrance (Pate's Creek) is another spot to look for migrants in season, but make sure you pull completely off the road onto the shoulder if you want to bird. The Newman Wetlands Center is open every day except Sunday (also closed Saturday in winter) from 8:30 A.M. to 5 P.M.; it has restrooms and lots of interesting exhibits. The gate to the parking lot and the trail are open every day at the same times.

The trail starts on the far side of the parking lot and is about 0.5 mile long. It travels through mostly swampy woods on a nice boardwalk and then finishes as a dirt trail along the forest edge. In spring the boardwalk area is generally the first place in Atlanta to report Louisiana Waterthrushes and Prothonotary Warblers, which both breed here. Lots of other spring and fall migrants come through this area; it is also a good place to just walk around and enjoy the scenery.

In winter the boardwalk is good for woodland winter birds like Winter Wrens and Dark-eyed Juncos, and the feeders around the center should be checked for finches. There are also hummingbird feeders near the center from spring through fall, and there usually are a few of these winged jewels zipping around. The tall, mature pines around the center are also a good place to look for Brown-headed Nuthatches, a common resident but sometimes difficult to find. A small flock of Wild Turkeys is resident here, and a few of them are frequently seen casually strolling around the grounds near the parking lot.

There are several lakes nearby that can be checked for waterfowl in winter or can be used as nice places to do some general birding. **Lake Shamrock** and **Lake Blalock** are right next to each other and very close to the Newman Wetlands Center; simply go back to Freeman Road, turn left, and quickly turn right on Shamrock Road. This area is operated as a fee-fishing lake by the water authority, which charges a $5 admission. Through a special deal worked out by the water authority, birders may enter for free but can stay only 20 minutes. If you wish to bird longer, you must pay the fee. Lake Shamrock has nice birding around its edges and a fairly dependable Red-headed Woodpecker colony to the right and downhill from the entrance. The larger lake at the bottom of the hill is Lake Blalock; it's worth scanning. Ospreys sometimes nest here, and there are frequently Bald Eagles in the area. Great Blue Herons have nested in recent years, along with dozens of Double-crested Cormorants. In migration this is another good spot for swallows. Both lakes usually have some ducks in winter. The Shamrock Lake and Blalock Lake area is open all year from 7 A.M. to 7 P.M.

General information: Newman Wetlands Center staff member Carol Lambert is very knowledgeable about birds and current conditions. Any rarities found should be reported to her as well as to the RBA. There is a list of recent sightings posted on the trail bulletin board you pass to get to the boardwalk. The Atlanta Audubon Society has 8 A.M. field trips at the E. L. Huie ponds every Sunday during migration. There are many restaurants and gas stations all along Tara Boulevard, although they thin out to the south near E. L. Huie. The Atlanta South Lakes Loop (Site 16) starts at US 19/41 here if you want to do some more birding in the area.

ADDITIONAL HELP

DeLorme map grid: page 26, F3, and F4.
For more information: Newman Wetlands Center, (770) 603-5606; Clayton County Water Authority, (770) 603-5605; Atlanta Audubon Society, (770) 955-4111.

16 Atlanta South Lakes Loop

See map on page 87

Counties: Henry, Clayton, Fayette, and Spalding.
Habitats: Pine forest, mixed pine/hardwood forest, upland hardwood forest, floodplain hardwood forest, weedy field, grassy field, reservoir.
Key birds: Waterfowl, sparrows.
Best times to bird: November through March.

The birding: This loop is about 50 miles long, and will take about four hours. The loop starts at the E. L. Huie Land Application Facility (Site 15), and takes you to three different lakes for an all-around waterfowl day. Sometimes this loop can be very productive, with ten or more species of duck and various other species around the lakes, but sometimes the ducks are more scattered. All of the lakes have deep enough water to attract divers, and one has shallow weedy edges favored by dabblers. Two of the lakes have good landbirding habitat around them as well. A scope is very helpful for distant ducks.

(A note of caution: Do NOT try this loop if there is a race at the Atlanta Motor Speedway, as the traffic is atrocious for hours before and after.) This is also a good loop to try in summer for typical lower Piedmont brush breeders such as Indigo Bunting, Blue Grosbeak, Orchard Oriole, and Yellow-breasted Chat.

Directions: Start at the intersection of Freeman Road and Tara Boulevard (US Highway 19/41). This is within a mile of the E. L. Huie Land Application Facility, (Site 15), and can be done in conjunction with a winter visit to that site. (See that site for directions to the starting point.) From Freeman Road, drive south on US 19/41 for 2 miles to McDonough Road. Turn right, and go 1 mile to Panhandle Road. Now turn left, and in 3.5 miles you will cross **J. W. Smith Reservoir.** Immediately after crossing, turn left into the parking lot of the Clayton County Fire Station Number 10. Birders have permission to park here while they scan the lake. Scan both ends of the lake—the shallower portion is behind the fire station—and walk across the road to scan the deeper portion toward the dam.

This won't take very long. When you are finished, turn left back onto Panhandle Road. In 2.9 miles you will dead-end into Woolsey Road. Turn right, and note Wildwood Road on your left in 0.4 mile. This road will take you back to US 19/41 if you don't have enough time to do the whole loop; you can also backtrack from Lake Horton to here. To follow this shortcut back, drive 0.5 mile on Wildwood to Lower Woolsey road. Turn left; in 3.6 miles you will come to US 19/41 at the Atlanta Motor Speedway. (See later in the directions on how to bird there, if desired.)

Back on Woolsey Road, after turning right from Panhandle, drive 3.3 miles to Georgia Highway 92. This is the town of Woolsey. Turn right and go only 0.1 mile, then turn left on Hampton Road for 0.7 mile. Turn left again on Antioch Road, which goes right into **Lake Horton** (literally). The gate for the reservoir is in 1.5 miles, and there is a boat ramp on your left 0.2 mile past that. This is an excellent spot from which to scan the east side of the lake; you can also walk around the shoreline a little. Some ducks may be partly hidden in vegetation in the water, so look carefully. This is a good spot for sparrows in the grass around the lake edge and in the nearby bushes. Vesper Sparrows are frequently found in late fall.

After leaving the boat ramp and returning to Antioch Road, turn left again; the road ends in 0.4 mile at a large guardrail just before the lake. You can scan toward the dam, to the right. This is the most likely area for divers.

To access a shallow, weedy arm of the lake, drive back out Antioch Road 1.7 miles and turn left on Brooks Woolsey Road. In 0.5 mile you will cross this part of the lake and you can park on the dirt area on the left, on the far side of the arm. Scan both sides of the road, primarily for dabblers and Pied-billed Grebes.

Turn around, and go back to GA 92 and the town of Woolsey. Turn right on GA 92; in 1 mile Fletcher Ford Road is on your right. This dirt road ends in 0.4 mile at the lake, and is another good area to look for landbirds, including sparrows along the edge. You can turn around at the lake.

Continuing along GA 92 from here, drive south 2.6 miles to Lowery Road. Note that you will pass the other end of Antioch Road on the right, which affords another view of the lake, covering the same water you have already searched. There is a great landbird spot on Lowery Road, but no more ducks. To view this spot, turn right on Lowery; in 1.4 miles you will be below the dam at a great wetland. Find a place to park on the shoulder of Lowery, and search here for more sparrows or woodpeckers in the area of dead trees.

To continue the loop, go back to GA 92 and turn right again. In 2.2 miles turn right on Cheatham Road. This intersection will sneak up on you, so look for the large building at the Pirkle Memorial Campground on the corner. After turning right on Cheatham, which is south, turn right again on Vaughn School Road in 0.5 mile. You will cross two shallow arms of the **Heads Creek Reservoir** in 0.4 and 0.8 miles; both are worth scanning, but beware the "No Parking" signs. At 1.5 miles, turn left on New Salem Road. In 0.3 mile, turn left again into a boat ramp parking lot. This is the reservoir dam, the best spot for divers. You can scan well up the lake from here. There is also a small wet area below the dam that can be searched for landbirds. Return to Cheatham Road the way you came, and turn right onto Cheatham. Almost immediately, pull off to the left into a dirt parking area. From here you can scan the lake from both sides of the road. This is the last lake stop on this loop. There are also trails to bird through the woods.

To get back to the starting point, continue south on Cheatham 1.9 miles to West McIntosh Road, and turn left. In 1.4 miles you will rejoin GA 92; turn right for 1.4 miles until you get to US 19/41; turn left. To go straight back to the beginning, drive 14.6 miles to the intersection with Freeman Road.

To make a short stop at the **Atlanta Motor Speedway,** drive 7.4 miles to Richard Petty Boulevard on your left. Turn left, and scan any open area for a flock of Rusty Blackbirds that sometimes winter here. This includes all grass parking areas at the speedway. In 1.1 miles, turn right on Speedway Boulevard. The next 0.5

mile on the right is very good for Horned Larks anywhere in the grass. You can also try on the left after that. Follow this road all the way around in a big circle to US 19/41, still scanning for blackbird flocks. At US 19/41, turn left and you will reach the starting point in 5 miles.

General information: Development is proceeding rapidly in this area, so there may be unforeseen road changes in the future. These reservoirs should remain as they are, however. The shortcut into or out of the middle of the loop runs between the motor speedway and Wildwood Road, just after Smith Reservoir on the loop.

ADDITIONAL HELP

DeLorme map grid: page 26, F3/4, G3/4, H3/4.
For more information: Atlanta Motor Speedway, (770) 946-4211; Clayton County Water Authority, (770) 603-5605.

17 Dawson Forest Wildlife Management Area

County: Dawson.
Habitats: Pine forest, mixed pine/hardwood forest, floodplain hardwood forest, freshwater marsh shrubland, river.
Key birds: Blue-winged Warbler, Louisiana Waterthrush, Kentucky Warbler, Yellow-throated Warbler, Whip-poor-will, passerine migrants.
Best times to bird: April through October.

The birding: This area of Dawson Forest WMA is called the City of Atlanta tract. It is a large area of maturing second-growth forest near the Etowah River with many interesting breeding warblers and other neotropical migrants, including a few Blue-winged Warblers. The Etowah River itself is good to bird during migration, and there is a nearby sometimes-flooded area to check for waterfowl or shorebirds. Inside Dawson Forest you'll bird along a paved road; there are also several good dirt roads to bird for more variety. For non-birders who like to shop, there is a huge outlet mall close by.

Directions: To reach this area from Atlanta, go north on Georgia Highway 400 for 30 miles from the Perimeter, Interstate 285. The first stop light you come to (yes, after 30 miles) is GA 369. Continue 6.6 miles to Dawson Forest Road, and turn left. The outlet mall is on this corner. Drive 3.9 miles to GA 9, and continue another 1.5 miles to the always-open gate into Dawson Forest. This entire area is good birding, so I will offer a few generalities and you can bird along this road for as far as you like.

The open or cut areas such as that along the powerline near the gate are the places to look for Blue-winged Warblers, Prairie Warblers, Yellow-breasted Chats, Blue Grosbeaks, and Indigo Buntings. Most of the northern Piedmont upland hardwood forest breeders occur in the forest here, such as Ovenbird, Scarlet Tanager,

17 Dawson Forest Wildlife Management Area

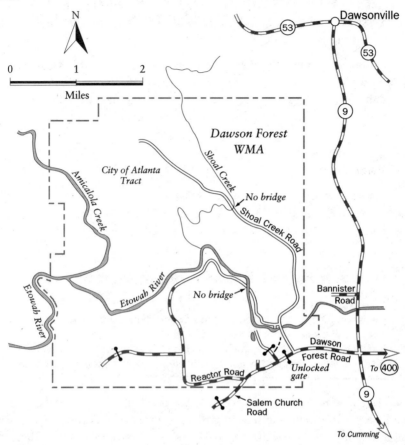

and Hooded Warbler. Check along the numerous streams for Louisiana Waterthrushes, Kentucky Warblers, and Acadian Flycatchers; and Northern Waterthrushes during migration. Check any areas of mature pine for Yellow-throated Warblers. Both Chuck-will's-widows and Whip-poor-wills also occur, and a few American Woodcocks. Eastern Screech-Owls are common; Great Horned Owls are near the open areas and Barred Owls near the river.

You have several options from here. From the gate, continue ahead 0.1 mile and turn right. Park in the lot immediately on your left, and walk up the road a short distance. On your right is a dirt trail that goes by a wooded swampy area always worth checking. On the left side is a pine stand and then a stretch of privet hedge also worth checking, especially during migration. After another pine stand is a fenced area and a gate across the road. Just beyond that, still on the left, is a pond that may have a few ducks in winter. This road is very popular with horse-back riders on weekends, and when there is much activity, it is less productive.

Return to Dawson Forest Road, and turn right. In 0.3 mile is another short road to the right worth checking for forest species. Continue on Dawson Forest another

0.3 mile to Salem Church Road on the left. This area is pretty open and has fewer forest species, but can be worth driving down until you reach a closed gate in about 0.5 mile. Dawson Forest becomes Reactor Road and continues almost 3 miles until the pavement ends near the Etowah River. There are several good patches of forest along this stretch, so stop wherever you find good habitat or see some birds. At the small hill where the pavement ends, the road continues as a rough dirt road (not suitable for passenger cars even when dry) for just over 1 mile, roughly paralleling the Etowah River until it ends at the river. This stretch can be very good during migration, as flocks follow the river on their way north or south. It is worth walking if you are here fairly early in the morning. When you have gone as far as you care to, return to the original gate.

If you still want to explore, 0.1 mile past the gate on your way out is a dirt road to the left. There is no sign, but this is Shoal Creek Road. This dirt road crosses the Etowah River in 0.4 mile, another area to check for migrants. Just past the river is another dirt road to the left, which roughly follows the river about 1 mile. This area has been logged more heavily than the area at the end of Reactor Road, and is not as productive. Shoal Creek Road continues for about 2.5 miles past the river; then you reach a ford across a creek, impassable even for four-wheel-drive vehicles. Trees along this stretch of road are pretty well cut, but it's good for species that like this habitat such as Prairie Warbler, Yellow-breasted Chat, White-eyed Vireo, and Field Sparrow. If you are here during winter, this can be good for sparrows as well.

The last spot to check is an area that may be wet after rainy periods and can hold shorebirds or waterfowl temporarily. Continue out Dawson Forest Road 1.5 miles from the gate to GA 9, and turn left. Drive 0.8 mile, crossing the Etowah River again, and turn left on Bannister Road. Immediately park on the wide shoulder. Look back down GA 9 the way you just came, in the field in front of you. After rain, the depression out in this field has had numerous shorebird or waterfowl species at various times. This is a bit of a long shot, but takes only minutes to check.

General information: This 10,000-acre site is the property of the city of Atlanta, but was formerly owned by Lockheed Aircraft Corporation. Lockheed had a research site here called the Georgia Nuclear Aircraft Laboratory, as well as a small test nuclear reactor. Though the facilities are long gone, you may run across some unusual fences with dire warnings to keep out; these are remnants from that program. Stay out of these areas, of course! They may have some remaining radiological activity. These areas are fenced and are not near any of the roads listed for this location.

ADDITIONAL HELP

DeLorme map grid: page 20, B5.
For more information: Georgia Department of Natural Resources; Dawson County Chamber of Commerce, (706) 265-6278.

18 Lake Lanier

Counties: Forsyth, Gwinnett, and Hall.
Habitats: Pine forest, mixed pine/hardwood forest, weedy field, reservoir.
Key birds: Common Loon, Eared Grebe, Horned Grebe, gulls.
Best times to bird: November through March.

The birding: Lake Lanier is a 38,000-acre deepwater lake northeast of Atlanta. It has numerous parks and boat ramps affording viewing access to large areas of the lower lake. While this lake is heavily used in warm weather, during the winter it gets less boat traffic and is a good place to look for waterfowl and gulls. Numerous rarities have been found, including gulls and a few Red-necked Grebes, so it pays to be alert for anything. Of the gulls, Ring-billed are the most common, followed by a few Herring and sometimes Bonaparte's. A scope is a necessity. Many of the parks and ramps have wooded areas nearby for landbirding possibilities. This route starts on the east side of the lake and works around the south side to the west side. If you do not have a full morning, you can start in the middle of the route at the dam by following the directions in reverse and going to only a few spots near the dam as time permits. The dam and spots near it are the most productive.

Directions: The first stop is Aqualand Marina, on the east side of the lake. Take Exit 12 (old 3) off Interstate 985, which is the Spout Springs/ Flowery Branch exit. Turn west toward the lake, bearing left at the fork, and drive 0.8 mile to Church Street, and turn left. This is just past an intersection and railroad track. In quick succession, turn right on Tanner Street and right again on Mitchell Street to Lights Ferry Road. Turn left, and note McEver Road as you cross it at 0.9 mile (this is where you turn on the way out). Continue on Lights Ferry Road 1.9 miles to a three-way intersection with an Aqualand sign on the left hillside. The left fork takes you to a lake view in 0.3 mile, next to a convenience store and heated restrooms. The right fork has no lake view. The center road has the best view, found by turning right 0.2 mile past the three-way stop at the Docks X-ZD sign. Drive to the end of this short road, and park. Walk to the left-hand edge of the lot (away from all the boats), and scan.

After trying these two spots, turn around and drive back to McEver Road. Turn right 4 miles to Holiday Road, Georgia Highway 347, and turn right. In 1.4 miles turn right on Big Creek Road, and drive 0.5 mile to Big Creek Park. Here you will find a boat ramp and another good lake view. After scanning, return to Holiday Road. A right turn will take you out to Lake Lanier Islands, which has some good lake views but costs $6 to get on, so most birders don't bother.

To continue, slightly to the right but almost directly across Holiday Road, is New Bethany Road. Follow it 1.1 miles to Waterworks Road, and turn right for 0.2 mile to Buford Dam Road (Waterworks veers left). Follow Buford Dam Road for 3.5 miles and note Sycamore Road on your left. In 0.3 mile on your right is

18 Lake Lanier

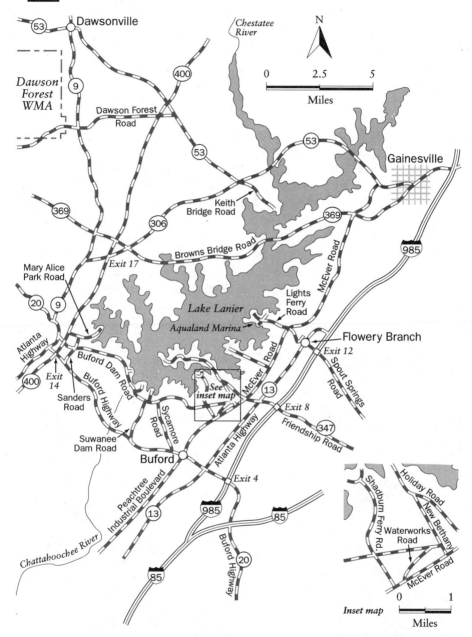

Lanier Park, one of the best viewing spots on the lake. There is no sign, but there is a large entrance. This park is closed for driving, unfortunately, so the only way to get to the lake is to walk in from East Bank Park (below).

In addition to good lake viewing, there are many pine trees for Pine Warblers, Brown-headed Nuthatches, and, rarely in winter, Brown Creepers. Continue 0.4

mile on Buford Dam Road to Suwanee Dam Road on the left and the East Bank Park on your right (no sign). Turn into the park 0.3 mile to a boat ramp, park, and scan the lake. You can also follow the shoreline, walking to the right to get out to the point in Lanier Park, but this is a bit of a hike and if the water level is high you may have to bushwhack your way in.

Continue on Buford Dam Road 0.7 mile to a large Lanier Project Management Office sign on the right, and turn right 0.6 mile to the visitor center, which has restrooms and maps. This used to be one of the best places to scan the lower lake, but due to what will surely become a case study in bureaucracy in action you cannot engage in any recreation here other than walking in and walking out of the visitor center. Just past here on Buford Dam Road is a road to the left down to the dam and powerhouse, worth a quick look but not very birdy. If you are here in spring or fall, it's worth checking for migrants along the river, but in spring there are lots of people as well. Another 0.3 mile on Buford Dam Road is the Lower Overlook on the right, another scanning spot when the gate is open. Buford Dam Road goes over the dam itself, and the best viewing spot is the parking lot in 0.4 mile. Scan carefully here for grebes, Eared Grebes in particular. Although they are rare in Georgia in winter, they're seen somewhat regularly here. When finished, continue on Buford Dam Road to West Bank Park, on the right in 0.5 mile. Follow the road to the right as far out as you can (0.5 mile), then walk 100 feet through the trees to scan the lake on both sides of this point.

Back on Buford Dam Road, continue 1.1 miles to a sign on the right for Little Ridge Boat Ramp. Turn right on Lanier Beach South Road to the ramp in 1.1 miles

The Lower Overlook at Lake Lanier. BRUCE HALLETT PHOTO

and scan. The last spot on this tour is another 1.9 miles along Buford Dam Road, then turn right on Sanders Road (no sign) for 0.7 mile to Mary Alice Park Road. Turn right, and follow the road 1.5 miles to another boat ramp, and scan.

You now have several choices to leave Lake Lanier, all from the corner of Sanders and Buford Dam Road. You can follow Buford Dam Road back around to the beginning and hit any of these spots again. To get back on an interstate, continue on Sanders Road across Buford Dam Road 0.8 mile to Buford Highway, GA 20. A right turn takes you to GA 400 in 0.6 mile at Exit 14 near Cumming. A left turn takes you back to I-985 in 10.3 miles at Exit 4 (old 1). Be aware that GA 20 changes names several times, so just follow the signs for GA 20.

General information: If your time is limited you can access the dam portion of this route quickly by exiting Interstate 985 at Exit 4 (old 1), Georgia Highway 20. Go west toward the lake and the towns of Buford and Sugar Hill. In 3.1 miles you will see Sycamore Road on your right. A right turn here gets you to Buford Dam Road in 2.6 miles. You can also access Buford Dam Road farther west by continuing past Sycamore Road on GA 20 for 2.3 miles to Suwanee Dam Road, where a right turn takes you to Buford Dam Road in 2.2 miles. At either of these two points, pick up the route from the main text above. All of the small parks and ramps mentioned have differing hours of operation, but all are open from 8 A.M. to at least 4:30 P.M. Some have a day use fee, usually $3. Many of the parks offer camping, but are only open April through August for that purpose.

ADDITIONAL HELP

DeLorme map grid: page 21, D6/7, E6/7.
For more information: U.S. Army Corps of Engineers Visitor Center, (770) 945-9531; Cumming-Forsyth Chamber of Commerce, (770) 887-6461.

19 Piedmont National Wildlife Refuge

County: Jones.
Habitats: Pine forest, mixed pine/hardwood forest, floodplain hardwood forest, young pine shrubland, weedy field, pond.
Key birds: Red-cockaded Woodpecker, Bachman's Sparrow, Cliff Swallow, Great Crested and Acadian Flycatchers, Eastern Wood-Pewee, Brown-headed Nuthatch, Wild Turkey, Blue-headed Vireo, Prairie, Hooded, and Kentucky Warblers.
Best times to bird: May to July for key species, otherwise all year.

The birding: Piedmont NWR is a 35,000-acre refuge with large areas of mature loblolly pine forest managed for Red-cockaded Woodpeckers (RCW), and is one of only two public-access areas for this endangered species in Georgia. There are several walking trails to try for woodpeckers and other interesting breeding species as well as a self-guided wildlife drive, and in winter there are ponds for waterfowl and fields for sparrows.

19 Piedmont National Wildlife Refuge

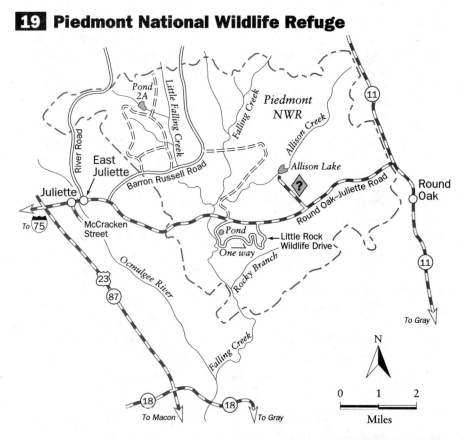

Directions: From Interstate 75 north of Macon, take Exit 186 (old 61) for Juliette Road to the east toward the town of Juliette. In 9.1 miles you will reach Juliette at McCracken Street on the right. Continue 0.3 mile on Juliette Road to the Ocmulgee River. Cliff and Barn Swallows nest under this bridge, and can be watched by pulling safely off the road on either end of the bridge and walking back to midriver. Continue on the same road, now named Round Oak–Juliette Road, to the refuge another 8 miles (stay to the left at 12.6 miles) and turn left at the Piedmont NWR sign (17.4 miles) to go 0.8 mile to the visitor center first. This is the best place to get current information and a map to whichever Red-cockaded Woodpecker cluster is the easiest for finding birds. The visitor center is open Monday through Friday, 8 A.M. to 4:30 P.M., and 9 A.M. to 5:30 P.M. on weekends, except federal holidays.

If your main goal is the woodpeckers, follow the directions you get at the visitor center, and expect Bachman's Sparrows. You can also expect to hear and see Summer Tanagers, Yellow-throated Vireos, Eastern Wood-Pewees, Great Crested Flycatchers, Prairie Warblers, Field Sparrows, and Yellow-billed Cuckoos. There are lots of Red-eyed Vireos here, and this is the southern limit of the nesting range for Blue-headed Vireos in Georgia, so you may have a chance to compare these two similar-sounding species. Both species are typically found in areas with slightly greater tree densities. All these pine trees are loaded with Pine Warblers and Brown-headed Nuthatches. Listen for the squeaky-toy calls of the foraging nuthatches. As you walk or drive along the gravel roads of the refuge you will also cross a few small streams; these areas have Acadian Flycatchers, Hooded and Kentucky Warblers, and Louisiana Waterthrushes. Keep in mind that this refuge is loaded with both ticks and chiggers, and protect yourself accordingly. If this is your first trip to the South and you don't know what chiggers are, see the introduction to this book or just believe me that you don't want any! Tall grass is the worst place for them.

The visitor center is on a paved road that continues 0.5 mile down to Allison Lake, worth checking in winter for waterfowl and for sparrows around the edges in weedy fields. This is true of any pond you find on this refuge, including the one on the wildlife drive. From Allison Lake you can walk several short trails, including the 2.9-mile Red-cockaded Woodpecker Trail. This takes you through at least one active cluster, with benches near active trees and plaques describing various aspects of RCW behavior and biology. During late May and early June the parents are busy feeding young and are most easily seen. DO NOT approach any active nests! This is also the easiest time to find Bachman's Sparrows, as they are singing constantly. Keep in mind that these sparrows act somewhat differently than most sparrows and usually sing from high, exposed perches. In winter the only time the woodpeckers are near the cluster is at dawn and dusk, and they are most difficult to see then. See the General Information section below for more details about this fascinating woodpecker.

If you have a four-wheel-drive vehicle, or if you want to enter another way, you can approach this cluster from gravel roads. Go back to Juliette Road and turn right. Note the entrance to the Little Rock Wildlife Drive (past the exit) at 2.7 miles, and turn right on the next gravel road (about 0.1 mile). This road looks easy to drive, but in 0.8 mile there is a stream crossing with steep banks that cars can't manage. You can park here, though; the cluster is now only 1.1 miles ahead of you on this same road, on the right. Go back out the same way.

The Little Rock Wildlife Drive you passed to get here is also good general birding. Turn left on Juliette Road and take the next right (by the sign) for the entrance to the wildlife drive, and pick up a leaflet at the box there. This 4.7-mile drive is good for a variety of species, including Wild Turkeys (which may be seen anywhere on the refuge). There is another good pond on the left 0.6 mile into the wildlife drive, although you will be looking into the sun in early morning. Next to the pond is a greentree reservoir (a low area that floods in fall) that can hold numerous dabbling ducks in winter. Past the pond the road becomes one-way, and you may stop anywhere you like to walk through the forest. At 2.5 and 3.2 miles are small streams to check for Acadian Flycatchers or warblers. At 4 miles is an RCW cluster on the right just before the sign describing a tornado-damaged area. As with all RCW sites, look for the trees with resin dripping down the trunk and white rings of paint around the base.

You can also explore any road you want, although many are for foot travel only. Another good area is Pond 2A with a couple of RCW clusters. Go west (out of the refuge) about 4.5 miles from the entrance of the wildlife drive to Barron Russell Road, and turn right. You can do this before the visitor center opens; Barron Russell is 1.2 miles east of the railroad tracks at the town of Juliette. There is a gravel-road loop you can try here, on flat roads in good condition. Watch your mileages, as there are no road signs. Go along Barron Russell Road for 1.4 miles, and turn left. Go straight at the first intersection (0.3 mile). In another mile (total 1.3) start watching along the left for an RCW cluster, obvious by the trees with white rings. Go another 1.3 miles (total 2.6), and make a sharp right turn. Drive another 0.9 mile to a road on the left. Walk or drive the road to the left 0.2 mile to get to Pond 2A, good for the species listed earlier plus Orchard Orioles and Yellow-throated Warblers.

Back out on the original road, continue 0.2 mile to another RCW cluster on the left. In another 0.6 mile you will cross a culvert over a tributary for Little Falling Creek, a beautiful rocky stream with breeding Louisiana Waterthrushes. From here it's 0.9 mile straight back to Barron Russell Road. Before you turn right to return to Juliette Road, there is a large bridge over Little Falling Creek worth checking, only 0.1 mile to your left.

General information: Of the 35,000 acres at this site, about 19,000 are actively managed for Red-cockaded Woodpeckers. They require mature pine trees with red heart disease to facilitate excavating nest holes. Most nests are about 40 feet

Little Falling Creek from Barron Russell Road.

above ground, but the birds will excavate at whatever height the heartwood of the tree has been softened by the disease. Almost all the holes in use here are in loblolly pines; most cavities face west. The birds drill small holes around the nest hole to cause sap to flow down the trunk, which is thought to discourage predators and conveniently provides an easy way for birders to recognize nest trees. The primary predator is actually the southern flying squirrel, followed by black rat snakes. Accipiters also take fledglings when they can. The birds typically lay eggs in late April and early May, and then fledge by early June. They usually have only one brood per season here in the Piedmont region, although they may renest if they lose the first clutch early enough. A cluster is typically made up of a mated pair and one to several male offspring from the previous year. Females are often ousted from the territory before their second year.

There are approximately 36 active clusters. From 1980 to 1992 the population was stable with about 25 clusters. Then in 1992, 80 artificial cavities were installed in about 13 clusters, and by 1996, 11 of these clusters had been occupied by at least one active male. The technique is to add cavity inserts in an active foraging area one-quarter mile away, and eventually one of the older male helpers starts roosting in an insert, although he may still be helping in the old site. He will start calling and patrolling in the new area, and eventually attract a female who has been expelled from her natal territory. In 1997, 20 more inserts were installed in 4 clusters, and by 1998 two of them had become occupied. There are also about 12 to 14 clusters in use in the nearby Hitchiti Experimental Forest.

There is food, lodging, and gas in Forsyth at Interstate 75, and, as an interesting aside, the movie *Fried Green Tomatoes* was filmed in the town of Juliette. If overpriced touristy cafes are your style, you will love the Whistle Stop Cafe. There are also several small stores.

This refuge is right next to the Rum Creek WMA and Lake Juliette, which are covered in Site 22, but are best in winter. This area is about 30 minutes north of Macon, which has other good birding spots including Ocmulgee National Monument (Site 21) and Central City Park and Lower Poplar Street (Site 20).

ADDITIONAL HELP

DeLorme map grid: page 34, C5.
For more information: Piedmont NWR, (912) 986-5441; Forsyth–Monroe County Chamber of Commerce, (888) 642-4628.

20 Central City Park and Lower Poplar Street

County: Bibb.
Habitats: Mixed pine/hardwood forest, floodplain hardwood forest, freshwater marsh shrubland, grassy field, river.
Key birds: Baltimore Oriole, Common Ground-Dove, Painted Bunting.
Best times to bird: April through October.

20 Central City Park and Lower Poplar Street
21 Ocmulgee National Monument

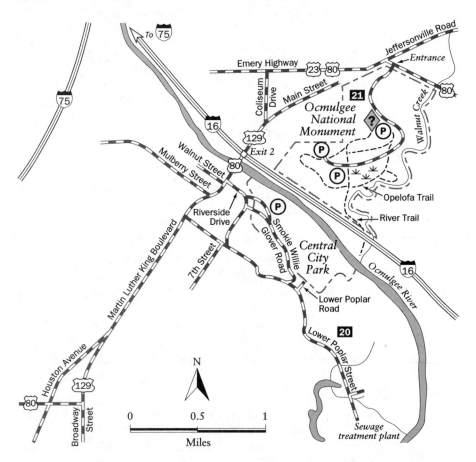

The birding: These two small areas offer some great birding right next to the city of Macon, and can easily be birded in a couple of hours from good paved roads. Central City Park is an open, manicured park on the bank of the Ocmulgee River with the only reliable nesting Baltimore Orioles in the state. Lower Poplar Street leaves the city behind and offers some excellent habitat for interesting breeding species as well as migrants. Brushy fields, wet pastures, and wet swampy woods occur right next to one another and can provide lots of migrants during spring or fall. This is the farthest spot north and inland to expect Common Ground-Doves (all year) or Painted Buntings (summer). Though this site description leads you to the park first, during spring migration you may want to pass by the park to check for migrants along Lower Poplar Street while it is early, and try the park later. This area is very close to Ocmulgee National Monument (Site 21).

Directions: Just east of Macon, take Exit 2 (old 4) from Interstate 16 and go south on Martin Luther King Boulevard, crossing the Ocmulgee River. This is also US Highway 80/Georgia Highway 87. In only 0.2 mile, turn left on Riverside Drive at the light and go another 0.2 mile. Turn left through a brick entrance into the park, and continue another 0.2 mile to park in a small lot on your left by the Macon Exchange Club building. Look for Baltimore Orioles around the large isolated trees in the park, especially sycamore and elm trees. Listen not only for their varied song but also for their harsh chatter. Birds this bright can be surprisingly difficult to find, so search carefully. Especially during spring migration, there may be other birds to enjoy, such as Eastern Kingbirds, swallows (Barn breed here, Rough-winged are seen commonly), warblers, or grosbeaks. Also watch for Mississippi Kites cruising above the river later in the morning. You can also walk the levee along the Ocmulgee River, soon to become the Ocmulgee Greenway Park. After you have birded the park, head over to Lower Poplar Street.

Turn left out of the parking area, and at the yield sign merge with Smokie Willie Glover Road (unsigned). Wind your way for 0.5 mile through ballfields, looking for shorebirds in any puddles during migration and Baltimore and Orchard Orioles in spring and summer. In winter there may be a few Ring-billed Gulls loafing here also. Cross the railroad tracks for another 0.1 mile and turn left on Lower Poplar Street. If you can't get here because a gate is closed, retrace your path along Willie Glover Road past the parking lot to Seventh Street, and turn left. Drive 0.3 mile and turn left again onto Lower Poplar Street. In 0.6 mile you are back at the intersection of Willie Glover and Lower Poplar.

Continue on Lower Poplar *Street,* and immediately start looking on the right shoulder for Common Ground-Doves, as locals frequently leave feed along the road for them here. You may have to look past all the House Sparrows, and if you don't see any doves, try again later as they are always nearby. You will reach Lower Poplar *Road* on the left in 0.1 mile; you can try the first 0.1 mile along this road for Ground-Doves. Both of these spots may have White-crowned Sparrows in winter.

When you are ready to continue, proceed down Lower Poplar Street—the next mile is worth walking. There is water along the left side of the road starting in 0.2 mile and continuing to a large, overhead powerline clearing in 0.3 mile. Breeding along here in the brush are Orchard Orioles and Indigo Buntings. Painted Buntings are frequently seen here in summer. Look for Yellow Warblers in the brush during migration, or Bobolinks in the powerline cut.

The next 0.5 mile to the small road on the left (0.8 mile from Lower Poplar Road) should be walked during migration for warblers and vireos, especially early in the morning. Look for either Louisiana or Northern Waterthrushes in the wet spots along the road. You can find up to 15 species of warblers here on a good day. Painted Buntings can be anywhere, and Yellow-billed Cuckoos and Blue Grosbeaks also breed along here.

You can also drive or walk 0.1 mile to the left along the paved road to some pastures at the end. Look for swallows flying over these fields; sometimes there are small pools of water to scan for shorebirds during migration. These fields are private property, so do not leave the paved road. A scope may help if the pools are too far out in the fields.

This is also a good area to check for hawks, mostly Red-tailed and Red-shouldered, with a few Broad-winged in spring or summer, and accipiters working the edges in winter. Also in winter, scan the blackbirds in the fields, as both Brewer's and Rusty have been (rarely) found among the Common Grackles, Red-winged Blackbirds, and Brown-headed Cowbirds.

Back on Lower Poplar Street the woods begin to thin out as you approach a sewage treatment plant, which offers more birding options. Go in 0.1 mile and turn left, and then go to the last building on your left. Report to the office for permission to bird (wearing your binoculars). Return to the entrance road, cross it, and drive a short way to the end of the pavement. There is a small pond to check for ducks, waders, or migrants in season, and you can bird the brushy areas in front of you. After you turn back toward the entrance road, you will immediately see another road on your right. This road, which is paved on your end, goes back down to the levee around the backside of the pond you just birded, to another area worth checking in any season, especially migration. This is also another shot at nesting Baltimore Orioles.

To exit, return the way you came and check again for ground-doves if you missed them on the way in.

General information: This spot is only minutes from downtown Macon or Ocmulgee National Monument (Site 21), and only about 30 minutes from Piedmont National Wildlife Refuge (Site 19). There are restaurants, gas stations, and motels nearby in Macon. A long-time Macon landmark is Len Berg's restaurant for a Southern-style lunch, about five minutes away. To get there from Exit 2, take Martin Luther King Boulevard just past Riverside Drive to Walnut Street, and turn right. Go 1.5 blocks and turn left into the alley.

ADDITIONAL HELP

DeLorme map grid: page 34, G5.
For more information: Macon–Bibb County CVB, (800) 768-3401; Len Berg's, (912) 742-9255.

21 Ocmulgee National Monument

See map on page 104

County: Bibb.
Habitats: Pine forest, mixed pine/hardwood forest, floodplain hardwood forest, freshwater marsh shrubland, grassy field, river.
Key birds: Yellow-bellied Flycatcher, Mississippi Kite; Prothonotary, Kentucky, and Canada Warblers.
Best times to bird: April through October.

The birding: The Ocmulgee National Monument was created to preserve the remains of a Mississippian culture outpost dating from about A.D. 1000. In addition to the historical site, there is some great birding in the forest along the Ocmulgee River and Walnut Creek, especially during migration. Even during the summer it has interesting breeders. There are several trails and road access to good spots, as well as fascinating historical exhibits and remains.

Directions: This park is just east of the town of Macon, on Interstate 16. Take Exit 2 (old 4), which is Martin Luther King Boulevard and US Highway 80. Go north 0.6 mile to Emery Highway (bear left on Coliseum Drive) and follow US Alt 129/80 to the right. In 0.8 mile you will find the entrance to Ocmulgee National Monument on the right. Turn in and drive 0.4 mile to the visitor center. There is a great museum here, but since this park does not open until 9 A.M., you should probably bird as soon as you get in while it's still cool, and visit the museum and restrooms later. During migration there are often birds working the trees around the parking lot, so it's worth walking around the perimeter to look. Even without migrants, there should be Eastern Bluebirds, Pine Warblers, and Brown-headed Nuthatches.

Yellow-bellied Flycatcher.

The Southeast Mound Trail leaves from the far side of this lot and offers good upland hardwood forest birding down to the rest of the park, or you can drive down to the wetter areas.

In fall this trail is the place to look for Yellow-bellied Flycatchers from mid-September until early October. These flycatchers are extremely rare in Georgia, but they have been found here fairly consistently for several years. You will have a chance to test your identification skills, as there may be up to four Empidonax flycatchers here in fall. The most common are Acadian, which breed here, followed by Yellow-bellied, then Least (usually a little earlier in the fall); Willow is casual. There are usually lots of Eastern Wood-Pewees as well, just to throw you off. This trail runs mostly through solid forest, so there may be more migrants along forest edges or the creek, and in September, look for Canada Warblers.

If driving, continue down the entrance road 0.2 mile to several wet, swampy ponds on your left and park in the pullout on the right. Scan the ponds for waders or ducks, usually Wood Ducks. If the ponds are very low, there may be mudflats to check for shorebirds during migration. You can either leave your car here or continue another 0.5 mile to the large parking lots by the mounds. You will want to walk this stretch of road looking for migrants anyway. Look for Mississippi Kites whenever you have a clear view of the sky, as they may be cruising over any part of this area in spring and summer. Fish Crows are pretty easy to find near the river here—just listen for their nasal calls.

There are two trails off toward Walnut Creek, and they are both worth walking. This area is full of herps, including snakes, so watch your step. This is a great place to find broad-headed skinks as well as birds. If you start at the large parking lot, take the Opelofa Trail around the pond area to the left, scanning the trees for migrants. In summer you may find such typical species as Yellow-billed Cuckoo, Wood Thrush, Hooded Warbler, or Summer Tanager along the way. Just around the corner, the River Trail goes off to the right and continues for 1 mile toward the Ocmulgee River, but it is frequently underwater and impassable in spring. If passable, look for Kentucky and Prothonotary Warblers, and Louisiana Waterthrushes down this trail, and there are even a very few Swainson's Warblers to hope for.

When finished with this trail, turn right to continue down the Opelofa Trail. This trail returns to the road in 0.5 mile where the Southeast Mound Trail comes in. It runs past several small ponds worth investigating for waders and Prothonotary Warblers as well as anything else that moves! Close to the road end is a 0.3-mile loop trail that goes down to Walnut Creek, also good for Kentucky and Swainson's Warblers. Other breeders to watch for are Great Crested Flycatcher, several species of woodpeckers, White- and Red-eyed Vireos, and Northern Parula. In open areas watch for other hawks, as both Red-tailed and Red-shouldered Hawks breed here; you might see Broad-winged Hawks in summer or fall. Other species in the open areas are Chimney Swift, Purple Martin, and Barn and Rough-winged Swallows. Brushier areas should have many Indigo Buntings, and a few Blue Grosbeaks, Yellow-breasted Chats, and Orchard Orioles. Eastern Kingbirds patrol the edges of the fields, feeding on the numerous insects you may not appreciate as much as they do. Exit the same way you came.

General information: The park is open from 9 A.M. to 5 P.M. daily, and it has a very interesting museum. This is an excellent place to bring a companion who is more interested in archaeology than birding. The park is very near downtown Macon and all its restaurants, hotels, and service stations. Also nearby are Central City Park and Lower Poplar Street (Site 20), and the Piedmont National Wildlife Refuge (Site 19) is about 30 minutes away.

ADDITIONAL HELP

DeLorme map grid: page 35, G6.
For more information: Ocmulgee National Monument, (912) 752-8257; Macon–Bibb County CVB, (800) 768-3401.

22 Piedmont Lakes Central

> **Counties:** Putnam, Hancock, Baldwin, Jones, Monroe, Butts, and Jasper.
> **Habitats:** Reservoir, pine forest, mixed pine/hardwood forest, upland hardwood forest, floodplain hardwood forest, weedy field, grassy field.
> **Key birds:** Migrant waterfowl, Horned Grebe, gulls.
> **Best times to bird:** November, December, March.

The birding: This site is a loose collection of several lakes and some nearby areas for other good birding opportunities. It is set up as a huge loop, one that would take all day to run, but each of these spots can be birded alone, or in any combination. All of the lakes with dam access can hold some ducks during migration, but Lake Oconee and to a lesser extent Lake Juliette are the only ones that almost always have a few birds somewhere. All the deepwater areas can have Common Loons or Horned Grebes in winter, and if you can get below the spillway you may find gulls as well, usually only Ring-billed in winter or Bonaparte's in migration. Directions to a couple of WMAs with good duck habitat are also included. All these lakes are worth exploring if you have time but will require a local map to do so. If you can only go to one of these sites, it should be Lake Oconee.

Directions: Checking a map before you start these directions will make them easier to follow. To get to **Lake Oconee** with a stop at **B. F. Grant WMA,** start near the town of Madison at Exit 114 (old 51) on Interstate 20, which is US Highway 441/129. Drive south on US 441/129 10.3 miles to Union Chapel Road, and turn right. This is where US 441/129 goes from four lanes to two. If you plan to be in the area for a while, you could also continue on US 441/129 another 2.2 miles to the Oconee Forest Ranger Station, which has maps and additional information during business hours on weekdays. Once you are on Union Chapel, drive for 6.4

22 Piedmont Lakes Central

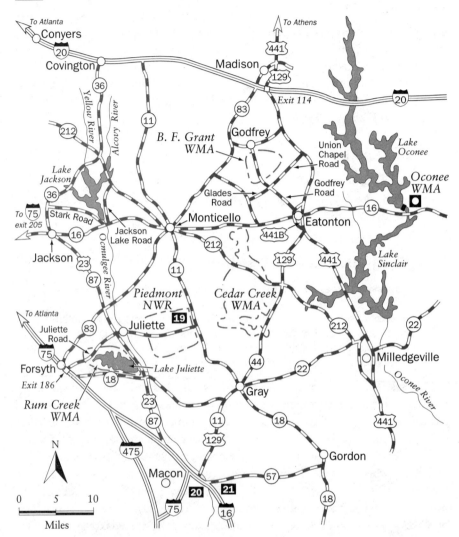

To Atlanta
Conyers
20
Covington
36
Yellow River
Alcovy River
212
11
Lake Jackson
36
To 75 exit 205
Stark Road
16
Jackson 23
87
Ocmulgee River
Jackson Lake Road
Monticello
212
Glades Road
B. F. Grant WMA
Godfrey
83
Exit 114
Madison
129
441
To Athens
20
Union Chapel Road
Godfrey Road
16
Lake Oconee
Oconee WMA
Eatonton
441B
129
441
Lake Sinclair
11
Piedmont NWR 19
Juliette
To Atlanta
Juliette Road
75
Forsyth
Exit 186
83
18
Cedar Creek WMA
Lake Juliette
44
212
22
Milledgeville
Oconee River
22
Gray
Rum Creek WMA
23
87
11
129
18
475
Macon
20 21
75
16
57
18
Gordon
441
N
0   5   10
Miles

miles to Godfrey Road (as you are doing this your road becomes Glades Road). Turn right on Godfrey Road. In 1.8 miles the check station will be on your right, just past Indian Creek Road. WMA maps are available here if you want one. Just past this building is a pond on your right, worth checking briefly for anything on or around it. Continue 1.2 miles from the check station to Hearnville Road, a good dirt road on the right.

Turn right, and in 0.8 mile (just past overhead powerlines), park at the trail that goes to your left. This trail runs up the west side of three successive ponds, which almost always have a few dabbling ducks in winter. Ducks frequently found here include Wood and Ring-necked, and Gadwalls as well as Pied-billed Grebes and Canada Geese. The marshy area below the pond closest to the road is good for Swamp Sparrows and Common Yellowthroats. The mixed woods here are also worth birding, as are the fields in winter for sparrows. Check the pine trees for Pine Warblers and Brown-headed Nuthatches. As you follow the trail away from the road, remember that the ponds are not all on the main trail, so it's worth taking each spur trail to the right to get to each pond. When you are finished, return to Godfrey Road.

You have to get around Eatonton to get to **Lake Oconee,** which is harder than it sounds. Take Godfrey Road to the left for 7.6 miles to US 441/129. Turn left for 1.2 miles, and turn right on Business US 441. Drive 1.5 miles to GA 16, and turn left. Drive 13.1 miles to Wallace Dam Road, and turn left. You have several options: Go up to the dam and walk a 2-mile trail to some ponds, or drive near the ponds and walk in for a short distance. To get to the dam, drive up Wallace Dam Road for 0.7 mile and check out the area above the dam from there. This area is only open weekdays, from 8:30 A.M. to 4 P.M. The road you passed on the right with the Tailrace Fishing Area sign takes you either 0.8 mile to an overlook of the spillway or another 0.3 mile (total 1.1 miles) down to the Oconee River. The area below the dam is not worth much time except to scan for gulls, although there may be Bald Eagles here.

The Wildlife Education Trail is also on Wallace Dam Road, on the right near GA 16. It consists of two interconnecting trails that form a loop about 1.9 miles long, and it goes through some decent mixed forest with a couple of fields and brushy areas for sparrows. Study the map at the beginning of the trail. The best area for ducks is the Oconee Waterfowl Area near the end of the Education Trail, a series of ponds on the west side of the Oconee River with an observation tower. If you don't want to hike that far, you can return to GA 16 and turn left. Park at the Oconee Waterfowl Area sign on the left in 0.9 mile. Walk the trail in to the ponds, scanning them through the trees as you approach so you don't spook any ducks by getting too close. This area is good for dabbling ducks, although you might see anything during migration. The brushy and weedy areas around the ponds are good for sparrows in winter. Across GA 16 is another trail that leads to two more ponds worth checking, although they are more out in the open. Any of these shallow ponds should be checked for shorebirds during spring or fall. Check with DNR if you are here in fall, in order to avoid hunting dates.

One last place worth checking here in winter is to continue on GA 16 for 1.7 miles to the entrance to the **Oconee Wildlife Management Area** on the left at the sign. The paved access road goes 2 miles to an overlook from this side, also open during weekdays only. There is a Bald Eagle nest near this overlook, so keep your eyes open for one of the pair to be flying around. The wooded areas along this road are always worth checking for woodland birds and sparrows in the brushy areas, mostly White-throated and Song Sparrows and Dark-eyed Juncos. There are more pines here to check for Pine Warblers and Brown-headed Nuthatches. Return to GA 16 when through, and drive back to Business US 441 at Eatonton. There are restaurants and gas stations here.

You now have another decision to make. **Lake Sinclair** is south toward Milledgeville, but it has no above-dam access on the west side and very limited below-dam access with a poor view of the river that does not usually produce many gulls. You do pass over arms of the lake on US 441 and can pick up a few birds that way, but this is generally not very rewarding. Your other choice is to bypass Lake Sinclair and head toward Lake Juliette, which is much more productive although not as good as Lake Oconee.

If you want to go to Lake Sinclair, go south on Bus. US 441 back to US 441, and turn left. Go 12.6 miles to Log Cabin Road, and turn left. In 4.4 miles the Georgia Power road to the dam is on your left, but there is no birding access. You can get below the dam by continuing along Log Cabin Road as it becomes a rough dirt road and joins the river in less than a mile. The birding here is generally poor.

To continue this trek toward **Lake Juliette,** take Bus. US 441 south 2.2 miles from GA 16 to US 441 and continue just past here around the loop to US 129/GA 44. Turn left, and drive about 21 miles to the town of Gray. On the way there you will be driving past Cedar Creek WMA on the right, and you can get a map at the check station. Turn right on GA 212; the check station is 6 miles on the left at the WMA sign.

To get to Lake Juliette from Gray, follow US 129 out of town to the west for 2.5 miles to GA 18 and turn right. In 12.8 miles you will reach US 23/GA 87. Reset your odometer, as the entrance to the dam overlook is easy to miss. Continue on GA 18 for 1.1 miles, looking for a dirt road on your right with a black metal gate. This gate is usually closed, but even if it is open this road is pretty rough and not suitable for passenger cars. Park well off GA 18 and walk 0.6 mile to the top of the dam. You are not allowed to walk across the dam itself, but you can scan the area above the dam from the end of this trail. The trail goes through some brushy areas worth checking for sparrows in winter, including Field Sparrows.

At the dam, a spotting scope is required since most of the ducks may be quite far out. There are usually Common Loons, and Pied-billed and Horned Grebes in winter. You will probably see rafts of dark "ducks" well off in the distance toward the power plant, and the good news is that they are virtually all American Coots. This lake has had several rare ducks over the years, mostly during migration, so check everything you can see. Lesser Scaups and other divers are regulars. Bald Eagles may be found, along with other raptors such as Red-tailed and Red-shouldered Hawks. When finished scanning, walk back to GA 16 and turn right toward I-75.

There is yet another WMA to check, the **Rum Creek WMA.** If you want a map, the check station is 2.7 miles down GA 18 on the right. The Non-Game Office for DNR is also here (with feeders), and there is a 0.5-mile trail through the woods to Lake Juliette. Back on GA 18, continue right for 4.7 miles to Colvin Road on the right, and turn right. Follow this paved road, bearing right at 0.3 mile, to Ebenezer Road at 1.3 miles from GA 16. This road becomes dirt and crosses upper Lake Juliette at 1 mile. This area is worth a quick stop for landbirds, but you won't usually find any ducks. Continue 0.5 mile to Holly Grove Road, and turn left for 0.2 mile to Juliette Road. This site is set up for winter birding, but in summer, Holly Grove is just lousy with Blue Grosbeaks and Indigo Buntings. At Juliette Road, turn left for 0.5 mile to the entrance to part of Rum Creek WMA and park at the closed gate on your right. There is no hunting allowed, and this area can be very good for ducks (what a coincidence). As you walk in, on your left is a swampy area and then two ponds. The birds can be pretty skittish, so proceed slowly and scan any water from as far away as you can to avoid spooking them. These are shallow areas best for dabbling species, including Wood Ducks. The hardwood forest you are walking through is also good for landbirds in any season. When satisfied, continue west on Juliette Road and drive 3.6 miles to I-75 at Exit 186 (old 61).

The last stop on your journey is **Lake Jackson**. Go north on I-75 19 miles to Exit 205 (old 67), which is GA 16. Proceed right (east) on GA 16 for 7.5 miles to the town of Jackson. Continue through Jackson, and at 8.7 miles from I-75 you will have to turn left to stay on GA 16. This is 1.2 miles past the intersection of GA 16 and US 23. From this left turn continue 7.1 miles to Stark Road, which is just before the Ocmulgee River. Incidentally, this is about 26 miles west of Eatonton from the Lake Oconee portion of this route. Turn left on Stark Road, and drive 1 mile to an unsigned road on the right with a convenience store. Turn right and drive 0.6 mile ahead into Lloyd Shoals Park, which loops around to give you a nice lake view that you might enjoy from picnic tables. This lake is pretty heavily developed, so it is not great for ducks, even during migration. There may be a few grebes and occasionally Common Loons. A few Ring-billed Gulls will be here, and sometimes Double-crested Cormorants, but that's about it. There is a small day-use fee of $2.

You can get below the spillway by taking the Fishing Pier road 0.3 mile down to the water, but this road gets a little bumpy in spots. Return to GA 16, and turn left. Cross the Ocmulgee River (Cliff Swallows breed here in summer) and quickly turn left on Jackson Lake Road just past the river. In winter, head up this road 1.1 miles to Riverside Park on the left, and pull in. There are restrooms at this small park, another lake view, and usually a few birds, including Dark-eyed Juncos. There are numerous pullouts along the river between this park and GA 16, and this area can be a pretty good spot for birds moving up or down the river during migration.

This concludes this tour, and you can return to I-75 the way you came. If you are going north from here, take US 23 right (north) from the town of Jackson, and drive 10.2 miles to the small town of Locust Grove. Turn left on Bill Gardner Parkway, and follow the sign 0.6 mile to I-75 at Exit 212 (old 68).

General information: Birding for ducks in Georgia can be pretty frustrating, but all of these lakes get a few of them in winter. In order from best to most duck-challenged, they are Oconee, Juliette, and Jackson. Sinclair gets some ducks but you can't get to the dam, so it doesn't make the list. Both B. F. Grant and Rum Creek

WMAs usually have at least a few ducks and can be quite good. Several other sites from this book are in this general area. Dyar Pasture WMA (Site 24) is on upper Lake Oconee, and Watson Spring (Site 23) is nearby. Piedmont NWR (Site 19) is very near Lake Juliette and Rum Creek WMA. This is also just north of the several Macon-area sites. Services while making this large loop are found in all the larger towns and along the interstates, which have your pick of lodging, gas, and restaurants.

ADDITIONAL HELP

DeLorme map grid: B. F. Grant WMA; page 28, G2. Lake Oconee; page 28, H5. Lake Sinclair; page 35, C10. Lake Juliette; page 34, D4. Rum Creek WMA; page 34, D3. Lake Jackson; page 27, H8.

For more information: Georgia Power Land Department Field Office (Lake Oconee), (706) 485-8704; Georgia Department of Natural Resources, Oconee National Forest, Oconee Ranger District, (706) 485-7110; Milledgeville–Baldwin County CVB, (800) 653-1804; Forsyth–Monroe County Chamber of Commerce, (888) 642-4628.

23 Watson Spring

County: Greene.
Habitats: Pine forest, mixed pine/hardwood forest, floodplain hardwood forest, weedy field, grassy field, river.
Key birds: Prothonotary, Kentucky, and Swainson's Warblers; Louisiana Waterthrush, American Redstart, Scarlet and Summer Tanagers, Grasshopper Sparrow, Cliff Swallow.
Best times to bird: April to October.

The birding: Watson Spring is a short trail that runs down from Georgia Highway 15 to the Oconee River, offering typical Piedmont woodland breeders along with migrants in spring and fall. It is a dirt jeep trail with a gentle slope and is easy walking. Nearby are a couple other small areas for roadside birding, including some different woods and weedy fields. This entire area can be birded thoroughly in a few hours. Morning is, of course, best.

Directions: This area is in northern Greene County, about midway between the town of Watkinsville and Interstate 20 on Georgia Highway 15. Since this trail is hard to find, we will start at the large bridge over the Oconee River on GA 15. To approach from the south, take Exit 130 (old 53) off I-20, onto GA 44. Go north 2.6 miles to US Highway 278. Turn left and go 0.3 mile, then right on GA 15. The bridge is about 10 miles from this corner. From Watkinsville, drive south about 12 miles to the bridge, then drive south 1.2 miles to the Watson Spring trail at a gate on the right. The trail you want is a dirt two-track, which goes off to the left and downhill inside the gate, just past the small overhead utility lines. If you reach a

23 Watson Spring
24 Dyar Pasture Wildlife Management Area

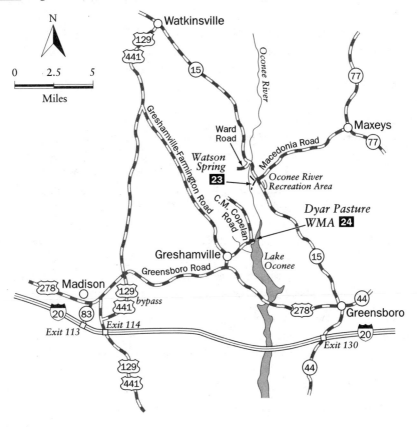

paved road to the left off GA 15 named Macedonia Road, you have gone too far. Park outside the gate but do not block it, and walk down the trail.

Look for Yellow-billed Cuckoos, Acadian Flycatchers, Red-eyed Vireos, Northern Parulas, and both Scarlet and Summer Tanagers. There is a small, swampy pond with dead trees 0.3 mile down the trail on the left, good for Prothonotary Warblers and Louisiana Waterthrushes. As you approach the river, there are Hooded and Kentucky Warblers, Wood Thrushes, and American Redstarts. In stands of cane and privet, look for Swainson's Warblers, although they are uncommon and should not be expected. The distance to the river is 0.7 mile. During migration you may see many other species of warblers and vireos as well. Return to your vehicle, and turn left (north) on GA 15.

In 0.7 mile you will see the road for **Oconee River Recreation Area** on the right. Take this road for 0.6 mile to the entrance, and park. There is a boat ramp, restrooms, and camping (for a fee). Check around the entrance for Eastern Wood-Pewees, Yellow-throated Vireos, and Yellow-throated Warblers (in pines). Return to GA 15 and turn right. You will cross the Oconee River bridge again in 0.5 mile;

look under this bridge for nesting Cliff and Barn Swallows. There are also usually a few Northern Rough-winged Swallows cruising around. Immediately on the north side of the bridge is Ward Road, also called County Road 18. Turn left.

This gravel road is in good condition except after heavy rains. In the first 0.3 mile check the field on the right for Field Sparrows and Loggerhead Shrikes, and the woods on the left for the same species as at Watson Spring. Since you are at the forest edge, you will see fewer birds than at Watson Spring, where you are in the middle of the forest. At 0.6 mile from GA 15 the forest opens up again into several weedy hay fields. Listen for the insect-like song of the Grasshopper Sparrow, and look for them perched along the barbed-wire fence on the left side of the road. Look also for Indigo Buntings and Blue Grosbeaks. The swampy areas off to the right are private, so do NOT leave the road, but watch for herons or ducks flying by. There are also several species of woodpeckers at this site, including Red-headed and Pileated.

In the large wet area in the field on the left you might see a Great Blue Heron. In late summer there may be other herons, usually Great Egrets and Little Blue Herons. Green Herons breed here but may be hard to find. At 0.9 mile the road enters the forest and marks the end of this tour. Yellow-throated Warblers and Brown-headed Nuthatches breed here. If you are here very early or very late in the day, Chuck-will's-widow may be heard, along with the three common owls (Eastern Screech-Owl, Barred, and Great Horned). The Barred Owl is more often heard near the river.

General information: This area is near Dyar Pasture Wildlife Management Area (Site 24). The closest services are either in Watkinsville, about 12 miles north on Georgia Highway 15, or south in Greensboro and at the intersection of GA 44 and Interstate 20.

ADDITIONAL HELP

DeLorme map grid: page 28, C4.
For more information: Oconee National Forest, Oconee Ranger District, (706) 468-2244; Greene County Chamber of Commerce, (800) 886-5253.

24 Dyar Pasture Wildlife Management Area

See map on page 115

Counties: Morgan and Greene.
Habitats: Mixed pine/hardwood forest, upland hardwood forest, floodplain hardwood forest, freshwater marshland, river, mudflat.
Key birds: Wood Stork, waders, Cliff Swallow, ducks, shorebirds.
Best times to bird: July through December.

The birding: This wetland was formerly a forest that was transformed by the filling of Lake Oconee. The rising water drowned the trees, and the seasonal rising and falling water level created a mudflat. In late summer this area is managed for waders—and there can be dozens and dozens on any given day. A cooperative

Little Blue Herons and Snowy Egret at Dyar Pasture.

project of the USDA Forest Service, Georgia DNR, Georgia Power, and Ducks Unlimited, Dyar Pasture now has a dike and water control system to maintain water levels at optimum for the habitat. If the summer has been very rainy, however, this area may have too much water for waders. Although it is part of Redlands WMA, this is a sanctuary with no hunting allowed. The surrounding forest also has good landbirding possibilities in spring through fall.

Directions: From the west, take the Georgia Highway 83 Exit off Interstate 20, which is Exit 113 (old 50). Drive north 1.4 miles to US Highway 278. Turn right toward Greensboro. In 0.8 mile, you will come to a stop sign. Turn left; you will still be on US 278. In 8.6 miles from the stop sign (total 9.4), you will cross Lake Oconee. After crossing the lake, take the third left. This intersection is 1.5 miles from the lake, a total of 10.9 miles. This is Farmington Road, although this sign tends to disappear. If there is no street sign, look for a sign on the right for Greenville Baptist Church, and a sign at the intersection that says "Greshamville 1 Mile."

To arrive here from the east, take Exit 130 (old 53), which is GA 44. Drive north 2.6 miles past several restaurants and gas stations to US 278. Turn left, and drive a total of 9.5 miles to Farmington, and turn right. Along the way, you will cross the bridge referred to at the end of this section for Cliff Swallows at 5.7 miles. After turning on Farmington, you will pass the ostentatiously named Greshamville Mall on your left, which consists of one small building. At 0.7 mile from US 278, turn right on C. M. Copelan Road (the red brick New Hope Baptist Church is at this intersection). After turning right, in 2 miles you will cross Lake Oconee again; although it is very small at this point, it can be quite good for swallows, including

Bank, in August. The second road to the right occurs in another 0.2 mile, where there is a large sign that reads "Dyar Pasture." Turn right onto the gravel road and drive 0.5 mile to the parking area and boat ramp. There is also a primitive toilet here.

At this point you have a couple of options. A five-minute walk to the left takes you to the wildlife viewing deck. This well-marked trail follows the river through nice hardwood forest, and has the typical middle Georgia floodplain forest breeding species. Excellent flycatcher habitat, the forest has Eastern Wood-Pewees and Acadian Flycatchers; at the edges there are Great Crested Flycatchers, and in the more open areas you can find Eastern Kingbirds. Yellow-billed Cuckoos and several species of woodpeckers are here, along with Gray Catbirds and Summer Tanagers. Vireos include Yellow-throated and Red-eyed in the woods and White-eyed in the open areas. Breeding warblers include Northern Parula, Common Yellowthroat, Hooded Warbler, and Yellow-breasted Chat. Both Indigo Buntings and Blue Grosbeaks nest here. Because you are near the water, this is also a good place to look for migrants during spring or fall.

During late summer and early fall, this is excellent for migrating swallows, and during August especially there can be impressive numbers of Purple Martins, and Northern Rough-winged, Barn, and Bank Swallows. Cliff Swallows breed nearby (see directions below); watch for them, although they are uncommon at best. Take care as you start to exit the woods because there are frequently waders and shorebirds in the mudflat at the end of the short trail, and a careless approach will flush them.

There is a wooden deck on your right, but the best viewing is at another deck at the end of the trail; it allows you to scan the extensive flats. To reach this deck, follow the short path to the left along the edge of the forest. This is the farthest northwest spot in Georgia to find Wood Storks in late summer, and although they are not always present, you have a good chance of finding these prehistoric-looking birds. They are most likely mid-July to late August, and as many as 40 have been seen here at once. In late summer there should be many Great Blue Herons and Great Egrets, and a few Snowy Egrets and Little Blue Herons. Green Herons breed here. You may see a Black-crowned Night-Heron if you are lucky. If you are really lucky you might find a Tricolored Heron, another species difficult this far inland.

There are frequently White Ibises here, although they tend to be the browner immatures. In fall and winter, depending on the summer water level, there are varying numbers of ducks. A very wet summer will provide poor growing conditions for duck food crops, but there are usually a few dabblers around anyway. The most common ducks here are Mallards and Wood Ducks, but as this site continues to be managed for waterfowl, the viewing opportunities should improve. You can explore along the dike to the right as long as the vegetation hasn't grown too high, but remember that chiggers are plentiful in the grass.

A nearby spot worth birding from early May through late July is a Cliff Swallow colony on Lake Oconee. Retrace your way to US 278, and turn left for about

3.8 miles to the old bridge. The swallows nest under this bridge. To leave from Dyar Pasture, retrace your route back to I-20, and from the Cliff Swallow colony drive back on US 278 from whichever direction you came.

General information: There are numerous restaurants and gas stations in Greenville and Madison.

ADDITIONAL HELP

DeLorme map grid: page 28, D4.
For more information: Walton Game Management Office, (770) 918-6416; Greene County Chamber of Commerce, (800) 886-5253.

25 Piedmont Lakes East

Counties: Hart and Columbia.
Habitats: Reservoir, pine forest, mixed pine/hardwood forest, upland hardwood forest, floodplain hardwood forest, weedy field, grassy field.
Key birds: Common Loon, Horned Grebe, migrant waterfowl, gulls.
Best times to bird: November, December, March.

The birding: This site consists of two of the large lakes on the Georgia/South Carolina border, Lake Hartwell and J. Strom Thurmond Lake (formerly Clark Hill Reservoir). As is typical in Georgia, neither of these lakes really has large numbers of waterfowl during the winter, but the areas of deep water near the dams are worth checking during waterfowl migration. They both have at least a few Common Loons and Horned Grebes throughout the winter. You can also check below both dams for gulls in winter. Most of the gulls will be Ring-billed, with a few Bonaparte's and rarely a Herring. Rare gulls have also been spotted below various Georgia dams, so check them all.

Though only directions to the dam are given, a local area map may allow you to explore the large areas of public lands nearby both lakes if you will be here for a while. The months given above are the best for duck migration, but a few ducks will be in both lakes all winter. At times when lake levels are down, the upper reaches may have enough mudflat habitat to attract shorebirds during migration.

Directions: **Lake Hartwell** is located northeast of Athens in Hart County, and is accessed from the town of Hartwell. From town, take US Highway 29/Georgia Highway 8 east toward the dam. From the point where four lanes become two on the east side of town, drive 5.8 miles to the visitor center on your left at Dam Road. The center has maps and additional information if you want to stay in the area. To view the area above the dam, turn left on Dam Road and follow it 0.2 mile into a large parking area and boat ramp. The best viewing is from here; be careful to check around both sides of the island in front of you. To access the spillway, go back to US 29/GA 8 and turn left for 1.1 miles to the Lake Hartwell Dam and Powerplant Road and turn right. Follow the road down to a parking

25 Piedmont Lakes East

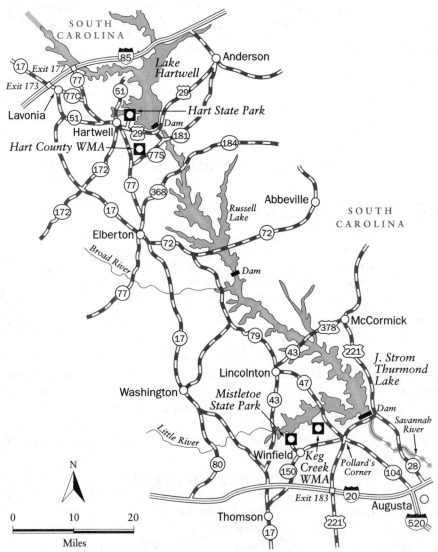

area and scan for gulls. This works better when the turbines are running to create some gull food out of fish unfortunate enough to be caught in the blades.

Some nearby spots worth checking include Hart State Park, with camping and other facilities but below average birding, and Hart County Wildlife Management Area, with some decent hardwood forest and beaver ponds. To get to the park, take Ridge Road north from US 29/GA 8 just outside town on the way to the dam for about 1.5 miles and turn left on Hart State Park Road into the park. For Hart County WMA, take GA 181 from the intersection of Dam Road and US 29/GA 8 for 2.1 miles to GA 77 Spur and turn right for 4.2 miles to the WMA entrance. Pick up a map at the WMA check station.

J. Strom Thurmond Lake is just north of Augusta on the border with South Carolina. Like Lake Hartwell, it has good viewing areas above the dam but with better access and usually more waterfowl and it has access below the spillway to check for gulls. From Augusta, go west on Interstate 20 to Exit 183 (old 61) and take US 221 to the right (north). The dam is 14.5 miles ahead (make sure you take the right jog in the road after 1.5 miles). The visitor center is actually across the dam in South Carolina; you can go there first, if you wish. To bird the area above the dam, park just before the dam at the road to the spillway, by the Below Dam, Ga. sign. Walk across US 221 to the West End Recreation Area (closed in winter), and scan any available water. Loons and grebes are usually in deeper water out in the middle and ducks are more likely around the shoreline. You can also walk around the shoreline to the left (away from the dam) to check a couple of small, productive coves. This area generally has more waterfowl all winter than Lake Hartwell, and during migration the duck species-mix changes daily. To check below the dam, drive down the road you are parked on for 0.6 mile and turn left into an overlook area (restrooms are available). This is the best viewing for gulls below the dam, again, best when power is being generated. You can also take the road all the way to the end (another 0.2 mile) to get down to the river.

Some nearby spots include Keg Creek WMA and Mistletoe State Park. Keg Creek WMA is 800 acres of mostly rolling mixed pine/ hardwood forest with only fair birding. Return on US 221 about 5 miles to Pollard's Corner and turn right on GA 47. The entrance to Keg Creek is on the left in about 2 miles. If you are trying this, you can also continue another 4 miles along GA 47 to cross the lake again. There are usually a few ducks here, although spots to scan from are few. To get to Mistletoe State Park, take GA 150 west from Pollard's Corner about 6 miles to the town of Winfield, where you should turn right and follow the signs for the park. Birding is limited, but there is camping and lodging.

General information: Both of these lakes can be checked at the dam in just a short time, or you can spend several hours birding the surrounding areas. Lodging, food, and gas can be found in the towns of Hartwell and Augusta. Several of this book's other sites that offer excellent birding are near J. Strom Thurmond Lake. They are Site 26, Merry Brothers Brickyard Ponds; Site 27, Savannah Lock and Dam; and Site 28, the Augusta Levee.

ADDITIONAL HELP

DeLorme map grid: Lake Hartwell; page 23, F10. J. Strom Thurmond Lake; page 30, C4.

For more information: Hartwell Lake Natural Resource Management Center, (706) 376-4788; Hart State Park, (706) 376-8756; J. Strom Thurmond Lake Natural Resource Management Center, (706) 722-3770; Mistletoe State Park, (706) 541-0321; Georgia Department of Natural Resources.

26 **Merry Brothers Brickyard Ponds**

See map on page 126

County: Richmond.
Habitats: Mixed pine/hardwood forest, upland hardwood forest, floodplain hardwood forest, cypress-tupelo swamp, freshwater marsh shrubland, weedy field, freshwater marshland, pond.
Key birds: Painted Bunting, Prothonotary Warbler, Least Bittern, White-crowned Sparrow, Bald Eagle, Anhinga, Redhead, and other ducks, passerine migrants.
Best times to bird: All year.

The birding: The Merry Ponds are a collection of ponds of varying sizes and ages crisscrossed with dikes that provide relatively easy access. There are also a couple of small streams with riparian wooded sections along them, and several mostly overgrown fields. This selection of good birding habitat attracts a wide variety of birds all year long and is a great single location for many sought-after species.

Directions: To reach Merry Ponds (as it is usually called), take the Bobby Jones Expressway (Interstate 520) south from I-20 at Exits 196 (old 64). Take I-520 9.9 miles to Georgia Highway Spur 56, Exit 10 (old 8). Turn left, and drive 2.9 miles to an unsigned paved road on your right. Some hints to help you find this road are to note the appearance of ponds on your right, and to realize that Spur 56 intersects Gordon Highway at a major intersection just 0.1 mile past this turnoff. This road is called Inner Plant Road, and runs along the north side of the complex. Turn right and drive 1.7 miles to a well-maintained dirt road called Fish Shack Road; it is also unsigned, but note the sign pointing right to the fish shack. Turn right and stop at the shack for permission to bird. These ponds are leased as a fishing area to the owner of the shack, and while he allows birders in for free, you must stop here to ask. DO NOT BIRD anywhere, even along the road, without permission.

There are many ways to bird this wonderful area, depending on the season and on what you are looking for. Refer to the map for the following roads and areas along them. Inner Plant Road is paved, and always in good shape. Mining Haul Road is dirt but is almost always in good shape, too. Long Ponds Road is usually good to Mining Haul Road. If it has rained recently, be very careful where you drive. The lease manager at the shack reports that a percentage of his income is from people who get their vehicles stuck and need a tow! A general way to bird this is to start at the shack and work toward the other end. Read the entire section first; see which spots you wish to bird, and make up your own game plan.

At the shack there is a small pond good for Black-crowned Night-Herons in winter. To get there, walk directly away from the shack on the right side of Fish Shack Road. Cross the dirt road, then cross another dirt road called Foster's Lane. If you follow Fish Shack Road past the shack, turn right on Long Pond Road in 0.1 mile. The continuation of Fish Shack Road may be passable in a four-wheel-drive vehicle but is not recommended for passenger cars. This road eventually loops around to Mining Haul Road and is 1.2 miles long. If you follow Long Ponds Road, check the ponds on both sides of the road for ducks and waders.

26 Merry Brothers Brickyard Ponds

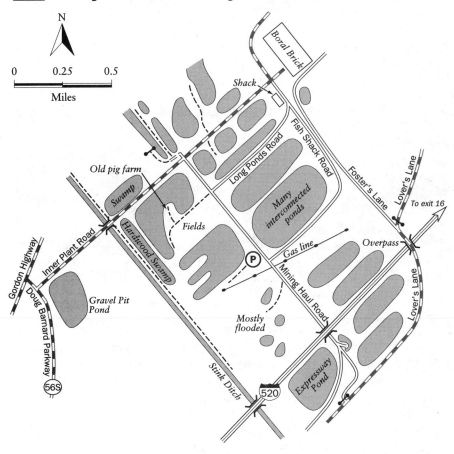

There are usually lots of Great Egrets, Great Blue Herons, and Double-crested Cormorants, and at least a few Anhinga. These ponds are fairly shallow and are better for dabbling ducks.

In 0.7 mile you will reach Mining Haul Road. Pig Farm Road is directly across; it's an undrivable dirt path good for seeing sparrows in winter, including White-crowned. Common Ground-Doves are sometimes found here but are not reliable. Turn left on Mining Haul Road, scanning any pond you can see. The pond on the right can be very good for ducks, but they may be in the back away from the road, so you should scan down the parallel rows of trees. In 0.4 mile there is a dirt turnoff on the right. Park here. A trail continues to your right along a row of trees, good for migrants in spring and fall.

Across Mining Haul Road is a very short path through some brush to scan a large pond good for more waders, ducks, and gulls. This is also a good pond for Bald Eagles. The brush should be checked in winter for sparrows and Orange-crowned Warblers. Continuing along Mining Haul Road, in 0.1 mile Fish Shack Road comes in on your left. Just past here is a powerline right-of-way that can be

Expressway Pond at Merry Brothers.

very good for sparrows. In another 0.2 mile a dirt road goes off to the right. This is one of the better areas, but you may have to walk in if the road is muddy. It's a patchwork of fields and marshy ponds—look for Least Bitterns and King Rails in spring and summer. In winter, it's a great place for sparrows, including Vesper and White-crowned, and Orange-crowned Warblers.

Back on Mining Haul Road, in 0.3 mile you will pass under a new section of I-520. The main road veers right, but stop at the small stub road farthest to the left about 100 feet beyond the overpass. A short path leads you to a deep pond usually good for Common Loons, Horned Grebes, and diving ducks such as mergansers. Back to the main road, continue to a large and deep pond on your right from 0.4 mile to 0.8 mile beyond the overpass. This is the best pond for divers, and it is fairly reliable for Redheads. The area beyond here is undergoing a lot of change due to road construction, but any scraped field or muddy area should be checked for shorebirds (this is true of the entire ponds area).

This is the end of the complex. Turn around and go back to the intersection with Long Ponds Road and continue 0.2 mile to Inner Plant Road, scanning on both sides. Cross Inner Plant Road, and park. This side of the road offers access to some older ponds that frequently have more ducks on them because fishermen don't use them as much. You will have to walk away from the road down the small trail to have a decent view. Another similar spot is 0.3 mile toward the shack area (left turn off Mining Haul Road). Again, you will need to walk back away from the road for good views. The large trees at this spot produce Baltimore Orioles in winter, reported almost annually from this exact spot but only a few times each winter at the most. The powerline area that runs along Inner Plant Road is another great place to look for sparrows. Continue in this direction 0.4 mile to the entrance to the shack, and continue across the intersection 50 to 100 feet. In summer the brushy willows on both sides of the paved road are excellent for Painted Buntings, as are other similar areas in the pond complex.

You are at the beginning again, and there is still one good place left to bird. Turn back around and follow Inner Plant Road to Mining Haul Road. Just past here is a great cypress-tupelo swamp area on your right, good in spring and summer for Barred Owls, Hooded and Prothonotary Warblers, Louisiana Waterthrushes, and Northern Parulas. In winter Rusty Blackbirds are rare but worth looking for. At 0.5 mile from Mining Haul Road, park on the left just before a small canal. Known locally as Stink Ditch due to the offal-dumping habits at a meat-processing plant upstream, it is one of the best areas in the entire complex. A gated-off jeep trail runs along the ditch and is great for migrants spring and fall. Swainson's Warblers sometimes breed somewhere along this ditch, although in very low numbers. Check Stink Ditch (and other canals) for Yellow-crowned Night-Herons in summer. The brush on the right-hand side of Inner Plant Road after the ditch is also good for Painted Buntings and Blue Grosbeaks. This is essentially the end of the ponds, but you can check the large pond on your left as you drive back to Spur 56 (0.5 mile in front of you). This pond is not part of the Merry Ponds, so you have to scan from your car.

General information: This area was created by many years of digging clay for use in making bricks, which is how it got its name. Though now leased by the Boral Brick Corporation, birders continue to refer to it by its old name.

ADDITIONAL HELP

DeLorme map grid: page 31, F7.
For more information: Augusta Metropolitan CVB, (800) 726-0243.

27 Savannah Lock and Dam

County: Richmond.
Habitats: Mixed pine/hardwood forest, floodplain hardwood forest, weedy field, grassy field, river.
Key birds: Mississippi Kite, Yellow-throated and Prothonotary Warblers.
Best times to bird: May through July.

The birding: The Savannah Lock and Dam is actually in Augusta, and gets its name from the Savannah River. This park is right on the river and is a great place to look for Mississippi Kites soaring over the water, as well as a few other interesting breeding species. A small park, it can be birded in less than an hour. It is dominated by large hardwoods, with a few pines and some swampy areas. At the far end of the park are some fields worth checking in winter for sparrows.

27 Savannah Lock and Dam
28 Augusta Levee

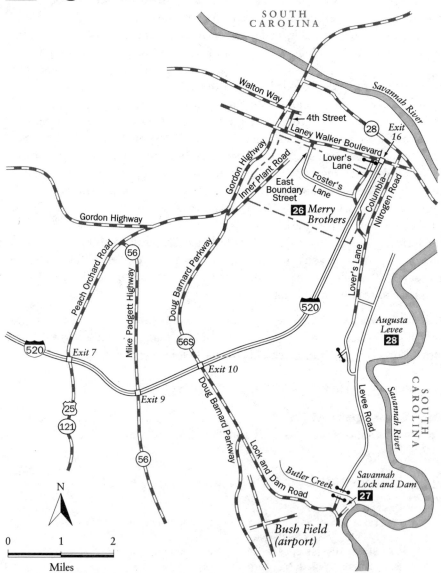

Directions: To reach the Savannah Lock and Dam Park, take the Bobby Jones Expressway (Interstate 520) south from I-20 at Exits 196 (old 64). Take I-520 9.9 miles to Georgia Highway Spur 56, Exit 10 (old 8). Turn right on Spur 56, also called Doug Barnard Parkway, for 1 mile. Turn left on Lock and Dam Road, and follow the road around the airport on your right for 2.2 miles to the entrance. If the grass at the airport is not too high, you might find Upland Sandpipers in spring and fall, although they are rare. Eastern Meadowlarks are common, and you may see Red-tailed Hawks or Loggerhead Shrikes hunting from the perimeter fence. Scan over the airport for soaring Mississippi Kites from midmorning on.

At the park entrance, there is a $2 fee. Once inside, turn left and follow the road through the park. Park anywhere that looks good, and scan for any movement in the mature hardwoods throughout the park. The small stream on your left 0.1 mile past the entrance usually has breeding Prothonotary Warblers. Yellow-throated Warblers also breed here, but they are frequently pretty high up in the trees, so it is important to listen for their clear, cascading song to find them. This park is swarming with Northern Parulas during breeding season as well. The last several years have seen a pair of breeding Swainson's Warblers. During spring and fall the park is good for migrants following the river, so look and listen for feeding flocks anywhere in the trees.

To look for Mississippi Kites, drive through the wooded area to the river, and pick a spot to scan upstream and down. The kites are best seen midmorning, when the sun heats up enough air to create the thermals these birds love to ride, although you may see them any time of day. In winter you can check the field at this end of the park for sparrows, but you have access only to the near end.

General information: This park is close to both the Augusta Levee (Site 28) and the Merry Brothers Brickyard Ponds (Site 26), and can be combined with either one of them. There are no amenities at the park, but any exit on Interstate 520 has several restaurants and gas stations.

ADDITIONAL HELP

DeLorme map grid: page 31, G7.
For more information: Augusta Metropolitan CVB, (800) 726-0243.

28 Augusta Levee

See map on page 126

County: Richmond.
Habitats: Upland hardwood forest, floodplain hardwood forest, cypress-tupelo swamp, grassy field, river.
Key birds: Yellow-crowned Night-Heron, Prothonotary and Swainson's Warblers, Louisiana Waterthrush, Painted Bunting, migrants.
Best times to bird: April through October.

The birding: This site is on a large levee along the Savannah River near Augusta, and it involves birding along the river for migrant passerines. A dirt road is birdable for about 3 miles along the river, and since many migrants follow the large rivers on their way north or south, this can be an excellent spot to look for them. There are also a couple of nearby sites to check for other interesting species, including some swamp breeders.

Directions: To reach the Augusta Levee, take the Bobby Jones Expressway (Interstate 520) south from I-20 at Exit 196 (old 64). Take I-520 14.4 miles to Laney

Walker Boulevard, Exit 16. Turn right at the end of the exit ramp, and almost immediately turn right again onto Columbia-Nitrogen Road. The chemical plants along this road may assault your nose, but beyond them lies good birding, so press on! In 0.6 mile take a short dirt road to the right. Drive 0.1 mile to the top of the small hill and bird this brushy corner for sparrows in winter or scrub breeders such as Orchard Orioles and Painted Buntings in summer. Continue along Columbia-Nitrogen Road another 0.8 mile to the northern end of Lover's Lane, which comes in on the right. Columbia-Nitrogen Road now becomes Lover's Lane, and continues for 1.1 miles to an unmarked dirt road on your left. This is one of the two roads up to the levee. If they are planted in crops, the fields you have just driven past can be good for Bobolinks in spring. The road up to the levee is only 0.2 mile long and the wet pastures are worth checking as you drive by. Sedge Wrens are sometimes found here. Up on the levee you have the choice of going either direction. Most birders head right first, as there is much more habitat in that direction. The dirt road on the levee can be really slick for days after rain; exercise caution. Lots of hunters use this road to access private land, so watch for other vehicles and under NO circumstances cross a chained-off side road.

Turning right first, just watch and listen for flocks of migrants as they forage along the levee. There are several interesting breeding species here, including Wood Duck, Red-shouldered Hawk, Prothonotary Warbler, Swainson's Warbler, and Louisiana Waterthrush. Listen for the last three species' songs as you pass by the swampy areas they prefer. A river oxbow 0.4 mile along the levee on your left has breeding Yellow-crowned Night-Herons, and if you are lucky you might spot one of their messy stick

The Savannah River.

nests in a tree. Another 0.9 mile past the oxbow is the old road to the levee on your right, which is the other road access. The road along the levee continues another 2.3 miles to Butler Creek, where it is permanently chained off. Search for migrants anywhere along this road, and when you are finished, return to the starting point. The levee can be birded another 1 mile in this direction, but the mature trees soon give way to chemical plants and the levee becomes much less interesting. Return to the original starting point on the levee and go back to Lover's Lane.

If you have time, turn left on Lover's Lane to continue birding (or turn right and retrace your route to exit). The road becomes dirt and heads toward a couple of good cypress-tupelo swamps. The first is 0.5 mile on your left down a short dirt spur (walk-in only), and you drive right into the second area another 0.2 mile farther down the road. The birding is great for typical swamp species, but also great for snakes, so watch your step. Another 0.3 mile past here is the old levee road on your left, so you can either return to the levee or retrace your path and bird anywhere you think needs more attention on the way back.

One last area to check is to go back to where Columbia-Nitrogen Road turns into Lover's Lane, and turn left on Lover's Lane. This road is paved for just more than 1 mile (until you cross over I-520). There is good scrub birding for sparrows in winter or Painted Buntings in summer all along the road, and a large wet area on your right about 0.5 mile in. After you cross over I-520, the old Lover's Lane goes off to your right but is chained off. This dirt road is about 0.6 mile long, and offers more of the same habitat for walk-in birding. You can also continue down what is now Foster's Lane for 1.0 mile to a sharp right turn. This corner is excellent for Painted Buntings. The area before this turn on the left is the Merry Brothers Brickyard Ponds, Site 26, but it is not accessible from this road. If you follow the road to the right it is now East Boundary Road, and it takes you back to Laney Walker Boulevard in 0.6 mile. A right turn on Laney Walker will take you back to I-520. If you want to go to Merry Brothers, turn left on Laney Walker for 0.5 mile and turn then right on Fourth Street. After 0.4 mile, turn left on Walton Way and then left again quickly on Gordon Highway. In 1.9 miles turn left on GA Spur 56, and then left in 0.1 mile on Inner Plant Road. From here follow the directions in the Merry Brothers section.

General information: This area has lots of great habitat, but is not a place to be after dark or before light. These particular dirt roads can be pretty treacherous after rain, which is common in spring. If the roads cannot be driven, the birding is just as good while walking along the levee. The Savannah Lock and Dam (Site 27) is also nearby.

ADDITIONAL HELP

DeLorme map grid: page 31, F7, G7.
For more information: Augusta Metropolitan CVB, (800) 726-0243.

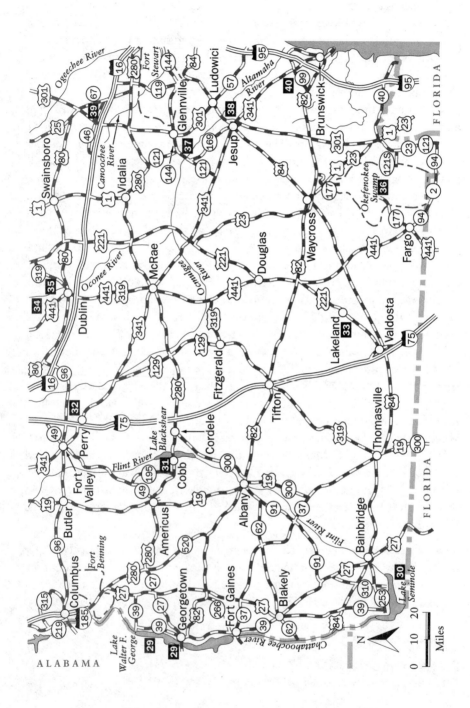

Coastal Plain Region

29 Eufaula National Wildlife Refuge and Lake Walter F. George

Counties: Stewart, Quitman, and Clay.
Habitats: Diked ponds, reservoir, hardwood floodplain forest, pine forest, freshwater marsh shrubland, weedy field, grassy field.
Key birds: King Rail, Purple Gallinule, Prothonotary Warbler, Anhinga, Least Bittern, Greater White-fronted Goose; sparrows, including LeConte's; waterfowl, gulls.
Best times to bird: May through July for first five species, October through February for others.

The birding: Lake Walter F. George is a 48,000-acre deepwater lake on the Georgia and Alabama border. In winter there are often gull concentrations below the spillway, and above the dam the lake is good for ducks, especially divers and species that prefer large bodies of water, such as loons. During migration just about any duck could show up, and several rare gulls have been spotted. The Eufaula NWR is mostly in Alabama, but the Bradley Unit is in Georgia and offers great fall and winter birding around two large diked impoundments. The walking is easy around the impoundments, and many rare species have been found. During fall these areas have great potential for species often very difficult to find in Georgia.

Directions: Drive south on Interstate 185 until it ends in Columbus. Take Exit 1B (old 1) on US Highway 27/280 to go east through Fort Benning for 11.4 miles to where US 27 splits off. The speed limit is vigorously enforced here. Turn right on US 27. After 2.2 miles, you will reach Riverbend Road on the right. If you have time, travel 8 miles down this road to Riverbend Park, good for ducks and Bald Eagles in winter or landbird migrants in spring and fall. Back at US 27, turn right and travel 8.9 miles to GA 39, then turn right again (total 11.1 miles from US 280). After 12.4 miles from US 27, GA 39 turns left and the road you have been on becomes GA 39 Spur. Turn left to continue on GA 39. At 3.8 miles Florence Marina State Park will be on your right. You can view the river from the marina for gulls or lingering Forster's Terns in winter. Across the water at the marina, to the right, is a small sandbar that may have a few shorebirds on it. In winter these might be Dunlins or Least Sandpipers, but in migration they could be anything. For turtle fans, the very rare Barbour's map turtle may be found in the marina. There is camping and cabins, and some nice pine habitat for Brown-headed Nuthatches or Pine Warblers. Back on GA 39, in another 2 miles you will pass through a sod farm that should be checked for shorebirds in fall. At 0.8 mile past the sod farm (6.8 miles from the turn) is a boat ramp access road on the right, offering another view of the Chattahoochee River above the lake.

29 Eufaula National Wildlife Refuge and Lake Walter F. George

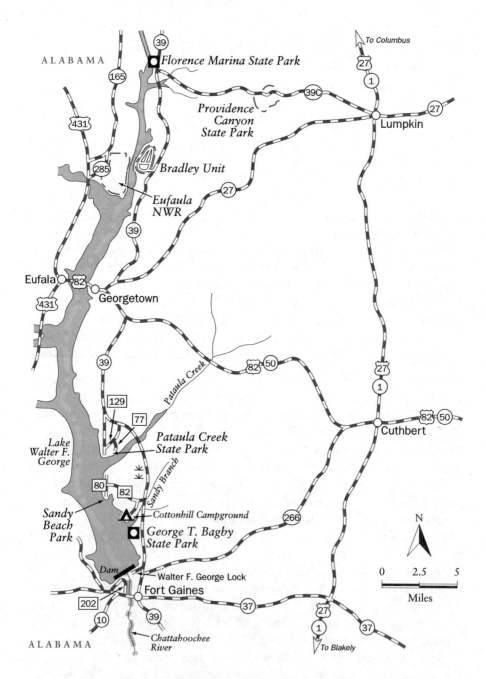

ALABAMA

To Columbus

Florence Marina State Park

Providence Canyon State Park

Lumpkin

Bradley Unit

Eufaula NWR

Eufala

Georgetown

Pataula Creek

Cuthbert

Lake Walter F. George

Pataula Creek State Park

Sandy Branch

Sandy Beach Park

Cottonhill Campground

George T. Bagby State Park

Dam

Walter F. George Lock

Fort Gaines

N

0   2.5   5

Miles

Chattahoochee River

To Blakely

ALABAMA

Another 3.9 miles (10.7 miles from the intersection) is the sign and access road for the Bradley Unit of the Eufaula NWR. The dirt access road, 0.5 mile long, leads you to the parking area and the dike road loop around the 3,000-acre Bradley Unit at the game check station. Walking is the only way in, so park here. The entire loop is just under 5 miles, with a 0.75-mile long cross-dike. If you have time, the entire loop is worth walking, but if not, you can go in either direction and cut across the cross-dike to create a 3.5-mile walk.

The habitat changes from year to year, so here are a few particular spots to concentrate on. In summer look for King Rails and the elusive Least Bittern in the marshy areas along the cross-dike. In winter this area may have other rails, Sedge Wrens, and sparrows, including LeConte's. Look for Common Ground-Doves as well. Also in summer, water with surface vegetation could house Common Moorhens and Purple Gallinules.

The first 0.5 mile to the right from the check station is good for Prothonotary Warblers, and Northern Parulas are everywhere. However, most of the action at the Bradley Unit is in winter for waterfowl and sparrows. Check any water for ducks. Dabblers can be found in the shallow channels along some of the dikes, and in pools in the impoundments. Watch for birds flying overhead (including gulls), and check the river whenever you can. Many Canada Geese winter here, and there are always a few Greater White-fronted Geese around, although they may not be easy to find. Most of the time they are somewhere on the river side, but they may be in any of the small bays, out of sight. This is probably the best place in Georgia to look for these geese and the only one that's close to reliable.

Sparrows can be anywhere, so look at all the different types of brush and fields for the different species, including White-crowned Sparrows. This area is loaded with Song, Swamp, White-throated, and Savannah Sparrows, with a few Field Sparrows mixed in, but the rest of the species are less common. The LeConte's Sparrow has recently been found in the fields with tall standing vegetation, such as brooms edge. The best areas seem to have ground that is damp but not underwater. As always with this very secretive species, your best shot at seeing one is when you accidentally flush it. There is hunting here in fall and winter, and there is no access during hunting season, so call ahead. When you are through here you may continue south to the lake itself and several access points.

Turn right off the Bradley road to continue on GA 39. In 8.3 miles you will join GA 27; turn right for 0.8 mile to US 82. To the right is the town of Georgetown, with many restaurants, motels, and gas stations, and a large bridge across midlake. Most of these businesses are across the lake on the Alabama side. To continue birding, turn left to stay on US 82/GA 39 for 2 miles until GA 39 turns right. To get to the dam, you will follow GA 39 for 19.4 miles to GA 37. However, there are several places to stop along GA 39 before then. The first one is signed as Pataula Creek State Park, 7.8 miles from US 82 on GA 39. This is not a state park anymore, but does give lake access at a boat ramp. To bird, turn right on County Road 129 for 1.1 miles to the unsigned entrance on the left. Drive through the

Great White-fronted Geese. JIM FLYNN PHOTO

entrance for 1.2 miles to the boat ramp. If your time is limited, this is the least productive spot along GA 39.

The next spot is a marshy pond 3.8 miles farther down GA 39. On the right side of GA 39, check for both gallinules in summer and ducks in winter. Another 1.5 miles brings you to CR 82 and Sandy Branch Park. Turn right, and drive west on CR 82. Cottonhill Campground is on your left, and there are several small ponds to scan as you drive 2.8 miles to a stop at CR 80. Turn left, and continue, checking the numerous ponds until you see the sign for Sandy Branch Park in 0.7 mile. Continue past the sign 1 mile to the end of the road at the lake, where you can scan for ducks and gulls. Back on GA 39, in 2.1 miles you reach the Bagby State Park entrance road. This is a very large and developed state park with boat ramps, a marina, and a large lodge with restaurant, and like all state parks there is a $2 daily use fee. There are numerous roads, but the main access road has several ponds on the left in the first 0.5 mile and the lodge is 1 mile beyond that. The best scanning is at the boat ramp or the beach picnic area; follow the signs from the main road.

Back on GA 39, another 2.2 miles gets you to the Walter F. George Lock, which takes you out to the dam. As you drive toward the dam, check the several small ponds along the road, before it ends up on the dam at 1.1 miles. This is the best place to scan for ducks, best done with a scope.

During fall migration from late October to early December there could be almost anything here, so scan carefully. Loons, grebes, and divers are the most likely, and so are good numbers of puddle ducks. This is a good place to look for scoters if you feel lucky, as Surf is annual, and Black is semiannual. Look for gulls on the lake, especially during cold winters. Bald Eagles are frequently seen. A small road goes below the dam to some good fields to check for sparrows, and there may be a Northern Harrier working the area as well. The state line between Georgia and Alabama is the middle of the dam.

The best place to view below the dam, which is the best place to look for gulls, is actually in Alabama (although you are looking back into Georgia). To get there, continue down GA 39 for 2 miles to GA 37. Turn right, and cross the Chattahoochee River into Alabama in 0.4 mile. Another 0.3 mile takes you to the Walter F. George Dam Road (signed CR 202); turn right and drive 1.4 miles to a stop sign. The road to your right leads to a small parking lot and dam spillway overlook. There is also a fishing area where you can get right down to the water. This is the best place to look for gulls, especially during cold winters and when the turbines are running. Most will be Ring-billed, with a few Herring mixed in. This spot has produced a couple of Franklin's Gulls in recent years, but they are extremely rare in fall. There are also usually scores of Double-crested Cormorants and large groups of Great Blue Herons and Great Egrets. Scan the exposed mud for shorebirds. All of the far shore here is Georgia. You can also drive right up on top of the dam on this side, another good spot to scan for ducks, this time in Alabama. This is the end of this tour; you can go back to Columbus the same way you came.

General information: The Eufaula NWR office is in Alabama, and can be reached at (334) 687-4065; this is the number to call about hunting times. The bulk of the refuge is in Alabama (8,000 acres), and if you want to bird there you can cross over the lake at Georgetown, Georgia to the town of Eufaula, Alabama. Go north on US Highway 341 for 7 miles to Alabama Highway 165 and turn right. Drive 1.5 miles and turn right on AL 285. The office and an auto tour loop entrance are immediately on your left. The lodge and cabins at George T. Bagby State Park are very popular and take reservations. Providence Canyon Conservation Park is nearby; it's very interesting geologically, but not for birds.

ADDITIONAL HELP

DeLorme map grid: page 48, A1 through G1.
For more information: Florence Marina State Park, (912) 838-6870; Eufaula NWR, (334) 687-4065; Georgia Department of Natural Resources; George T. Bagby State Park, (912) 768-2571; Providence Canyon Conservation Park, (912) 838-6202.

30 Lake Seminole Wildlife Management Area

Counties: Decatur and Seminole.
Habitats: Pine forest, mixed pine/hardwood forest, young pine shrubland, weedy field, grassy field, reservoir, lily pond.
Key birds: Canvasback, Purple Gallinule, Bald Eagle, Bachman's Sparrow.
Best times to bird: November through March for ducks and wintering sparrows; May through June for Purple Gallinule and Bachman's Sparrow; April, May, and August through October for passerine migrants.

The birding: Lake Seminole WMA consists of a series of discrete parcels of land along the shoreline of Lake Seminole in the extreme southwest corner of Georgia. There are two major river systems entering the lake (Chattahoochee and Flint), and the portions of the WMA along these rivers are excellent in spring and fall for migrant landbirds. In winter the lake gets a good population of ducks and sparrows at various locations, and although it is very hot in summer there are some breeding species worth looking for.

In general, each location in this section will be identified as a migrant, duck, sparrow, or combination spot. For migrant landbird spots, walk whatever trails are available for such species as flycatchers, thrushes, vireos, warblers, and tanagers. Look for mixed flocks of birds moving through the woods searching for food, and concentrate along wood edges or waterways. For ducks, scan whatever water is available. At sparrow spots, work the brushy or wood edge areas. As you drive the roads, scan ponds for ducks, waders, or Anhingas, if you have a wide enough road shoulder to stop on. Many of the fields and pastures may have interesting birds in them, and as long as you can scan from the shoulder some may be worth looking at, such as sod farms for shorebirds in spring and fall.

In winter harvested peanut fields are especially favored by pipits and other birds, and if you are lucky, Horned Larks. This area is full of good habitat for Bachman's Sparrows, so be sure to look and listen for them when you are in the open pine woodlands they favor. In no case should you leave the road or road edge, as this is all private property away from the lake. The first portion of the directions below covers the northern section of the lake, and the last portion covers the south side and the dam area. Overall, the northern portion is more productive in all seasons, but if you have time there are good spots on the south side also.

Directions: US Highway 27 forms a loop around the south side of Bainbridge, Georgia. To access the north side of the lake, take Georgia Highway 253 2.8 miles from the US 27 loop to the southwest, toward the lake. Ease left onto Ten Mile Still Road, and drive 2.3 miles to Hale's Landing Road. One mile to the left is Hale's Landing, which is good for landbird migrants on the Flint River, but has no lake view for ducks. Back on Ten Mile Still Road, continue 5.8 miles to Ten Mile Still Landing while checking the ponds on your right at 3.2 and 5.7 miles. Turn left and go for 0.3 mile to Ten Mile Still Landing, which is another good landbird migrant spot on the Flint River without a good lake view.

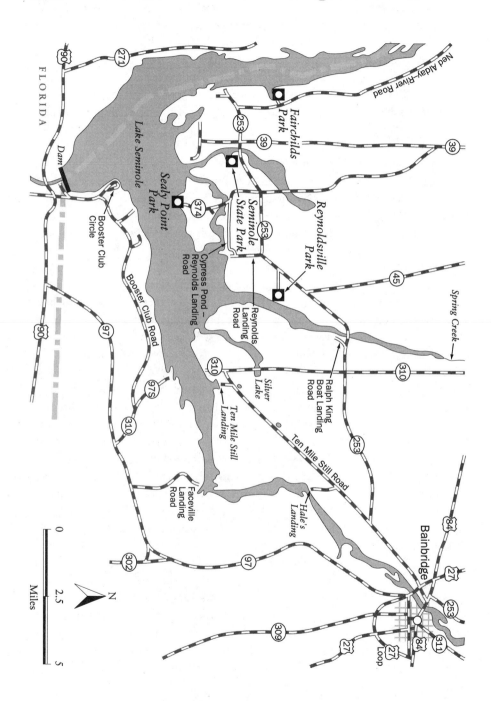

Continue 0.7 mile on Ten Mile Still to GA 310, and turn left. The road ends abruptly in 0.7 mile at the lake, at one of the best places to scan for ducks, especially Canvasbacks. This and Sealy Point Park later in this section are the best spots in Georgia to look for these majestic ducks. There will also be thousands of American Coots, so be prepared to scan through them for ducks such as Ring-necked, Lesser Scaup, or dabbling duck species. Double-crested Cormorants are very likely, and look for Ospreys and Bald Eagles. There is a great pine forest on both sides of the road for pine-loving species such as Brown-headed Nuthatches. There are several ponds with surface vegetation good for Wood Ducks along this end section of GA 310.

When you are finished scanning here, go back north on GA 310, passing Ten Mile Still Road. Silver Lake will appear 1.4 miles past that road, mostly on your left; it's the most likely location in summer for Purple Gallinules and Common Moorhens. The gallinules may require some patience, as they spend most of their time around the weedy edges and can be difficult to see. Any pond with wide-leaved surface vegetation should be checked for these shy birds. In winter this is the best pond for Ring-necked Ducks.

Continue along GA 310 for 3.4 more miles to GA 253, watching the sod farm you pass through during spring or fall migration for rare shorebird species such as American-Golden Plovers, and Upland or Buff-breasted Sandpipers. You would be lucky to find them, but they are worth looking for. Turn left on GA 253, and in 0.8 mile turn left again on Ralph King Boat Landing Road, which is dirt. In 0.4 mile, a short road leads off to the right to the boat landing, where you can look for ducks. Just 0.1 mile past this road, park on a wide bluff overlooking Spring Creek. You can scan for ducks, and in spring and fall this can be good for landbirds. This is a popular hunting area, so do not go any farther in hunting season. In spring, however, you can walk along the bluff and farther down the road (it continues for almost 3 miles) to look for small flocks working the edge of Spring Creek.

When finished here, return to GA 253. Turn left, and in 0.6 mile pull off to the right and park just before Spring Creek. This is part of an old dam, which you can walk out to the end of (0.1 mile) for ducks upriver. The sides of the old dam are steep, so you are actually looking at the tops of the trees. This can be easy on your neck if you can find some birds during migration! Continue on GA 253 over the bridge for 3.9 miles to an unsigned dirt road and turn left. Look for a green sign facing you with "108" on the back of the stop sign. This road dead-ends in 1.2 miles at Reynoldsville Park, a good viewing site for the Spring Creek arm of the lake, and at times for large numbers of ducks, including Canvasbacks. This dirt road also can be good for sparrows. Go back to GA 253, turn left for 0.5 mile to Reynold's Landing Road, then turn left again. The landing (variously called Reynold's or Spring Creek) is 1.3 miles ahead, yet another landbird migration spot with a limited lake view.

As you go back out, note the dirt Cypress Pond–Reynold's Landing Road on your left. If the weather has been dry, this is a shortcut to the next spot. If this road is wet, do not use it! Follow it 2.4 miles to GA 374—or, go back Reynold's Landing Road to GA 253 and turn left. In 2.6 miles, turn left on GA 374. At 1.5 miles, Cypress Pond–Reynold's Landing Road will come in from the left. Continue 1.7 miles to Sealy's Landing and Sealy Point Park and turn left into the park. This is excellent for ducks, along with the end of GA 310 mentioned earlier, and should be scanned for the same species. There is so much water it may take a while to scan it all; a scope is very helpful. There are restrooms, but they may be in bad shape because of repeated vandalism.

When you are finished, return to GA 253 and turn left. In 1.7 miles you will reach Seminole State Park. After you pay the Georgia State park fee, drive past the office to a loop road on your right (0.7 mile from GA 253), and follow it around to scan the water. There are also lots of mature pines to search for Pine Warblers or Brown-headed Nuthatches. When finished, return to GA 253 and turn left for 1.6 miles to Ned Alday–River Road. Turn right, and look for Fairchilds Park on your left in 1.5 miles. This park has dirt roads, so check their condition before birding. The park is on the Chattahoochee River, and offers great migrant possibilities in spring and fall. It's also a good area to bird in winter for resident landbirds.

Turn into the park, and in 0.4 mile take the right fork. This short road loops back on itself and returns to the entrance road, with a good water view at the end of the loop. Turn right after you return to the entrance road, and follow another short loop to water. After exploring, return to GA 253 and turn right for 0.5 mile. At the house, turn left for 0.4 mile and park at the gate just ahead of you (this road is called Ranger Station Road). You can walk past the gate and down the road for

The view from the end of Georgia Highway 310 with Oscar Dewberry.

migrants in spring and fall, and there is a partial lake view at the end of this 0.8-mile-long road.

This is the last spot on the north side. You can follow GA 253 all the way back to Bainbridge, about 21.3 miles to US 27. To access the south side of the lake and the dam, take GA 97 south from the US 27 loop. There is a direct exit from the west, but from the east you need to exit on the nonloop US 27 north for 0.1 mile, and turn left on GA 97, which crosses the loop in 0.2 mile.

However you get on GA 97, follow it south for 12.8 miles to Faceville Landing Road. A right turn for 3.1 miles takes you to a small picnic area with restrooms and a limited lake view, but it's not one of the better spots on this side of the lake. Continue on GA 97 for 1.8 miles to GA 310, and turn right. This road is also signed "Spur 97." In 1.8 miles turn left on Booster Club Road, which follows the top of a ridge; Bald Eagles can often be seen from here. Follow this road for 9.4 miles to Booster Club Circle, and turn right. The road ends at the lake in 0.8 mile; scan for ducks. Then drive the one-way loop to the right as you leave the water, good for Wild Turkeys in winter. There is a 0.3-mile nature trail called the Turkey Flight Trail, but it is pretty slow birding in winter.

After returning to Booster Club Road, continue right 1.4 miles to the dam area on your right. The resource manager's office on the left-most road has maps, exhibits, and information. The right-hand road leads down to the dam in 1.1 miles. There are several spots to scan for waterfowl, including Canvasbacks. This is an excellent area to check during duck migration, like most deepwater dams in the South. Check for Ospreys and Bald Eagles, too. You can drive out on the dam and scan below it for gulls and terns; the area below the dam is all in Florida. This is the end of the southern part of birding; retrace your route back to Bainbridge.

General information: Parts of this area are hunted during fall and winter, so you may want to check with Georgia Department of Natural Resources before you bird. There are lots of gas stations and restaurants around Bainbridge, but once you get toward the lake, there are very few of either, especially in winter.

ADDITIONAL HELP

DeLorme map grid: the entire upper half of page 64.
For more information: Lake Seminole Resource Management Office, (912) 662-2001; Seminole State Park, (912) 861-3137; Bainbridge–Decatur County Chamber of Commerce, (800) 243-4774; Oscar Dewberry is an experienced local birder who is willing to help visitors. His address is 909 Elizabeth Place, Bainbridge, GA 31717. His phone number is (912) 246-1890.

31 Cobb Owl Fields

County: Sumter.
Habitats: Weedy field, plowed field.
Key birds: Short-eared Owl, Northern Harrier, Vesper Sparrow.
Best times to bird: December through February.

The birding: This is the only spot in Georgia that has been reliable in recent years for Short-eared Owls. It is a series of cotton and other fields that has had this species in winter for at least the past five years. Included in this section are other nearby spots also worth birding. The Cordele Fish Hatchery has several small ponds to bird for sparrows or ducks when the ponds have water, and Lake Blackshear has a few gulls and ducks, although it is fairly developed. A small golf course pond frequently has Redhead ducks.

Directions: The main spot is the owl fields; get to them toward the end of the day. During midwinter, it gets dark around 6 P.M., and you may see owls as much as one hour before then. It is worth getting here at least by 5 P.M. to get the lay of the land. You can also see the owls just after dawn, but most people bird the area until dark.

Take the US Highway 280 Cordele exit from Interstate 75, Exit 101 (old 33). Go west, toward Cordele. The only gas or food is in Cordele, near the interstate. To get to Cobb, go west across Lake Blackshear on US 280 for 14.3 miles from the exit. The town is not as vibrant as perhaps it once was, so it's easy to miss. Watch your mileage and look for Cobb Cheek Road in an area of abandoned buildings. Turn right, and drive north 1.4 miles to Tim Tucker Road. Cobb Cheek Road becomes dirt and may be impassable after periods of rain, unless you have four-wheel drive. If the road is driveable, the best spot is about 1 mile in front of you, but the best areas shift a little year to year with different crop usage. Look for fields with some standing dead vegetation but not plowed flat or any higher than your hips. Probably the best way to find good owl habitat is to look during daylight for fields with the most Northern Harriers. This will tell you where the prey is. Other raptors will be present as well, mostly American Kestrels and Red-tailed Hawks, but Harriers are the most reliable indicators. This association holds up wherever these two species both occur, and you may find your own Short-eared Owl field someday by watching for large numbers of daytime Harriers. Of course, not all fields with Harriers have Short-eared Owls, but very few fields without Harriers do.

Back to Cobb—if the road is not passable, you have two options. Walk in or try to get in from the other side. This may prove to be impassable also, but if you have time it's worth a shot. Return to GA 280, and turn right. The small town of DeSoto is 4.3 miles ahead; turn right on GA 195. Go north 2.7 miles to Cobb Cheek Road, and turn right. The best part of the fields is 2.6 miles ahead (total of 3.6 miles to Tim Tucker Road, where the road becomes paved again). The approach from this side is flatter, so it tends to stay a little muddier, on average, but

31 Cobb Owl Fields

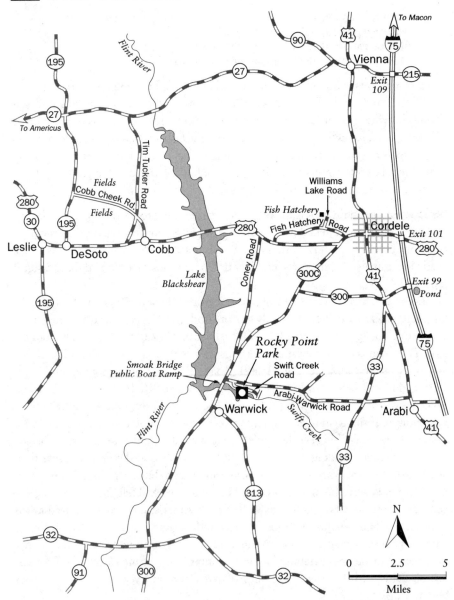

it doesn't usually get the really large puddles you can't cross in a truck, like the Cobb side does.

However you get to the better areas, there are plenty of birds to look for while waiting for sundown. These fields are full of sparrows, including scores of Song and Savannah Sparrows. There are quite a few Vespers to look for and a very few White-crowned. Look for the White-crowns in areas of brush or small saplings. Sometimes Sandhill Cranes feed in the distant fields; listen for them and scan with your scope to find them—they are rarely near the road. There are a few small ponds in the various fields, so there may be a few ducks flying around. Occasionally you may hear King Rails calling, but you may not leave the road to look for them because this is all private property. Once it starts to get dark, look for the owls with their moth-like flight low over the fields. Sometimes they will even give their distinctive *"bark"* call while flying around. If your chosen fields do not have any owls as it starts to get dark, try different ones. The best strategy is to pick a high point that allows you to scan several fields at once. If you have several people, you might station them at different points along the road to look, as long as you have a way to communicate with each other. There are probably only six to eight owls here in any given winter. Once you have had your fill or it is totally dark, return to GA 280 and to the interstate by turning left.

If you are in the area early, here are a couple of other spots to bird. Just west of Cordele (2.9 miles from I-75 on GA 280) is Fish Hatchery Road. Turn north (right turn if coming from the interstate) and drive 1.4 miles. In winter there may be sparrows in the fields along this road, including a few White-crowned Sparrows. Turn right on Williams Lake Road into the hatchery and find someone to get permission from to wander around the ponds. Things to look for include herons, kingfishers, or ducks. Except in midwinter, you might find a few shorebirds such as Least Sandpipers or possibly American Pipits in empty but still wet ponds. Look for sparrows as well.

For those with more time, Lake Blackshear offers a few possibilities. Although it is developed and the dam area is not very attractive to waterfowl, it does have a few interesting areas. To bird the lake, go south one more exit on I-75 to Exit 99 (old 32), which is GA 300. Before you go down to Blackshear, there is a pond visible from this exit which is fairly consistent for Redheads in winter. Since the pond is located on the southeast corner of this exit, turn left off the exit ramp to cross over I-75 and park immediately on the wide, right shoulder. The pond is visible on your right, and as usual, a scope is very helpful. If they are there (slightly more than half of the time), they will be toward the right side of the pond from where you are, near the dam. There should be Pied-billed Grebes there at least, and sometimes other ducks, but never large numbers. To go to the lake, turn around again and head southwest on GA 300. From the exit, note in 5.9 miles on your right the 300 Connector, which takes you up to the business section of Cordele. Continue 5 miles; Coney Road is on your right—this is what you'll take later to get up to GA 280 to head for Cobb.

Continuing southwest on GA 300, in 2.1 miles is the lake. The only safe viewing spot here is the Smoak Bridge public boat ramp on your left, immediately before you cross the water. You are not likely to see much besides Ring-billed Gulls, although there are a few Bonaparte's in winter. Turn right out of this park back on GA 300 for 0.4 mile and turn right on Arabi-Warwick Road, which is also County Road 33. Proceed only another 0.4 mile and turn right on Swift Creek Road. Follow this road around a sweeping left turn for 0.9 mile to Rocky

Point Park on your right, and turn in. Despite its curious name (there isn't a rock in sight), this park offers a view of the lower lake, which is shallow and dotted with cypress trees. In winter there are more gulls here, and lots of Double-crested Cormorants and American Coots. There are no facilities other than a large covered area with picnic tables.

One final spot for landbirds is another 0.9 mile farther down Swift Creek Road where it dead-ends into a dirt road. Park, and walk 0.2 mile to your right toward the creek. This takes you into an area of floodplain hardwood forest with a nice cypress-tupelo swamp at Swift Creek. This area is good general birding in winter and offers the chance for migrants moving up- or downriver in spring and fall. There are Prothonotary Warblers in spring and summer. This is the last spot; retrace your path back to Cordele or to Cobb. If you want to go to Cobb, go back up to Coney Road. GA 280 is 6.2 miles left (north) on Coney Road, then turn left on GA 280 6.1 miles to proceed to Cobb.

General information: Most of the food and gas here is in Cordele, just west of Interstate 75, although there are a few stores on Georgia Highway 300 near Lake Blackshear. Though you cross the lake on GA 280, there are no safe spots to scan the lake. Also, there are no stores in Cobb or DeSoto, so fuel yourself and your car before you head west.

ADDITIONAL HELP

DeLorme map grid: page 50, B2, C2/3.
For more information: Cordele-Crisp Tourism Committee, (912) 273-5132.

32 Perry Super Sod Farm

County: Peach.
Habitats: Grassy field, plowed field, pond.
Key birds: Buff-breasted, Upland, Pectoral, and Least Sandpipers; American Golden-Plover, Horned Lark, American Pipit, swallows.
Best times to bird: Mid-July through September.

The birding: This sod farm is just south of Macon and is fairly small in comparison with the other sod farms in this book, but it gets a lot of the same great species and is very easy to bird. There are two sections, only a couple of miles apart, both birded by driving down good dirt roads and scanning the sod. Like all sod farms, during weekdays you must check in at the office for permission to bird, but on weekends you can just drive in. As at other sod farms, remain only on established roads and stay out of the way of workers and equipment.

Directions: This sod farm is just barely off Interstate 75 in Perry, Georgia. Use Exit 142 (old 44), which is both Georgia Highway 96 and Houser's Mill Road. Go east 0.3 mile to Sod Farm Road and turn right at the "Super Sod" sign. Drive this dirt road another 0.3 mile to the office and check in.

32 Perry Super Sod Farm

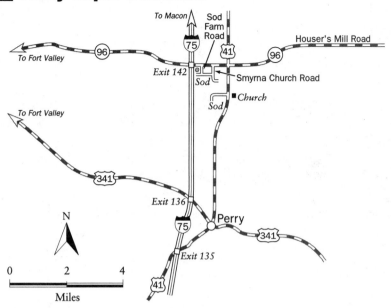

You can quickly check the area west of the office by going back in the direction of the interstate on the dirt road right in front of the office. Check the sod to your left, and if you are here on a weekend when no work is being done you can drive to the left side of the large equipment barn on the right to check a pond in the small valley. Go back to the office and continue along this main road while checking the sod on both sides. If you have a scope, it's worth setting up and panning the whole area as you go. Pay special attention to areas of standing water, whether from rain or the large sprinklers. If you can get here after a large rain has passed through in fall the birds can be spectacular!

All the shorebirds listed under the Key Birds section can be found anywhere on the sod, so scan carefully. Check the ditch on both sides of this road for shorebirds that prefer wetter areas, such as Yellowlegs or Solitary Sandpipers. There are always a few Killdeer here, and American Golden-Plovers may be mixed in with them. Check the same areas of sod for American Pipits in winter and Horned Larks all year long. In fall there may be large numbers of swallows, including Bank (mostly late July and August). Barn and Northern Rough-winged Swallows are common.

This dirt road ends in 0.6 mile. Turn left and follow Smyrna Church Road 0.3 mile back to GA 96, scanning as you go. If you haven't found what you are looking for, there is another section to check. Turn right on GA 96 for 0.5 mile to US 41. Turn right again for 0.9 mile to an unnamed dirt road on the right across from the Christ's Sanctified Holy Church. This is the second dirt road on the right since you have turned onto US 41. Turn right. Follow the road for 0.5 mile until it bends left and deteriorates into grass. Scan all the sod to your left for the same species as

Start scanning!

in the other section of sod. At this point you have covered all the sod there is, but you can bird the scrubby brush for landbirds along the back of the sod farm. You can also go back to the main section to cover that area again.

General information: This sod farm is about 20 minutes south of Macon and all the great birding sites there. Just about every exit along Interstate 75 has food and gas except Georgia Highway 96, which has only gas. However, there is a large fruit packing company nearby that has food, drinks, and just about any peach product you can imagine. The Lane Packing Company is 4.9 miles west of I-75 on GA 96, and is open 8 A.M. to 8 P.M. daily.

ADDITIONAL HELP

DeLorme map grid: page 42, C4.
For more information: Perry Area CVB, (912) 988-8000; Lane Packing Company, (800) 277-3224.

33 Grand Bay Wildlife Management Area

Counties: Lowndes and Lanier.
Habitats: Cypress-tupelo swamp, freshwater marsh, floodplain hardwood forest, upland hardwood forest, pine forest, weedy fields.
Key birds: Sandhill Crane, Purple Gallinule, American Bittern, King Rail, Prothonotary Warbler, Wood Stork, Bachman's Sparrow, Anhinga.
Best times to bird: All Year.

33 Grand Bay Wildlife Management Area

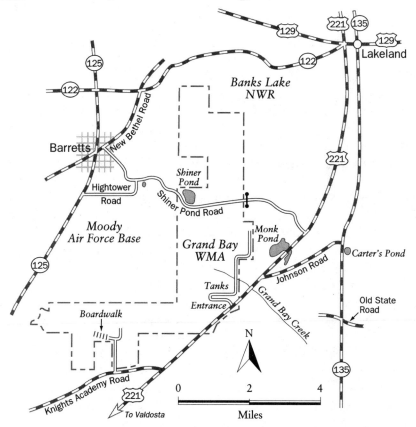

The birding: Grand Bay Wildlife Management Area is a wonderful area just east of Valdosta, with many great birding habitats. The main attraction is the large cypress swamp and associated freshwater marshes, where Georgia's largest number of Sandhill Cranes are found in winter. A boardwalk into the swamp leads to an observation tower overlooking hundreds of acres of swamp and marsh. There are also areas of wet and upland forest for interesting breeding species and good habitat for winter sparrows.

Directions: Just north of Valdosta, exit Interstate 75 at Exit 22 (old 6) on US Highway 41/Georgia Highway 7. Go east 4 miles to Inner Perimeter Road, and turn left. In 3.8 miles you will reach US 221; turn left again. At 5.3 miles, look for Knight's Academy Road on the left; turn left once more. To get to the boardwalk, drive 1.5 miles to the entrance on your right, and turn in. As you drive this 0.8-mile road, you can watch for landbirds, including sparrows (in winter) on both sides of the road.

Turn left at the end and park in the parking lot in front of you. There are exhibits about the area in the education center, and straight ahead there is a 0.4-mile boardwalk that leads through a small marshy area and into the edge of the swamp to a large observation tower with a commanding view. This tower is good at any time of day, especially in winter when you may see cranes and other waders, including herons, egrets, and White Ibises. Toward dusk there is usually an impressive show of all of those species returning to a nearby hammock to roost, along with hundreds of both Turkey and Black Vultures. In summer look for Wood Storks. Back at the entrance road, a right turn takes you to a canoe trail (you must supply the canoe!) that snakes through the swamp out into the more open prairie area. The swamp is full of woodpeckers at all seasons, and typical breeding species include Prothonotary Warblers. There is a gate just past the entrance road preventing you from driving in, but you can walk almost a mile around the berm of the swamp. The hardwood floodplain forest is worth birding in all seasons. When you are finished, return to US 221, and turn left.

Another entrance to the WMA is on your left in 2.3 miles, but it is open only on weekends. Take the dirt entrance road in for 0.4 mile, turn right at the campground, and travel 0.1 mile. Turn right again at the tanks, and follow a turn to the left. Note that the area on the other side of the fence on your right is private and off-limits. At 0.7 mile you will cross Grand Bay Creek, an area worth birding for floodplain forest species. Continue another 0.3 mile to the beginning of an open longleaf pine forest on your left, good for Bachman's Sparrows for the next 0.3 mile. There is also a bay head behind the forest on the left with breeding Swainson's Warblers, but they are difficult to get to. Of course, any area here with good habitat is worth birding. When finished exploring, return to US 221.

Turn left again on US 221, and in 1.1 miles look for Johnson Road. You will cross Grand Bay Creek again just before Johnson Road; it's a good spot to stop for a few minutes to bird the floodplain forest around the creek. Acadian Flycatchers and Prothonotary Warblers are two species to search for. When ready, turn right on Johnson Road, drive 2.6 miles to GA 135, and turn right. Just past Carter's Pond immediately on your left is room to park on the left shoulder. You are not in the WMA here, so you must stay on the shoulder. In winter check this pond for Pied-billed Grebes, Common Moorhens, Wood Ducks, and any other ducks, including the common Ring-necked Duck. There are usually a few Tree Swallows in winter, and there may be landbirds around the small edge you can bird from the road. In summer scan for Purple Gallinules. This is one of the few reliable spots in Georgia for this elusive species. This is also good for Anhinga all year-round. Return to US 221 when you are done scanning.

Before you continue, there is one other spot nearby to check for Bachman's Sparrows. Continue south on GA 135 for 2.3 miles (from Johnson Road) to Old State Road, and turn left. Drive 1.4 miles to Good Hope Road and cross it. The area on the right side of Old State Road immediately past Good Hope Road for 0.3 mile is good for these sparrows in spring and summer. If you are staying near Grand Bay, return to US 221.

Turn right on US 221 again. Monk Pond is 0.9 mile on your left. Park on the shoulder, and realize that this area is pretty grown up for a pond but has many interesting species similar to Grand Bay Creek. In another 0.7 mile you will see the unsigned Shiner Pond Road on your left. It is worth checking the sod farm fields around this corner at any season, although you may not find anything but Killdeer. This dirt road is usually in pretty good condition for passenger cars. Turn left, reset your trip meter, and drive 1.9 miles to a gate. There is an impressive "Aerial Bombing Range" sign, and you may enter only if the gate is open as it usually is on weekends. The area you are entering is usually called Shiner Pond or the Bombing Range, and it has a variety of wonderful birding spots.

Just past the gate are two small ponds on the left worth checking for shorebirds. Park when you get to 2.3 miles (another 0.4 mile). This is always worth checking, and is the best general area on this tour. Walk up and down the road and along any of the dikes that you can travel on the left side of the road. Check all the small pools and ponds for just about anything. In winter there are usually a couple of American Bitterns, a very difficult bird in Georgia. Also look for Sandhill Cranes, Sedge Wrens, and various waders. There are sparrows in winter, and sometimes a few dabbling ducks. King Rails occur, but they are very difficult to find. Anhingas are present all year. In summer check for Common Moorhens and Least Bitterns (if you are lucky). In spring search for early arrivals like Prothonotary Warblers.

Continue along Shiner Pond Road through an upland area to another pond at 4.9 miles and check the open areas for Eastern Wood-Pewees, Purple Martins, and Orchard Orioles. At 5.1 miles you will reach Hightower Road on the left. There are a few more sparrow fields on Shiner Pond Road ahead of you, and a good field for Bobolinks 0.2 mile to the left on Hightower. This is the end of this tour, so bird your way back out the way you came.

General information: This area has more wintering Sandhill Cranes than any other spot in Georgia. Studies have shown that birds on their way south stage out of Hiwassee National Wildlife Refuge near Chattanooga and mostly make a beeline for Grand Bay. Banks Lake NWR is right next to Grand Bay but offers little access to good birding spots. The city of Valdosta has plenty of lodging, gas, and restaurants, but the area around Grand Bay WMA does not.

ADDITIONAL HELP

DeLorme map grid: page 67, A10; page 60, H1.
For more information: Georgia Department of Natural Resources; Valdosta–Lowndes County CVB, (800) 569-8689.

34 Beaverdam Wildlife Management Area

County: Laurens.
Habitats: Pine forest, mixed pine/hardwood forest, floodplain hardwood forest, cypress-tupelo swamp, young pine shrubland, weedy field, grassy field, river.
Key birds: Swainson's and Prothonotary Warblers, Louisiana Waterthrush, Common Ground-Dove, migrant warblers, wintering sparrows.
Best times to bird: All year.

The birding: Beaverdam WMA is a great area of mostly hardwood forest on the bank of the Oconee River. It offers miles of good trails for both breeding species and migrants. Many of the trails are driveable and those that aren't are easy walking.

Directions: From the west, exit Interstate 16 at Georgia Highway 338, which is Exit 42 (old 12). Go north on GA 338. In 1.9 miles you will cross US Highway 80; continue 7.2 miles to US 441. Cross US 441 and your road becomes Holly Ridge Road, dead-ending in 1.1 miles at Old Toomsboro Road. Turn left on Old Toomsboro and drive 4.2 miles to Oconee Church Road. Turn right, and go 1.4 miles to entrance one to Beaverdam WMA, a dirt road on your left.

From the east, exit I-16 at GA 19, which is Exit 54 (old 15). Turn right (north). As you approach downtown Dublin, your road becomes US 441 at 3.5 miles. Continue on US 441 for a total of 11.4 miles from I-16 and turn right on Holly Ridge Road. There is a sign on the left for GA 338 at the intersection, so look for that as a marker but remember to turn right on Holly Ridge. Drive 1.1 miles to Old Toomsboro, turn left, and follow the directions above to the entrance. The headquarters and check station is on the right 0.3 mile down the dirt road, which is usually in good shape but can be muddy after rain.

Two-tenths mile past the headquarters is a dirt road on your left that makes a short loop back to the main road; it's a good place to look for Common Ground-Doves and Wild Turkeys. The ground-doves may be seen feeding along the side of the road. If you stay on the main road, bird any open area in winter for sparrows, especially where you find brush piles or hedgerows. Field and Chipping Sparrows are year-round residents, and in winter you could find Song, Savannah, and White-throated Sparrows, or Dark-eyed Juncos. Vesper Sparrows are less likely but fairly common, and Fox and White-crowned Sparrows are uncommonly found. During summer look for Prairie Warblers and Yellow-breasted Chats. Look also for Common Ground-Doves at any season. At 1 mile on the main road, the loop road rejoins from the left.

At 1.9 miles you cross a small stream that has breeding Louisiana Waterthrushes and Kentucky and Hooded Warblers, and is a good all-around spot to bird at any season. Just past here a couple of dirt roads go off to the right. The farthest right dead-ends quickly. The middle one, which is actually straight ahead, is good for all-around birding at any season. It may be gated off, but you can walk in to bird if it is locked. In 2.6 miles it will connect with the main road from entrance two.

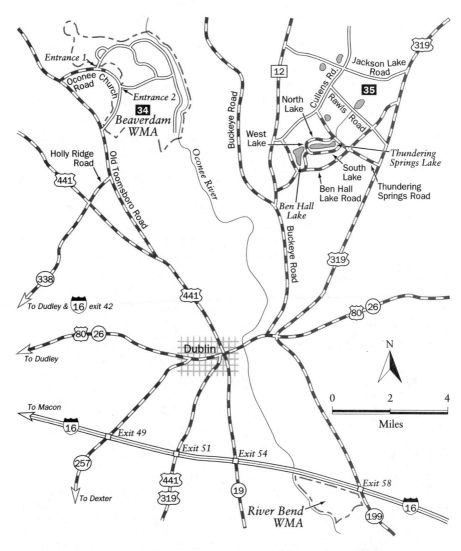

The main road you are on veers left and begins to follow a stream that sometimes overflows the road, at which point it will be gated off. You can still walk in, or drive in when the gate is open. Along this road are breeding Prothonotary, Northern Parula, and Yellow-throated Warblers, Acadian and Great Crested Flycatchers, and several species of woodpeckers. This is a good spot for White-breasted Nuthatches, very local this far south in Georgia. Bird the road along the stream until you come to a boat launch and a gate across the road that is usually locked.

This is a good spot for migrants (as is anywhere along the road or any of the creeks) or to hope for a soaring Mississippi Kite over the Oconee River, which you can now see on the left side of the road. The best habitat for the Swainson's Warbler is along the main road for a couple of miles past the locked gate. You can walk in at any season and find all the other species you have been looking for. For Swainson's Warblers, concentrate your search in the stands of canebrake, a preferred habitat for this secretive species. Listen for its loud "chip" or its song, which resembles that of the Louisiana Waterthrush but lacks the fading jumble of notes at the end. After birding here or along the main road beyond the gate, you can retrace your steps back toward the entrance or try any of the side roads you haven't yet birded. Be alert during migration for the soft "chips" and call notes that may signal the approach of a flock of feeding migrants, and remember that migrants will sometimes be found in the company of chickadees and titmice.

After you come back to the entrance, try the other section of Beaverdam. Turn left on Oconee Church Road and drive 1.3 miles to entrance two. Oconee Church Road becomes dirt after 0.4 mile; it could be slippery after rain but is usually in good shape. Entrance two is on your left; it is usually locked, except in the fall when most of the gates here are left open for hunters. Check with the game management office listed in the General Information section to find out if it is hunting season, and of course make your plans accordingly. You can walk in at any season, but the best birding spots are a little over 1 mile away.

Walking or driving, proceed down the dirt road from entrance two. At 1.1 miles you will come to an intersection. The road to your right goes a short way to

Swainson's Warbler.

a picnic area, and the road on your left goes 2.6 miles back to the part of Beaverdam discussed above. This road is always interesting birding but it's quite a walk. Continue on the main road to 1.3 miles from Oconee Church Road; a small concrete bridge signals the start of a nice swampy area on both sides of the road. This swamp requires three bridges to cross, 1.7 miles total, and is a great area for breeding species such as Hooded, Prothonotary, and Kentucky Warblers. If you are lucky, a few Swainson's Warblers might be found here or anywhere farther down the main road.

At 2 miles a road curves off to the left; it's the road that continued past the locked gate from the boat launch in the other section of Beaverdam. Continue on the main road to 3.1 miles, and you will see an open area on your left that is an oxbow from the Oconee River. It is the best place in Beaverdam to look for migrants during spring and fall. You can walk this section up and back several times until you find a flock crossing the road, but be advised that early and late during migration, a "flock" may consist of only a few birds. The main road continues on, but these are the most productive spots. From here there is a nice turnaround at 3.3 miles, so you can return to the entrance. A right turn on Oconee Church Road will take you back to the main entrance or to the interstate the same way you came.

General information: This 4,500-acre area offers excellent birding at any season. In fall, however, the WMA is hunted and should be avoided during deer and other large game hunting times. Call the Department of Natural Resources Game Management Office at (912) 825-6354 to find out when these hunts are scheduled.

ADDITIONAL HELP

DeLorme map grid: page 44, A2.
For more information: Dublin–Laurens County Chamber of Commerce, (912) 272-5546.

35 Laurens County Loop

See map on page 151

County: Laurens.
Habitat: Pine forest, mixed pine/hardwood forest, floodplain hardwood forest, freshwater marsh shrubland, weedy field, grassy field, freshwater marshland, pond.
Key birds: Brewer's Blackbird, Upland Sandpiper, American Golden-Plover, wading birds, ducks.
Best times to bird: April for Upland Sandpiper; April, May, July to October for migrant shorebirds; July to September for waders; November to March for ducks.

The birding: This loop route does't have much traffic, and follows numerous county and farm roads by a series of lakes and pastures. It has produced more than 250 species over the past 20 years, including many rarities, so be alert for anything. It can be good in any season, although for different mix of species. Though the latter portion of the loop is dirt roads, they are usually in very good shape. Care should be taken after rain, of course, and if the rain has lasted several days, don't leave the paved roads.

Directions: To follow the loop, exit Interstate 16 from either direction at Exit 54 (old 15), which is Georgia Highway 19. Go north 3.7 miles to US Highway 80/GA 26. Just before this point your road will become US 441; continue straight ahead. At the intersection with US 80/GA 26, turn right (east) and drive 1.7 miles to the second traffic light, which is Buckeye Road. You will cross the Oconee River. Turn left on Buckeye Road. At 3.8 miles from US 80/GA 26, there is a large wet ditch on your left that may have waders and rails. At 4.9 miles you will reach an unsigned Y intersection with several church signs and signs for Ben Hall and Thundering Springs Lakes. Take the fork to the right, and continue on this road to a T intersection 1.7 miles past the Y. Ignore the road that cuts off to the left in between these two intersections. Turn right at the T on Ben Hall Lake Road and immediately park near the dumpsters. Scan Ben Hall Lake for cormorants, ducks, or raptors. In the summer this is a great spot for swallows and martins, and during migration you may find swallows by the thousands here and at Thundering Springs Lake. There is also a small store for drinks or snacks.

Pull back onto Ben Hall Lake Road and turn left in 0.1 mile on South Lake Drive (no sign). Drive 0.9 mile, turn left on West Lake Drive, and stop between the two lakes to scan. The lake on your left is still Ben Hall, and the lake on your right is Thundering Springs. Scan for the same species as before, and if the lake levels are down during the late summer or fall there might be shorebirds around the edges. This road becomes North Lake Drive, and in 1.7 miles ends at another T at Thundering Springs Road. Turn left, and in 0.8 mile stop and scan the pasture on your right during April for Upland Sandpipers and American Golden-Plovers. This is the most reliable spot in Georgia for Upland Sandpipers, although they are not always near the road and can be difficult to pick out of the sometimes tall grass.

As you look at this pasture, there is a wet area to the right (past the fence) that may be a small pond, depending on recent rainfall. Check for ducks, waders, or shorebirds around the edges, especially in the spring when the vegetation hasn't grown too high. This is a regular spot in late September and early October for American Bitterns, but they are usually hidden in the tall vegetation. The field behind you (left side of the road) can be good in the winter for raptors or in the spring for Bobolinks. During summer, Grasshopper Sparrows breed in these fields in low numbers, and there are lots of Indigo Buntings, Blue Grosbeaks, Orchard Orioles, and Eastern Meadowlarks. Cattle Egrets are usually found somewhere in this area during summer and fall.

When you are finished, continue in the same direction another 0.3 mile to a stop sign and turn right on Cullens Road (dirt). Drive 1.8 miles to Jackson Lake

Road, scanning especially on your right for the same species—it's another view of the same pasture. The intersection at Jackson Lake Road is good all year for Common Ground-Doves, especially in the farm equipment area on your left. Turn left, and note Jackson Lake on the right in 0.3 mile. The lake may hold ducks and raptors or waders around the edges. Continue another 0.5 mile to a pond/marsh on your left, which is excellent for waders, shorebirds, and dabbling ducks. Wood Storks are sometimes seen in the late summer or early fall. From here back to Cullens Road is the only reliable spot for Brewer's Blackbirds in Georgia. The flock of usually a couple hundred blackbirds arrives around the end of November and stays until the end of March, but it roams quite a bit. The blackbirds are often found in the company of cows, so check all the fields where the cows are that day.

At this point, make a U turn, drive back to Cullens Road, and turn right. Drive 0.8 mile to Rawls Road, and turn left. At 0.2 mile is a small pond on the right with some dead standing trees. Look for Wood Ducks and Red-headed Woodpeckers. Continue to scan the pasture on the right side of the road for grassland shorebirds in spring and Cattle Egrets in summer. Continue past this small pond an additional 1 mile to Rawls Pond on the left. Scan for ducks in winter and Anhingas in summer and fall. When finished, continue on Rawls Road another 2 miles through a large field to US 319. This is good for Palm Warblers in fall, and there are usually a few that stay all winter. If you were unable to find Brewer's Blackbirds on Jackson Lake Road, you might try the dairy farm you pass on Rawls Road just before US 319, although they rarely stray there. US 319 marks the end of this loop. To return to the interstate, turn right on US 319 and drive 8 miles to where US 319 turns to the right and joins US 80/GA 26. In another 2 miles the road curves right, around the Laurens County courthouse; turn left immediately past the courthouse on US 441. Drive 3.7 miles to I-16, and you are back to the starting point.

General information: This is a loop route through private property on public roads. You MUST stay on the roads and cannot go into any fields or cross any fences, no matter how tantalizing a distant bird is. The landowners here are tolerant but wary of birders, so do not ruin things for others by leaving the road.

ADDITIONAL HELP

DeLorme map grid: page 44, A3, B3.
For more information: Dublin–Laurens County Chamber of Commerce, (912) 272-5546.

36 Okefenokee National Wildlife Refuge

Counties: Ware and Charlton.
Habitats: Pine forest, mixed pine/hardwood forest, floodplain hardwood forest, cypress-tupelo swamp, upland pine woodland, young pine shrubland, freshwater marsh shrubland, weedy field, pond, lily pond.
Key birds: Sandhill Crane, Red-cockaded Woodpecker, Bachman's Sparrow, Prothonotary Warbler, waders.
Best times to bird: October through May.

The birding: The Okefenokee NWR covers a huge area, but there is road access to only a small portion of it. The Suwanee Canal Recreation Area on the east side offers the best birding, followed by Stephen C. Foster State Park on the west side. A commercial area called Okefenokee Swamp Park lies close to Waycross on the north side; also near Waycross is Laura S. Walker State Park with different habitats and birds. If you have time for only one area, the most interesting from a birding standpoint is Suwanee Canal, with a nice observation tower and year-round Sandhill Cranes and Red-cockaded Woodpeckers. This is one of only two places with public access in Georgia for Red-cockaded Woodpeckers.

Directions: Starting in Waycross, north of the swamp, head south on US Highway 1/23. At 6.7 miles from Waycross you will reach Georgia Highway 177. A left turn for 4.7 miles takes you to Laura S. Walker State Park, where there is camping and lodging, as well as a lake for ducks. Be aware that this park is heavily used in summer and is better for birding in winter. Across the street from the entrance is a nice floodplain forest trail, about a mile long, called the Big Creek Nature Trail. Fields that have lots of sparrows in winter surround the park.

A right turn on GA 177 for 5 miles takes you to Okefenokee Swamp Park, a commercial area that abuts the north side of the swamp. Here you will find exhibits, boat rides, a boardwalk, and wildlife shows. It is a little touristy for my taste, but does give you a glimpse of the swamp, if you don't mind paying for it.

To get to less-developed parts of the swamp, continue southeast on US 1/23. The town of Folkston is 25.7 miles from GA 177 (32.4 miles from Waycross). This is your last chance for gas or food, other than from a vendor within the NWR. If you are planning on driving around the southern end of the swamp to the west, fill up on gas here.

If you wish to come directly to Folkston from Interstate 95, take Exit 3 (old 2). This is GA 40. Go west, away from the coast, for 19.6 miles to Folkston. The roads are a little tricky, so watch your turns. At 19.6 miles, turn left on Third Street (ignore the signs for the Okefenokee Parkway, which will strand you). Take your first right in 0.1 mile, which is Martin Street. Immediately cross US 301 and continue 0.2 mile to GA 23/121, then turn left and follow the directions below (only 7.3 miles to Spur 121).

Depart Folkston on GA 23/121 (also called Okefenokee Parkway) for 7.7 miles, and turn right on Spur 121 to the **Suwanee Canal Recreation Area.** At any

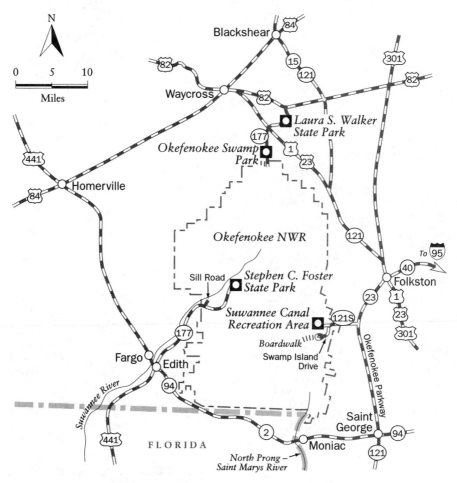

time you are near the swamp, keep your eyes open for Mississippi Kites and if you are very lucky, Swallow-tailed Kites in spring and summer. In 3.3 miles you will reach the gate, open daily from November 1 to February 28 from 30 minutes before sunrise until 5:30 P.M. and March 1 to October 31 from 30 minutes before sunrise until 7:30 P.M. In another 0.5 mile is a pay station. A seven-day pass costs $5; an annual pass is $12. There is an older Red-cockaded Woodpecker (RCW) cluster here, but these birds often range widely and can be difficult to find. As with other attempts to find RCWs, learning the distinct call-note is extremely helpful. Listen for Bachman's Sparrows as well, and bird from the road only. This refuge is mostly pine, and Brown-headed Nuthatches and Pine Warblers are widespread and common.

Continue another 0.1 mile until Swamp Island Drive turns off to your left. This is where most of the birding is, but for now continue straight ahead into the

The observation tower from the boardwalk at Suwanee Canal.

large parking lot. This nice visitor center opens at 9 A.M. and has maps, exhibits, and the latest information on RCW or other sightings. There is also a concession-aire with boat rentals, guided boat tours, and some food items. You can rent canoes for day trips or camping trips, but you need to arrange these in advance. The first part of the canoe trail is through a vegetated canal, and it takes a bit of paddling to get into good birding prairie habitat. Be aware that this is a swamp—in summer and fall it can be very buggy. In spring there will be Prothonotary Warblers and Northern Parulas everywhere.

To bird the rest of the area, return to Swamp Island Drive and turn right. Watch all along this road for the striking fox squirrels. In 0.8 mile you will reach the Upland Discovery Trail, which is the most likely spot for RCWs. Depending on the season (see discussion below), watch the nest holes, identified by the sap running profusely down the trunk of tall longleaf pines. These trees usually have rings of white paint around them as well. The cluster is on the left side of the road, but you may also find the woodpeckers on the right side of the road feeding in the trees on the far side of the small pond. As with other clusters, sometimes the birds range far from the colony and can't be found until they return to the cluster. You will find Bachman's Sparrows here as well, easiest to find when they are singing in spring from high, exposed perches. From here, continue 2.3 miles to a loop road, and turn right. Look for Wild Turkeys anywhere along this road. In 0.7 mile, you will reach the boardwalk to the tower. This is a great place to bird, and it's simply beautiful.

If you have a scope, it will be very useful. Walk out the boardwalk trail, which is about 0.8 mile long. Scan all the brushy areas for warblers in spring or sparrows in winter, and the open areas for Sandhill Cranes. The resident race of cranes is the "Florida Sandhill," and a few of them can be seen year-round. In winter their numbers are bolstered by migrants from the north. There may be a few ducks in winter; also watch for waders and the ever-present Common Yellowthroats. There are breeding King Rails, but they are hard to spot.

Continue out to the tower, and climb up for a magnificent view and to scan for cranes or other waders. In winter there are usually a couple of American Bitterns, and a few lucky observers actually get to see them. Continue around the loop for another 0.7 mile and rejoin Swamp Island Drive back out to Spur 121. You can stop anywhere along these roads to bird, but at some places the areas beyond the road are closed, so watch for signs.

To get to the other side of the swamp, return to GA 23/121. Keep in mind there is no gas available during the drive to **Stephen C. Foster State Park**. Turn right; in 14.9 miles you will reach the small town of Saint George (one small store with limited hours). Turn right on GA 94. In 11.5 miles you will enter Florida and the road becomes Florida Highway 2; in another 15.5 miles it reenters Georgia as GA 94. Continue 8.2 miles more and you get the town of Edith, again without services.

Total distance from Saint George is 35.2 miles. Turn right on GA 177, and you will reach the park boundary in 10.7 miles.

This area can be good for kites, though you will need some luck to spot a Swallow-tailed. The pay station is another 0.4 mile, and if you came from Suwanee Canal the fee you paid there is good here. Just before the pay station you will see Sill Road on your left. This road ends in 0.3 mile at a gate and a boat ramp, but you can park there and walk down the sill itself. This can be good birding if you have time. As you continue along the road, there are RCW trees at 1.4 and 2.4 miles past the pay station, but this cluster is currently not in use. The park entrance is 5.5 miles from the pay station, and the end of the road is another 0.7 mile. There is a museum here, boat and canoe rentals, a campground, and cabins. The Trembling Earth Nature Trail, about 0.5 mile long, is mostly within floodplain forest and cypress-tupelo swamp. In spring and summer, this area also is full of Prothonotary Warblers and Northern Parulas. Look for Wood Ducks in standing water.

General information: The following information concerning Red-cockaded Woodpeckers came from the refuge RCW biologist; there is more life history information about these birds in the Piedmont NWR section (Site 19). A cluster of RCWs (formerly called a colony) consists of year-round roosting and nesting trees, and is made up of one pair of adults, their offspring, and possibly male "helpers." Within Okefenokee NWR, there are 63 clusters, 31 of which have birds. They generally nest at the refuge from late April to mid-July, and the fledglings are usually around mid-June to early July. This is probably the easiest time to find RCWs, as the adults constantly return to the nest throughout the day to feed the nestlings. When they are not feeding birds in the nest, they may be near the cluster only at dawn or dusk.

ADDITIONAL HELP

DeLorme map grid: most of page 69 and the lower section of page 61.
For more information: Okefenokee NWR Visitor Center, (912) 496-7836; Suwanee Canal Recreation Area Concessionaire, (800) SWAMP-96; Stephen C. Foster State Park, (912) 637-5274; Laura S. Walker State Park, (912) 287-4900; Okefenokee Swamp Park, (912) 283-0583; Waycross–Ware County CVB, (912) 283-3742; Okefenokee Chamber of Commerce (Folkston), (912) 496-2536; *Paddling Okefenokee,* Falcon Publishing.

37 Big Hammock Wildlife Management Area

County: Tatnall.
Habitats: Mixed pine/hardwood forest, floodplain hardwood forest, cypress-tupelo swamp, river.
Key birds: Swainson's Warbler, Mississippi Kite, Prothonotary Warbler, Acadian Flycatcher, Hooded and Kentucky Warblers, Yellow-billed Cuckoo.
Best times to bird: April through October.

The birding: This 6,000-acre area is on the banks of the Altamaha River. It offers easy access to interesting coastal plain breeding species as well as a good place for migrants. There are several pairs of Swainson's Warblers here, so look for floodplain forest that is periodically flooded for feeding sites, and nearby stands of cane for breeding sites. The main road is driveable by passenger cars, and the many spur trails are easy walking. You can cover this site in a couple of hours; early morning is best.

Directions: The WMA is just northwest of the town of Jesup. From the intersection of US Highway 84 and US 341 in Jesup, go northwest for 0.9 mile on US 341 and turn right on Georgia Highway 169. Drive 20.9 miles and merge right on GA 121/144. Just after you cross the Altamaha River, turn right into the WMA at the sign (1.8 miles from GA 169). This entire WMA is good river-edge habitat for a variety of species, and you can work the roads and paths as quickly or slowly as you like. You may find Hooded and Kentucky Warblers anywhere you find floodplain forest, and other typical species such as Summer Tanagers and Yellow-billed Cuckoos can be found throughout the WMA. The main road is gravel, which is good traveling except after heavy rains; most of the side trails are impassable by almost any vehicle. A good technique is to drive along the main road until you find an area you wish to explore on foot. As with all WMAs, there is hunting in the fall, but the hunting season is after the good birding ends. A few sparrows and other species winter here, but it's not worth a trip to get here in that season.

One way to explore Big Hammock is to drive in the main road (Big Hammock Road). From the entrance, continue along the road to any habitat that looks good, or until you find some birds to check out. A small cypress-tupelo swamp 0.5 mile from the entrance is a good bet for Prothonotary Warblers (like all cypress-tupelo swamps here). After another 0.3 mile Dog Pen Road goes off to the right. This road is passable by truck but not by car, and gets you near the river at a T intersection in about 1.2 miles. Turn either way to explore on foot.

Back at Big Hammock Road, continue 0.6 mile to Middle Road on the right. The road you are on becomes Hammock Lake Road, and ends in 0.5 mile in an extensive swampy area. If you turn down Middle Road, you will pass several more small swamps alongside for Prothonotary Warblers or Acadian Flycatchers, and at 0.9 mile there is a small two-track spur on the right. You can walk down this trail for all the species listed above. There is also a good area for Swainson's

37 Big Hammock Wildlife Management Area

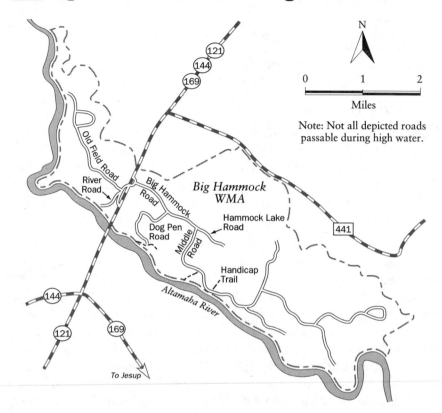

Warblers (on the left in 0.3 mile). Look for the stands of cane. Back on Middle Road, another 0.3 mile brings you to the river on your right. Scan the sky for soaring raptors, including Mississippi Kites and Broad-winged and Red-shouldered Hawks, especially later in the morning as the thermals begin. There may be migrants anywhere in the WMA, but they are usually concentrated in feeding flocks along the river edge. In another 0.2 mile is a side trail to the left with a "Handicapped Access Only" sign. This sign means to say that only vehicles of the handicapped are permitted; for others, this is a great trail to walk for all of the wetter-habitat species here, including Swainson's Warblers.

By now you should have an idea of the types of habitat in which to look for particular species; there are several more miles of road and side trail in front of you to explore. Bird as long as you want, and return to the entrance. If you want more options, there are also roads and trails on the other side of GA 121/144.

To access these areas, drive the loop under GA 121/144 for 0.3 mile to an intersection. The road on the left has two roads off it, both fairly short and in bad shape. The road farthest to the left dead-ends at Taylor Lake in 0.3 mile. This is a nice spot, but there may be lots of fisherman traffic in the area. River Road, the other road, runs into some nice floodplain forest worth checking on foot, if it isn't

37 Big Hammock Wildlife Management Area
38 Altamaha River Overlook

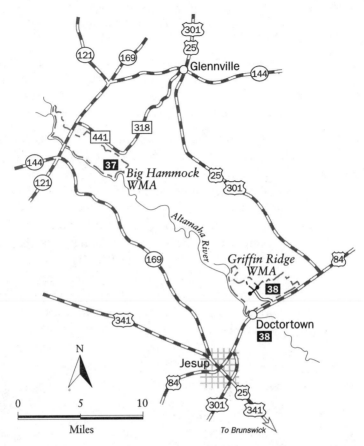

too warm. The main road is called Old Field Road and continues ahead. Though it too deteriorates in 1 mile, there is some nice habitat, including two small swamps and a few mature pine trees. Check them for breeding Yellow-throated Warblers. Like the south end, there are several more roads to explore, as long as your energy and water hold out.

General information: There are no services near this WMA, but Jesup has anything you might want. This area is also near the Altamaha River Overlook (Site 38), and not far from many good coastal birding sites.

ADDITIONAL HELP

DeLorme map grid: page 54, D1.
For more information: Georgia Department of Natural Resources; Wayne County (Jesup) Tourism Board, (912) 427-2028.

38 Altamaha River Overlook

See map on page 163

Counties: Wayne and Long.
Habitats: River, floodplain hardwood forest, lily pond.
Key birds: Swallow-tailed Kite, Mississippi Kite, Wood Stork.
Best times to bird: May to July.

The birding: This site is simply an overlook for the Altamaha River in an area that boasts more Swallow-tailed Kites than any other in Georgia. They are not guaranteed, but if you spend a few hours here in the right season you are likely to to see one. A nearby WMA offers additional birding in floodplain hardwood forest.

Directions: Basically, you need to get to the Altamaha River bridge on US Highways 25/84/301. This is just northeast of the town of Jesup. From Jesup, drive toward the river about 5 miles to Doctortown. Just before the river (0.5 mile prior), look for a sign on your left (north side of road) for the Jesup Jaycee Fairgrounds, with a smaller one for the Jaycee Landing. This is across the highway from a large paper mill. Turn on this road, and follow it around to the right toward the river for 0.2 mile. Before you go down the hill to the boat landing, there is a small park on your right called Altamaha River Heritage Park. Drive in here, and park wherever you want to scan. You want to be looking across the river at the forested floodplain area both above and below you on the river. This is the highest place from which to look, but you may have to work around the trees to make sure you are watching the entire area. You can also scan from down at the

Swallow-tailed Kite.

boat landing, but at that elevation you are able to cover less area. Midmorning to early afternoon is best, as the birds are more likely to be soaring then. You will probably see Mississippi Kites, and various waders and vultures flying around while you are watching for Swallow-tails. As usual, a scope is very helpful. When you are finished, a small store down at the boat landing offers drinks and some packaged food items.

For more birding nearby, go back to US 301 and drive over the main bridge. The entrance to **Griffin Ridge WMA** is 1.8 miles past the bridge on the left. If the gate is open, you can drive 1.7 miles in through a nice floodplain area with the usual Coastal Plain breeders in summer, including Northern Parulas and Prothonotary Warblers. If you are lucky you may find a few Swainson's Warblers in here as well. This area is more active early in the day, so you might want to come here before you go to the overlook. If the gate is closed, you can walk in to bird. Back out on US 301 and another 0.5 mile along is Forrest Pond on the left. This is a great lily pond, with Anhingas and sometimes Yellow-crowned Night-Herons. Purple Martins nest here as well, and you might see Wood Ducks, but they are usually pretty shy. Be careful parking, as this is a busy road, though there are a couple of areas where the shoulder is very wide.

General information: The kites can be found in most large river floodplain areas near the coast in Georgia, but this is one of the only areas with easy access. The town of Jesup has all the facilities you might want, such as motels, gas, and food. The town of Ludowici is about 6 miles farther northeast on US 301 and has restaurants and gas, but it is not as large as Jesup.

ADDITIONAL HELP

DeLorme map grid: page 54, G3.
For more information: Wayne County (Jesup) Tourism Board, (912) 427-2028; Georgia Department of Natural Resources.

39 East Georgia Turf Farm

County: Bulloch.
Habitats: Pine forest, mixed pine/hardwood forest, freshwater marsh shrubland, grassy field, pond.
Key birds: Buff-breasted and Upland Sandpipers, American Golden-Plover, Pectoral Sandpiper, Least Sandpiper, White Ibis, Common Ground-Dove, Horned Lark, American Pipit, Vesper Sparrow, swallows.
Best times to bird: Mid-July through September, although any time can be interesting.

The birding: This sod farm is just north of Interstate 16 near Statesboro. It offers a good opportunity to look for grassland shorebirds and herons in fall. A selection of adjacent habitats offers good birding at any time of year. Access is easy, and the

39 East Georgia Turf Farm

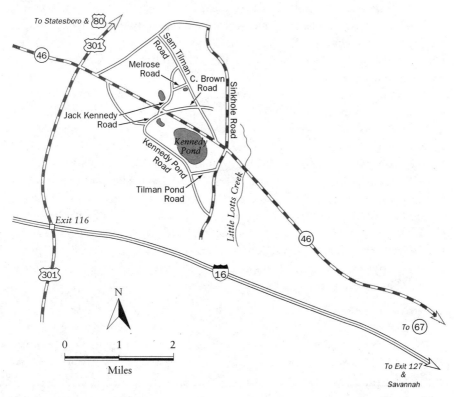

dirt roads are in good condition except after rain. Some parts can be accessed from paved roads, namely Georgia Highway 46 and Sinkhole Road. This area is private land, so birding is from the roads only.

Directions: This sod farm is located along Georgia Highway 46, which parallels Interstate 16 to the north, and is accessible from either end. These directions will bring you in from the west, but could easily be done in reverse from the east. From the west, take the Statesboro exit on US Highway 301, which is Exit 116 (old 25). Go north on US 301 for 3.6 miles from I-16 to GA 46, and turn right. In 2.1 miles you will reach Jack Kennedy Road. From this spot, refer to the map when deciding which spots to explore.

When birding this area, keep the following guidelines in mind. In fall look for shorebirds wherever you find areas of sod, especially when the sod is wet from watering or rain. These same areas will have Horned Larks and American Pipits in fall and winter. Check areas of standing water carefully for birds working the edges. Of the highly sought-after sod shorebirds, the most likely is the Buff-breasted Sandpiper, followed by Upland Sandpiper and American Golden-Plover. Pectoral Sandpipers are common in fall, and next common is the Least Sandpiper. The wet areas may have any of a number of species of shorebirds, including both Greater and Lesser Yellowlegs, Solitary or Spotted Sandpiper, either Long-billed (rare) or Short-billed Dowitcher, or Common Snipes (in winter). Many rare shorebirds have been found, so check everything. There are shorebirds in spring, too, but in general not as many as in fall.

Always watch for Common Ground-Doves, especially in areas of dirt, including partially tilled fields, roads, and places with low, scrubby plants. Loggerhead Shrikes and Eastern Bluebirds are found year-round, usually on telephone wires. In summer breeding birds of the open areas include Indigo Buntings, Blue Grosbeaks, Eastern Kingbirds, Red-winged Blackbirds, and Chimney Swifts. You can look for Painted Buntings, but there are very few. Check the areas of old pecan orchards for Orchard Orioles in summer (and for Yellow Warblers in migration). Herons build up in fall, mostly Cattle Egrets on the sod and Little Blue Herons and Snowy Egrets in wet areas. White Ibises occur here in fall also. Green Herons breed here, and there are usually a few Great Blue Herons and Great Egrets around. Look for large numbers of blackbirds in fall and winter, primarily Common Grackles, Red-winged Blackbirds, and Brown-headed Cowbirds. Check these flocks for rarities such as Yellow-headed Blackbirds, but they are casual in occurrence. American Kestrels are common in winter.

In late summer and fall check the ponds and sod areas for swallows. Barn and Rough-winged are common, and there are good numbers of Bank in late July and early August. Tree Swallows appear later, and a few are present all winter, mostly over Kennedy Pond. Check areas of unmowed grass or other weeds in winter for sparrows. Wet areas will have Swamp and Song Sparrows, and drier areas will have Field, Chipping, Savannah, and a few Vesper Sparrows. Brushy areas may have some of the above sparrows, as well as White-throated Sparrows. White-crowned Sparrows have been found here in fall, but rarely.

This sod farm is large, and many of the species mentioned can be challenging to locate. The following tour may help you cover this area systematically. Turn left on Jack Kennedy Road. In 0.2 mile there is a pond on your left, good in winter for Pied-billed Grebes but not much else. In fall check the sod area to your right for shorebirds and the open fields on both sides in winter for Savannah and Chipping Sparrows. Look for Melrose Road at 0.6 mile. The area just before Melrose on the right is usually left in low vegetation in winter; look for Common Ground-Doves and Vesper Sparrows there. Turn right on Melrose, and proceed 0.3 mile to Sam Tilman Road. Just before this corner is a small cypress-tupelo swamp on the left. Look for Prothonotary Warblers in summer and Anhingas and Wood Ducks all year. The pond on the right at this corner can be checked for ducks in winter, although generally only the Ring-necked Duck is found here.

Turn right on Sam Tilman Road, and continue to watch the pond on the right as you pass. In 0.2 mile from the corner, you are at the outflow of the pond; this wet area of scrub can be checked for landbirds in any season. In winter you can look here for White-eyed Vireos or the less-likely Blue-gray Gnatcatchers among the large numbers of Yellow-rumped Warblers and Ruby-crowned Kinglets present.

Continue another 0.3 mile to an intersection, and turn right onto C. Brown Road; the road on the left is Joe Robert Tilman Road. Follow this road 0.7 mile back to GA 46. As you drive it, carefully scan the sod on your left in fall, as this is the usually the best area for grassland shorebirds. Most of the shorebirds will be Pectoral Sandpipers or Killdeer, but this is the most reliable place for Buff-breasted and Upland Sandpipers and American Golden-Plovers. Of course, if these species are your goal, check all areas of sod throughout this farm.

To explore Kennedy Pond, go straight across GA 46 and join Jack Kennedy Road heading south. Check along here for Common Ground-Doves and sparrows, and scan the pond on your left in 0.2 mile, although it usually doesn't have much. At 0.4 mile from GA 46, turn left on Kennedy Pond Road. Follow this road for 1.1 miles, pausing near pine trees if Brown-headed Nuthatches or Pine Warblers are species of interest. When you reach 1.1 miles, look for a small blue sign on the left that reads "Dry Hydrant," and park. Walk out the very small area of grass on your left to the edge of Kennedy Pond, and scan. There will be lots of American Coots, with good numbers of Ring-necked Ducks and a few Wood Ducks and Blue-winged Teals. Many other duck species have been seen, though not regularly. Watch for Anhingas and in summer, Common Moorhen.

To scan the rest of the sod farm, return to GA 46 the way you came. Turn right on GA 46, and watch the sod areas on your left in fall. At around 0.8 mile, stop along the road and scan Kennedy Pond on your right for Bald Eagles or ducks in winter, and Anhingas all year. Continue another 0.5 mile to Sinkhole Road (passing Sam Tilman Road in the process), and turn left. The next 0.5 mile on the right is the best area of open sod for nongrassland shorebirds in fall. Look down the wet ditch for all species of shorebirds, and the wet area in the very back of the sod in front of you for more shorebirds and waders such as ibises or herons. This wet area is overflow from Little Lotts Creek. In times of wet weather, there may be dabbling ducks here. It is a good area for swallows also. This area is not close, and a scope will be helpful. At the end of this section along Sinkhole Road, check any wet areas of low weeds for other shorebirds. This is the last section of the sod farm, so return back to GA 46.

At this point you can either revisit parts of the sod farm or leave the area. If returning west, go back out to I-16 the way you came. If you want to go east toward the coast, turn left on GA 46. In 0.7 mile you will cross Little Lotts Creek, which may be worth a quick stop along the road if you have time. In spring and summer you can find (or at least hear) Yellow-throated Vireos, Acadian Flycatchers, and Yellow-billed Cuckoos. Barred Owls breed here. Continue another 6.1 miles (6.8 miles from Sinkhole Road) to GA 67, and turn right. You will reach I-16 in 1.4 miles at Exit 127 (old 26).

General information: This sod farm and golf course are privately run, and birders are allowed here through the generosity of the owners. Please respect their property by birding from the roads only. So far, the golf course has not really had an impact on the good areas of sod for shorebirds, but if the course ever expands some areas in this section could change from sod to golf course. This would, of course, have a negative impact on birding here. A small convenience store at the corner of Sinkhole Road and GA 46 has gas and food, and there are services available along I-16 as well, more at Exit 116 for US 301.

ADDITIONAL HELP

DeLorme map grid: page 46, E3/4, F3/4.
For more information: Statesboro–Bulloch Chamber of Commerce, (912) 764-6111.

40 Paulk's Pasture Wildlife Management Area

County: Glynn.
Habitats: Pine forest, hardwood floodplain forest, cypress-tupelo swamp, cleared pine flatwoods, weedy fields.
Key birds: Henslow's Sparrow, Sedge Wren, Prothonotary Warbler, Swainson's Warbler, White-breasted Nuthatch, Yellow-crowned Night-Heron.
Best times to bird: November to February for first two species, April to June for the rest.

The birding: Paulk's Pasture WMA is just inland from Brunswick and near many of the best coastal sites for birding. It is a timber-managed area with several smaller sections of good birding, including a wet powerline cut and a couple of very nice swamps.

Directions: From Interstate 95 Exit 36A or B (old 7A/B), drive inland (west) on US Highway 341/25. The main entrance is 7.9 miles from the interstate, on your left. The road, which is called Main Road, is open only seasonally and usually during hunting season, so you may need to walk in. At only 0.2 mile in is a large powerline across the road; park here. The best spot for Henslow's Sparrows is the cut area directly under the powerline to your left, an area that is always wet. This used to be pine flatwoods, and even though the trees are long gone, the structure of the habitat is enough to draw Henslow's Sparrows in winter. There will be many other sparrows as well, mostly Swamp and Song. As you walk through the grass (wear boots), watch for any bird that flies away from you. Most of them will fly away into the woods, which Henslow's rarely do. In flight, the Henslow's appears to have a much shorter tail than either Song or Swamp Sparrow. The Henslow's seems to prefer to fly a short distance and drop back into the wet grass, so concentrate on birds that act like this. If you watch where they land and get there quickly, you may be able to see them on the ground. They have a tendency to land and run away like a mouse, so you need to be quick! If you are really lucky, sometimes they will fly toward the woods but stop in a shrub right on the edge. They tend to just sit there when they do this, so if you think one has landed in a particular shrub, scan the whole bush very carefully.

40 Paulk's Pasture Wildlife Management Area

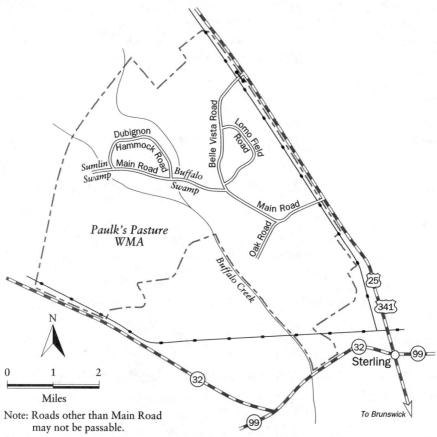

Note: Roads other than Main Road may not be passable.

LeConte's Sparrows have been seen here a few times as well, but they are even rarer. They act just like the Henslow's, which is not surprising, as they are closely related. A few Sedge Wrens occur here, and they tend to fly weakly off like Henslow's but are smaller and yellowish, even in flight. LeConte's will also appear paler in flight. Keep in mind that in any given winter there are only a few Henslow's in this entire powerline cut, and they are very difficult to see. Eastern Bluebirds and Pine Warblers are in the pines also, and in winter there are plenty of Yellow-rumped Warblers.

For spring migrant or breeding species, you need to get to the interior of this WMA. From US 341, take Main Road 1.1 miles to a fork, and bear right. Continue another 1.3 miles to another fork, and bear left. The fork to the right is Belle Vista Road, with some good woods for general birding and a small swamp about 1.5 miles up the road. After bearing left on Main Road, you will hit the first section of Buffalo Swamp in another 0.9 mile (total of 3.3 miles from US 341). This nice cypress-tupelo swamp is good for migrants along the edges in spring and to a lesser degree in fall, when more birds are on the actual coast. Swainson's Warblers

Henslow's Sparrow.

can be found here in spring, and probably breed. There are lots of Prothonotary Warblers and Northern Parulas then, too. There is a permanent resident colony of White-breasted Nuthatches that cannot be found anywhere else nearby. In summer a colony of Yellow-crowned Night-Herons breeds here. Barred Owls also love this type of habitat. This area is 0.2 mile wide; if you continue on Main Road another 1.4 miles you will reach Sumlin Swamp, with similar species. This area has been underbirded in the past, so you might find more interesting species as well.

General information: If you strike out here, there is another powerline cut on the west side of this WMA. Go back toward Brunswick on US 341 to GA 99 in the town of Sterling (just under 4 miles). Turn right to go west. Follow this road about 3 miles to GA 32, and turn right. In about 4 miles you will see another large powerline off to your right in the WMA. This habitat changes from year to year, so look for another area with wet ground and lots of grass and try again for the Henslow's. This side is not as reliable as the east side. When in the main section detailed above, watch for logging trucks, as they may not be watching for you. Most of the hunting takes place in the woods, which is not normally a problem because there isn't much to look for bird-wise there in winter. In any season, rain may turn these dirt roads into a quagmire, so be careful of that, although the short road to the Henslow's site is usually passable. There are many areas that have been clearcut, but those that were cut a year or two earlier may have enough brush to make them attractive to sparrows in winter and can be birded easily from the road.

The area back near the interstate has more restaurants, hotels, and gas stations than you would ever want or need, but there isn't much away from there, so plan accordingly.

ADDITIONAL HELP

DeLorme map grid: page 63, C6, D6; page 62, D5.
For more information: Georgia Department of Natural Resources; Brunswick–Golden Isles CVB, (800) 933-2627.

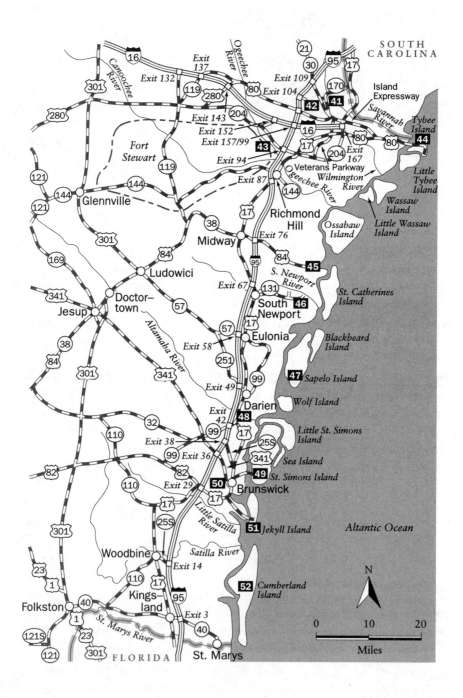

Coast Region

41 Onslow Island

County: Chatham.
Habitats: Coastal shrub, freshwater marsh shrubland, brackish marsh, diked spoil impoundment, river.
Key birds: American Avocet, Stilt Sandpiper, Mottled Duck, Common Ground-Dove.
Best times to bird: Anytime there is water. All year.

The birding: This small spoil site is not currently receiving fresh spoil, and is wet only after rain. This is crucial to birding, because when it is dry, the ducks and shorebirds are simply not here. The single impoundment is walk-in only, and the loop around it is 1.8 miles long. Shrub surrounds the impoundment, which can be good for sparrows in winter and migrants spring and fall. When wet, this is one of only two fairly reliable sites for avocets in Georgia. The surrounding marsh is always worth checking for ducks, waders, and rails, and the nearby Savannah National Wildlife Refuge just across the border in South Carolina is excellent for ducks in winter.

Directions: This site can be accessed from Savannah, but is easier to get to from Interstate 95. Take the last Georgia exit, which is Exit 109 (old 19) for Georgia Highway 21/30. Go south toward Savannah 2.7 miles to where GA 30 cuts off to the left, or east. This road is also called Bonny Bridge Road. Turn left, and in 0.9 mile, turn left on GA 25 (formerly US Highway 17) and follow it to a bridge at 0.8 mile. This is the Houlihan Bridge over the Front River channel of the Savannah River. The entrance to Onslow Island, a dirt road with a brown metal gate, is immediately past this bridge on the right. Park here. Even if this gate is open, you may walk in ONLY. Access to these spoil sites is always tenuous, so please obey ALL signs to keep this great area available. Some areas of the site may be closed seasonally for nesting birds, so heed all "Area Beyond This Sign Closed" signs as they are specifically for birders. Obviously, you enter at your own risk (I had to put that in! This is an open, easy-to-bird site). Again, whether there will be shorebirds or ducks here depends on whether the area is wet. The US Fish & Wildlife office, which oversees this refuge, has graciously allowed birders to call beforehand to check on the water level; their number is (912) 652-4415.

Park at the gate, and walk in the 0.2-mile entrance road. Watch for Common Ground-Doves anywhere on the road or in sandy areas. The brush that lines the road and continues around the loop should be checked in spring and fall for migrants and in winter for sparrows. In fall this scrub will be loaded with warblers such as Yellow, Palm, and Common Yellowthroat, and lots of Yellow-rumped Warblers in winter. Once you get to the loop, scan the open dirt area in front of

41 Onslow Island

42 Savannah Airport Ponds

43 Savannah-Ogeechee Canal

44 Fort Pulaski/Tybee Island

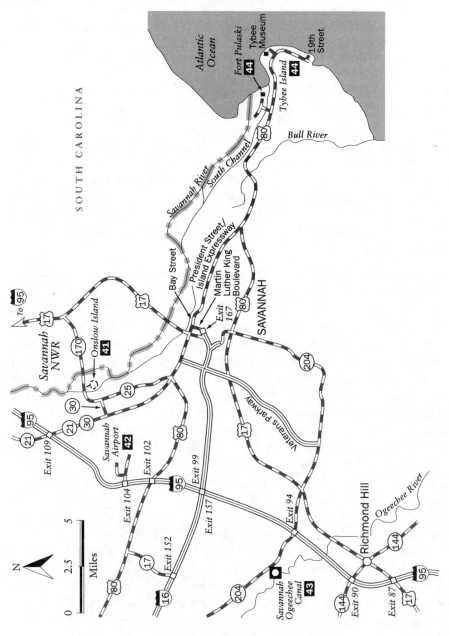

you. The area that is usually most productive is 0.4 mile to the left, so you can take the loop to the left first. The entire loop is 1.8 miles long.

As you walk around the loop, scan the skies for swallows and raptors. In mid-September through early November, there are lots of accipiters and falcons passing by, especially if there are other birds present. As you approach the wet area, start scanning for ducks in winter or shorebirds anytime. A scope is extremely useful, as you will spook the birds if you get too close. In winter most ducks will be dabblers such as teals and shovelers. The refuge just north of here is loaded with Mottled Ducks, and this is a great place to look for them in Georgia. Also in winter, the most common shorebirds will be Common Snipes, either Greater or Lesser Yellowlegs, and Least Sandpipers. Look also for Stilt Sandpipers in migration or in winter, as this is the only place in the state where they are regular in winter.

Other shorebirds in migration include all the peeps, including White-rumped Sandpipers in spring and the chance for Baird's Sandpipers in fall. Look for Wilson's Phalaropes in spring or fall; even though this is one of the best places to look, they are pretty rare. Semipalmated Plovers and Killdeer are the most common plovers. Look also for American Avocets all year or Black-necked Stilts in summer and fall. Just about any shorebird can show up, so keep your eyes and your options open! The much larger but inaccessible Barnwell spoil site in South Carolina is only a few miles away and has produced many rarities for the region, any of which could also come here. While walking around you can also scan the marsh for waders, or hope to see some of the rails that continually call. Brackish areas have Clapper all year round and King in winter, and freshwater areas will have King and Virginia Rails and Soras during winter. They usually stay pretty well hidden in the marsh. You can either continue the loop all the way around or go back the way you came when you are finished.

When you return to your vehicle, you can depart the way you came or continue east on GA 25. The next 4 to 5 miles run through great marsh habitat and are always worth checking. The first 1.1 miles are in Georgia and usually don't have much to see from the road. After you cross Back River into South Carolina, the next 3.2 miles are usually full of ducks in winter. At the border, GA 25 becomes South Carolina 170. You will find Common Moorhens in summer and, rarely, Purple Gallinules. There is a great wildlife drive on your right about a mile from the border for more impoundments and scrub areas. Return via GA 25 or take SC 170 to US 17 (4.4 miles from the Onslow Island gate). Turn left on US 17 and you will reach I-95 in 6 miles at Exit 5 in South Carolina.

General information: This is the only accessible spoil site on the Georgia coast; it has similar species to Andrews Island near Brunswick. The presence of water is key to both sites, but Onslow is not as buggy as Andrews. The only facilities near this site are along Georgia Highway 21/30 near Interstate 95.

ADDITIONAL HELP

DeLorme map grid: page 47, H10.

For more information: US Fish & Wildlife, Coastal Refuges, (912) 652-4415; Savannah CVB, (912) 944-0456.

42 Savannah Airport Ponds

See map on page 174

County: Chatham.
Habitats: Shallow pond, pond, cypress-tupelo swamp.
Key birds: Glossy Ibis, Common Moorhen, Anhinga, waders.
Best times to bird: All year.

The birding: This area, just off the interstate, consists of several small ponds visible from roads within Savannah International Airport. Although there is no birding out of your car, this is probably the most reliable area in the state for Glossy Ibises and it takes only minutes to check.

Directions: Take Exit 104 (old 18A) on Interstate 95, and follow signs to the airport. Only 0.9 mile from Interstate 95 is a crossroad named McKenna Drive; turn left. Pull over to the shoulder just after you turn left and scan the small shallow pond on your left. This is the most likely spot for Glossy Ibises, but they may be in the back of the pond and tough to see. There are usually a couple of the small herons and a few waders such as Greater Yellowlegs here. In winter there may be

Cypress-tupelo swamp along McKenna Drive.

Common Snipes along the edge. Do not get out of your car to bird as this is shoulder-birding only.

During extended periods of little rain, this pond may dry up and Glossy Ibises head elsewhere. They are the main attraction, but you can continue on McKenna Drive to check a couple of other areas as well. Continue around the corner for less than a mile and scan the swamp on both sides for Anhingas and Common Moorhens. Belted Kingfishers and Red-shouldered Hawks frequent the area as well. Just past this swamp is another pond on your left, where there are usually American Coots and sometimes other ducks in winter. This pond may have herons working the edges and sometimes you will find Glossy Ibises here instead of in the first pond. Just past the pond, turn left onto the dirt access road to turn around and exit the airport.

General information: This is a working airport, so to keep relations good with the airport authority, just check the ponds without lingering too long and head back out. There is a gas station at this exit, and other services at virtually every other exit.

ADDITIONAL HELP

DeLorme map grid: page 47, H9/10.
For more information: Savannah CVB, (912) 944-0456.

43 Savannah-Ogeechee Canal

See map on page 174

County: Chatham.
Habitats: Floodplain hardwood forest, cypress-tupelo swamp, river
Key birds: Swainson's, Prothonotary, Hooded, and Yellow-throated Warblers, Mississippi Kite, Acadian Flycatcher, Yellow-throated Vireo, Barred Owl.
Best times to bird: April through October.

The birding: This small park is an easy way to get into some prime floodplain habitat located just west of Interstate 95. A short, level trail offers easy birding down to the Ogeechee River and back, and it can be birded in only an hour or two. This is one of the best examples of this habitat that is both easily accessed and this close to the coast.

Directions: Use the Georgia Highway 204 exit from Interstate 95, which is Exit 94 (old 16), and head west away from the coast. Drive 2.3 miles and look on your left for the parking lot to the Savannah-Ogeechee Canal. This lot sneaks up on you and you may be past it before you see the sign for the park, so watch for it at the correct mileage. Turn into the lot and park. This park is open from 9 A.M. to 5 P.M. every day, and has restrooms as well as a small, interesting museum and nature center. Admission is free, but this park is self-supporting and could certainly use a small donation.

As you pass through the gate, the building is to your right and the trails are to your left. There are two ways to get to the river. One way is to walk on either side of the small canal, and the other way is to follow the Jenkes Road Trail through the forest. Although both are interesting, more of the key birds are found on the Jenkes Road Trail. Both trails are 0.5 mile long. About halfway to the river is a cross-trail that connects the Jenkes Road Trail and the Tow Path.

The Jenkes Road Trail goes right through some great floodplain forest and some small areas of cypress-tupelo swamp. Anywhere along this trail watch for any of the key species listed above, except for the Mississippi Kite, which is more likely to be seen by scanning above the Ogeechee River at the end of the trail. Prothonotary Warblers should be looked and listened for at the short boardwalk areas over the swampy sections. If you are lucky, you may hear Barred Owls calling, especially on cloudy days. Other birds along this trail are Northern Parulas, White- and Red-eyed Vireos, Great Crested Flycatchers, and Wood Thrushes. The thrush is more likely in the slightly upland habitat across the canal near the building. Once you get to the river, scan up and down for soaring kites, especially mid-morning. The Mississippi is far more likely, although a Swallow-tailed is occasionally seen here. They actually soar over this entire area, but you are under trees most of the time.

The canal is fairly small, with the old Tow Path down the east side and the Heel Path down the west side. Both offer good birding, although they are more open than the Jenkes Road Trail. You can cross the canal at Lock 5 near the building, but if you take the Heel Path you can't cross downstream. There is another lock (6) at the river, but no bridge. In spring and fall watch for small groups of migrant landbirds working the canal or the river.

If you're interested in a longer hike, the Holly Trail (0.5 mile) connects to the Sandhill Trail to the east (1 mile). This takes you through a much drier sandhill habitat. Trail maps are available at the nature center, which also has a few reptiles and amphibians from the area on display.

General information: This canal was built in the early 1800s to connect the Savannah and Ogeechee Rivers, and remains largely intact all the way to downtown Savannah. The museum has lots of interesting historical exhibits and literature. There are also restrooms, picnic tables, and vending machines. Back at Interstate 95 are many restaurants and service stations.

ADDITIONAL HELP

DeLorme map grid: page 55, B8.
For more information: Savannah–Ogeechee Canal Museum and Nature Center, (912) 748-8068; Savannah CVB, (912) 944-0456.

44 Fort Pulaski/Tybee Island

See map on page 174

County: Chatham.
Habitats: Coastal shrub, grassy field, brackish marsh, salt marsh, tidal flat, beach, ocean.
Key birds: Red-throated Loon, terns and gulls including Lesser Black-backed Gull, Purple Sandpiper and other shorebirds, salt marsh sparrows, and migrant passerines.
Best times to bird: October to February for coastal birds including key species above and sparrows; April, May, and August to October for passerine migrants.

The birding: Fort Pulaski is an excellent location for coastal passerine migrants in the scrub and myrtle thickets around the old fort. The salt marshes in this area are very good for wrens and sparrows, and there are several good beach roost sites on Tybee Island. The north end of Tybee is great for the more northerly winter seabirds, and this island is the best spot in Georgia for Purple Sandpipers. If you are not birding during migration, you may want to skip Fort Pulaski and go straight to Tybee Island.

Directions: Drive east on Interstate 16 from the intersection at I-95 for 8.5 miles to Exit 167 (old 37A), which is Martin Luther King Boulevard, and take the short ramp down to a traffic light. Turn left on MLK Boulevard, also called Connecticut Highway 25, and drive 0.8 mile through several lights. Turn right on Bay Street, which is the last major cross-street before you go down a hill. After turning on Bay Street, go through several lights in quick succession, and then get in the left-hand lane. Just at 0.7 mile, the left lane goes down a one-lane blind hill without warning, becoming General McIntosh Boulevard for 0.4 mile. If you are in the right-hand lane you cannot make this turn, so get in the left-hand lane on Bay Street as soon as possible. At the bottom of the hill on General McIntosh Boulevard, the road splits into two lanes; both can turn left at the light onto the multilane President Street. Stay on this road all the way to Fort Pulaski. At 6.1 miles from General McIntosh Boulevard, US Highway 80 comes in from the right, so stay to the left. Your road is now Island Expressway, US 80/GA 26.

In another 3.5 miles you will see a sign on the right for Fort Pulaski National Monument, which you have just entered. There is an old railroad line on the left, which has been made into a trail, nice for a walk but not very interesting birding. The marsh and waterway on your right can be scanned for waders or ducks, depending on tide and season, and the shoulder is wide enough to park on. About 1.4 miles from the sign, the marsh on your right becomes very good for Seaside and both Nelson's and Saltmarsh Sharp-tailed Sparrows. All three are easier to find at high tide when the rising water pushes them closer to dry land (and birders). They are usually responsive to "pishing" or squeaking sounds. After 2 miles of this habitat, a road on your left leads to **Fort Pulaski.**

Turn left here, and pay your $2 entrance fee. Keep in mind that the gate does not open until 8:30 A.M. If the small booth is unattended, you must pay at the visitor center at the fort. After the booth, cross a small bridge and note the many gulls and terns, especially Forster's, that roost on this bridge. If there are no cars, many of these birds will pose for photos if you don't make any sudden movements. The marsh at the base of the bridge on both ends is excellent for sparrows, Marsh Wrens, and Clapper Rails. At the far side of the bridge there is space to park, and you can then walk a dike around the marsh. The path is good, and frequently loads of birds inhabit the scrub and myrtle that line the inside of the path. Migrants can often be found here in season. This is also an excellent way to try for birds in the marsh if you don't have boots, especially at high tide, as you walk along the dike pishing.

Back at the entrance road, continue toward the fort. At 0.7 mile, a road to the left leads to a picnic area and the coast guard station. The picnic area is in 0.3 mile; it's a good place for lunch but not very birdy. The restrooms are open 24 hours a day. Continue another 0.2 mile to a T intersection with a sign for the coast guard station. Turn right, which is still part of the monument and not the station, and in 100 yards is a small parking area right on the bank of the Savannah River channel. You can scan for birds in the channel, and check the rocky riprap lining the shore for Purple Sandpipers or other shorebirds at any tide but high. This is not as good for Purples as Tybee Island, but it is a good secondary spot.

After birding here, go back past the picnic area to the entrance road, and turn left. In only 0.2 mile you will reach the main parking lot. The fort and a very nice visitor center are on your right; maps and restrooms are available. You have a few choices for birding. Several trails on the side of the parking lot away from the fort go through a nice area of coastal scrub on the north side of the island, and they're good during spring or fall migration. This area is very good for passerine migrants in season.

At the end of one of the trails is the North Pier, another good Savannah River viewing area. There is an additional rock jetty to your right along the shore, but it is exposed only at lower tides and can be checked then for Purple Sandpipers. The shell mounds along the river's edge are good for roosting shorebirds. In the parking lot area in late fall grass-loving migrants such as sparrows can be in the grass. You can also walk the dikes around the fort—there is a 1.9-mile Dike System Walk on the map. These walks are pleasant but not very birdy, unless you are willing to work hard at pishing birds out of the grass. When you are finished here, drive back out the entrance road to US 80.

To continue to **Tybee Island,** turn left, and in 1.1 miles you will be on the island. Be extremely careful about your speed on this island; the posted limits change often and there is always a radar trap somewhere. In another 1.7 miles (2.8 miles from Fort Pulaski), you will see Polk Road on your left. A small creek and marsh is 0.1 mile down Polk on the left, and it's worth a quick look for the close-up views of waders you can get. Back at US 80, continue another 0.3 mile to Campbell Street, and turn left. Campbell dead-ends at Van Horne Avenue in 0.2 mile; turn left and then take the first right, almost immediately, on Meddin Drive.

The beach along the north end of Tybee Island.

The parking lot you want is only 0.2 mile up Meddin on the right, but the entrance is tricky—it's sandwiched between Gulick Street on the right and Tom Lynch Loop on the left. The large structure here is the Tybee Museum. Turn into the parking lot, and drive around back. There is a parking fee booth, but this is a spot to bird in the winter and they do not charge for parking in the off-season. In season the charge is $5, and you would also have to contend with the massive beach crowds that keep both birds and birders away.

Drive past the booth and park in the farthest corner of the lot from the entrance to a wooden walkway over the dunes for beach access. On the backside of the parking lot you passed public restrooms that may or may not be open, on no apparent schedule. All of the following comments pertain to birding here October through February. The two top draws are Red-throated Loons and Purple Sandpipers. To get to them, walk over the boardwalk to the beach. Turn left when reaching the sand, and almost immediately you will see a rock breakwater. This breakwater is not large, and it's best at low tide. This is the best and most reliable spot in the state for Purple Sandpipers. If you find yourself here at high tide, do not despair, as there is a fairly reliable beach roost site described below. There are usually Ruddy Turnstones on this breakwater. Scan around the far end of the breakwater for diving ducks such as Buffleheads and Red-breasted Mergansers, and the numerous Double-crested Cormorants fishing here. Walk past the breakwater to the left, and scan the beach for roosting gulls, terns, and shorebirds. Lesser Black-backed Gulls may be anywhere on the beach.

The best way to try for Red-throated Loons is to stop here and scan out to sea. A scope is essential; it also helps you scan the resting flocks on the beach. Concentrate more on the ocean than the river. Unless they are in close, which is pretty uncommon, your best shot for loons is to spot them flying. There is usually a pretty large swell here, so it is very difficult to spot them sitting on the water. You can also look for scoters, although you won't see them very often, and rarely in winter Long-tailed Duck may be seen. Northern Gannet are usually seen, and when there is an onshore (easterly) wind, these large plunge-divers may be in the river channel. Continue walking on the beach in the same direction, looking for birds on the beach to your right and left. The changing small pools may have Semipalmated and Piping Plovers, and Savannah Sparrows in the grass.

The north tip of Tybee is marked by a green channel marker on a pole with the number "1" on it. If the tide is very high, the beach may be submerged and you will have to cut across the tip. From this point on (about a half mile from the boardwalk), the upper beach should be checked for roosting shorebirds. They may be pretty high up on the beach, and you should watch from a safe distance to avoid disturbing them. If the rock jetties are underwater, here is where the roosting Purple Sandpipers will be. They are usually mixed in with Ruddy Turnstones or Dunlins, so scan carefully any flocks of Turnstones or Dunlins. American Oyster-catchers are here at high tide. When you have walked as far as you want, return to the parking lot.

This is the best beach area on Tybee, but if you have more time you may want to try a couple other spots. Drive back out to US 80. If you are finished birding, turn right and follow the same route back to I-95, but if you want to bird more, turn left and follow US 80 around the corner and then parallel to the beach. Several signed beach access spots with parking areas lie along this road, but the beaches are pretty busy. In 1.9 miles US 80 ends; continue straight ahead on the same road for another 0.3 mile to a dead-end at Nineteenth Street. Turn left and park in one of the metered spots. Another boardwalk goes out to the beach, with one last rock jetty to scan for Purple Sandpipers. There is enough beach to sometimes have roosting flocks, and you can scan the water for loons and ducks. This is the last stop on the Tybee tour, so retrace your route back to the interstate. One caution: On the way back, about 8 miles after you leave Tybee Island, you get to the intersection of President Street and US 80. Stay to the right, and do not go under the overpass here or you will still be on US 80, which becomes very congested very quickly. Follow the same route through Savannah, and then out the interstate.

General information: Fort Pulaski National Monument is open every day except December 25, from 8 A.M. to 5:30 P.M., except in summer—Memorial Day to Labor Day—when it stays open until 7 P.M. The visitor center and fort are fascinating from a historical standpoint, and are worth some time. When built, Fort Pulaski was considered virtually impregnable by artillery, but in the early days of the Civil War, Federal rifled cannons decimated the fortification and the fort surrendered in 30 hours. This new weapon caused a tremendous change in the arts of fortification and bombardment, and rendered these forts obsolete. On Tybee Island, the Tybee Museum is also interesting.

ADDITIONAL HELP

DeLorme map grid: page 39, Inset B10.
For more information: Fort Pulaski National Monument, (912) 786-5787; Savannah CVB, (912) 944-0456.

45 Youman's Pond

County: Liberty.
Habitats: Mixed pine/hardwood forest, maritime mixed pine/hardwood forest, freshwater marsh shrubland, brackish marsh, lily pond.
Key birds: Wood Stork, Yellow- and Black-crowned Night-Herons, other herons, Anhinga, White Ibis, Osprey.
Best times to bird: All year, slightly slower in summer.

The birding: Youman's Pond is a large swampy area with some adjacent forest and marsh areas good for waders all year long. Even when there aren't many birds, it is a beautiful place to visit. Located just east of Interstate 95, it is very accessible to anyone transiting the interstate.

Directions: Take the Georgia Highway 38/US Highway 84 exit off Interstate 95, which is Exit 76 (old 13). This road is sometimes referred to as the Islands Highway. Head east toward the coast, keeping in mind that the only facilities are those right next to the interstate. After about 1.5 miles you will enter a large area of open fields that has resident bluebirds, and in another 3.3 miles (total 4.8) the partially clearcut woods on your left can be good for woodpeckers. Red-headed Woodpeckers are very local and hard to find near the coast, but sometimes occur here. Take Camp Viking Road on the left in 3.4 more miles (total 8.2). In 1.5 miles there is a road on the right, which is the loop-around of GA 38. The stretch of Camp Viking Road you are on has pretty good mixed forest on both sides of the road, and it's worth watching for small flocks of feeding birds, especially in winter or during migration. Near the turn, the forest on the left contains a wet area worth checking for passerines in all seasons. The camp in front of you is part of a fee fishing lake, and you can frequently see Cattle Egrets in the large field on the left side of the entrance road in summer. Back at the intersection, turn off Camp Viking onto GA 38 again (unsigned, but it's the only turn you passed coming in), and proceed 0.8 mile to Youman's Pond. The field on your right has nesting Ospreys in summer; look for their bulky nests in the trees. This is usually a good field for Loggerhead Shrikes also.

The road you are on becomes dirt in the last 0.5 mile before the pond, but is usually passable for all vehicles. At the pond, on your right, scan all the exposed

45 Youman's Pond
46 Harris Neck National Wildlife Refuge

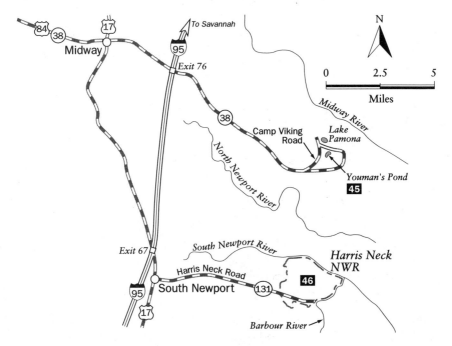

trees and even the bushes for perched waders. Both Black-crowned and Yellow-crowned Night-Herons are usually here, but they may be in low numbers and require careful searching to spot them hidden in foliage. They are often in the section to your left as you face the pond, roosting in the trees. Other breeding waders include Green Herons, Snowy and Great Egrets, and Anhingas. Just about any freshwater wader may be found at any given time, and toward evening you may get to enjoy the sight of herons and ibises returning to their nearby roost. In summer, scan for Purple Gallinules, but they are not here every year. Common Moorhens can be found all year long. In winter there may be a few ducks, usually dabblers, but never in large numbers. Swallows are frequently overhead, especially in migration.

The marsh on the opposite side of the road will have Common Yellowthroats, and maybe Louisiana or Northern Waterthrushes during migration. The brackish marshes along the road have Clapper Rails, and though you will rarely see one, you will often hear them. This is also a good place to listen for Barred Owls, which sometimes call during the middle of the day, especially when it's cloudy. The forest on either side of the pond can be checked for typical maritime forest species such as year-round Yellow-throated Warblers, and breeding Great Crested Flycatchers and Summer Tanagers. After you have had your fill, proceed straight ahead for 3 miles to the Camp Viking intersection and then back to I-95, or turn around and return the way you came.

General information: This area is privately owned, so please remain on the road. The owners have been very generous in sharing this delightful spot, and we want to keep it that way! The large lake at the end of Camp Viking Road, called Lake Pamona, can be pretty good for ducks in winter, but you can't bird there unless you pay the fishing fee of $3, so most birders usually don't bother.

ADDITIONAL HELP

DeLorme map grid: page 55, F9.
For more information: Hinesville–Liberty County Chamber of Commerce, (912) 368-4445.

46 Harris Neck National Wildlife Refuge

See map on page 184

County: McIntosh.
Habitats: Pine forest, maritime mixed pine/hardwood forest, coastal scrub, freshwater marsh shrubland, grassy field, freshwater marsh, salt marsh, pond, river.
Key birds: Wood Stork, Anhinga, Painted Bunting; waders, including Glossy Ibis; ducks.
Best times to bird: April through June for Wood Stork and Painted Bunting; April, May, and August through October for migrants including passerines and shorebirds; October through February for ducks and waders.

The birding: Harris Neck offers an auto tour loop through varied habitats, and is always worth a visit. Very few people come here; so you can usually just stop anywhere and walk around or bird an area that looks especially interesting. Wood Storks breed in good numbers, and the scrub areas are full of Painted Buntings. When the various ponds have water, as they usually do, they can be great for waders and ducks.

Directions: The exit off Interstate 95 is Exit 67 (old 12), US Highway 17. Go east (right turn if you were north on I-95, left turn if you were south), which turns south as this road curves around to parallel I-95. The first road after leaving the interstate is Georgia Highway 131, or Harris Neck Road; it is only 1.1 miles from I-95. Turn left on GA 131, and drive 6.4 miles south to the entrance to Harris Neck NWR. The entrance is on the left, and if there is nobody fishing at the bridge there are usually a few Black Vultures sitting on the pier to welcome you. There are portable toilets at the entrance.

You are at the beginning of the one-way auto tour loop, which is 4.2 miles long. Drive down the only road there, recently paved, and start birding. This large

46 Harris Neck National Wildlife Refuge

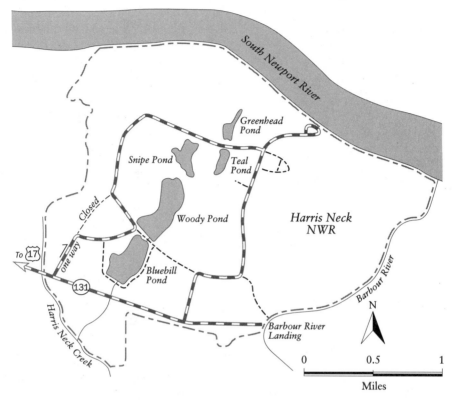

stand of maritime forest is good for typical coastal forest breeders, and you are likely to see them throughout your drive. Anytime you see some movement or hear some activity, stop and check it out. During migration, mixed feeding flocks sometimes move through. In 0.4 mile the road turns right, and there's a small information display that should have maps and checklists. A trail appears on your right after 0.2 mile; it goes around Bluebill Pond, which is frequently dry.

In another 0.2 mile the road turns left; park here. The large pond in front of you is Woody Pond, where most of the Wood Storks nest. Refuge personnel have built many artificial nesting platforms in the back of this pond, and if you walk out on the dike to your right you can see the nesting area. This is a great birding site in general, and at any season you should scan the pond for ducks or waders. After breeding season for the storks, the pond is usually drawn down and attracts lots of herons, egrets, ibises, and a few shorebirds. Common Moorhens are usually present somewhere, and rarely Purple Gallinules as well. The woods below the dike are frequently wet and can harbor bottomland species such as Hooded Warblers. The trail along the dike continues past the pond and connects with the last part of the auto tour in 0.5 mile. This area is also favored by woodpeckers for the many dead trees available.

Continue on the road for 0.3 mile, where the forest ends and the open scrub begins. The next 2 miles are excellent for Painted Buntings in summer, along with other scrub-preferring species. It can be brutally hot in summer, so try to come early. The road turns right in 0.5 mile; you can tell that you are driving in an old airport by the crumbling pavement runways. At another 0.5 mile, look for a small spur of faded asphalt off to your right, and park there. This is just past a white bluebird house with the number "8" on it on the left side of the road, and just past a large clump of scrub on the right. Walk away from the road to a small trail, sometimes almost overgrown with vegetation. Follow this trail to the left only 100 feet to Snipe Pond to your right. When this pond has water, it is great for waders and ducks, but it may be dry. In either case, this is a good place for Red-shouldered Hawks, or Great Horned Owls early or late in the day. If the pond is wet, there are usually Anhingas here, and King Rails in summer.

When finished, drive another 0.2 mile up onto an elevated section of the road. You are now on a dike between Teal Pond on your right and Greenhead Pond on your left. Actually, "pond" is something of a misnomer as there is rarely any water here. In any case, this is another good area to get out and look around. It's good for sparrows in winter. Down at the bottom of the dike in 0.3 mile, you have two choices. The road to the left is a 0.5-mile-long spur that takes you into a mature pine area on the bank of the South Newport River. This part of the road is two-way, unlike the rest of the loop. The view is not spectacular, but there is a vast expanse of salt marsh, and there are usually a few birds flying over it.

Snipe Pond.

The second choice back at the bottom of the dike is to continue on the tour loop road. In 0.9 mile the road turns right; there's a trail to the left that leads to the Barbour River Landing (also accessible by car, see below). Continuing on, in 0.3 mile the road turns left, and the trail across Woody Pond's dike goes off to the right. In 0.4 mile you are at the exit from the refuge, which is again GA 131, just 0.9 mile south of the entrance. You can access Barbour River Landing by turning left here and taking the dirt road to the left (the right-hand choice is private). The landing, at 0.7 mile, comes with a boat ramp and a good view of more marsh and the Barbour River. This is a great spot for swallows, especially in late summer as migrants are starting to push through. October brings hundreds of Tree Swallows daily. You are now finished at Harris Neck; drive back up GA 131 to US 17 and the interstate.

General information: Harris Neck is the site of a World War II–era training airfield, and part of the tour road is over long-abandoned runways. In addition to birds, this area is full of armadillos, and you should see a few of these invaders from Florida during your drive. This can be an excellent spot for butterflies. Harris Neck is a part of the Savannah coastal refuges complex, managed by the US Fish & Wildlife Service in Savannah.

ADDITIONAL HELP

DeLorme map grid: page 55, G9.
For more information: Harris Neck NWR/Savannah Coastal Refuges, (912) 652-4415; McIntosh County Chamber of Commerce, (912) 437-4192.

47 Sapelo Island

County: McIntosh.
Habitats: Maritime mixed pine/hardwood forest, coastal shrubland, brackish marsh, salt marsh, tidal flat, beach, ocean.
Key birds: Plain Chachalaca, Long-billed Curlew, Painted Bunting, shorebirds, gulls, terns.
Best times to bird: All year for Chachalaca, April through June for Painted Bunting, October through February for others.

The birding: Sapelo Island is a limited-access barrier island with lots of great beach and inland habitat. Unfortunately, for birding purposes it is difficult to get to. This is the only place in Georgia to find the Plain Chachalaca, and the only place in the United States to find them outside Texas. These birds were introduced in the 1920s. The beaches are long and have relatively few people on them, which is favorable for the very few Long-billed Curlews that winter on the Georgia coast. Other beach species are also found here, and receive much less pressure than their counterparts on more-developed islands. Painted Buntings are fairly common in spring and summer and can be easily found all over the island in the scrub areas between

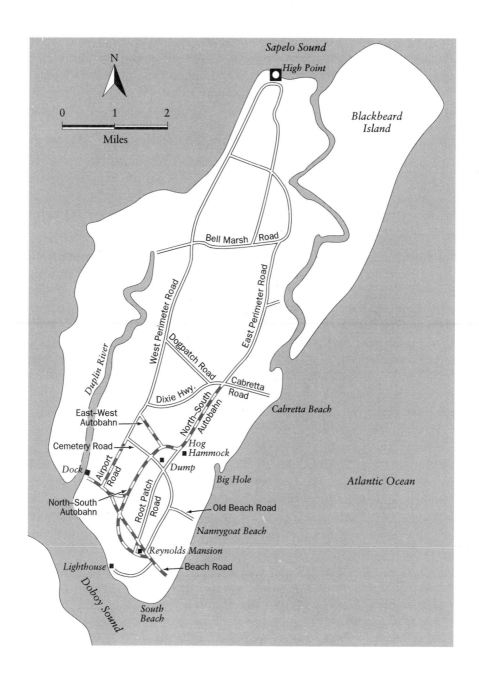

the forest and the beach. Just like any island on the coast, Sapelo is a great place to be for both spring and fall migration.

There are three ways to get out to the island, all of which require being on a tour or by being sponsored by someone or something on the island. Tours run by Georgia Department of Natural Resources do not allow much time for birding and usually don't go to the best spots. They are available at the Sapelo Island Visitor Center. Another option requires that you be part of a group eligible to stay at the Reynolds Mansion. This facility is reserved for groups with educational or scientific interests. The daily rate at the mansion is high, but it includes all meals and transportation. The third option is through a couple of relatively inexpensive ("nonluxury") places called the Weekender and Lula's Kitchen. Birders can arrange stays here or rent decent bicycles for day trips. A day trip can usually allow a few hours in some of the good habitat and a good shot at chachalacas, but isn't long enough to get out to all the beaches for Long-billed Curlews. See the General Information section below for details.

Directions: Once you have a sponsor to get on the ferry, the directions are pretty easy. The best way to get to the boat dock is to take Exit 58 (old 11) from Interstate 95, which is Georgia Highway 99/57. Go east, toward the coast, for 9 miles to Landing Road, and turn left. Drive 0.8 mile to the parking areas. Since GA 99/57 forms a big loop, you can also get here from the south by taking Exit 49 (old 10) from I-95, which is GA 251. Go east toward the coast 1.1 miles to US Highway 17 in Darien, and turn right (south). In another 1.1 miles, turn left on GA 99/57 and follow it 7.9 miles to Landing Road. Turn right and proceed to the parking area and the Sapelo Island Visitor Center, which has information, maps, and restrooms.

Once you are on the island, how you bird depends on what arrangements you have made. Maps are also available at both the Weekender and the mansion. The key spot for Plain Chachalacas is around the dump (yet another lovely birding hotspot). This is actually not as bad as it sounds; it's just an area with some dumpsters, located on Cemetery Road. Check all the trails in this general area, but keep in mind that for big, noisy birds, chachalacas can be surprisingly sneaky and quiet. The best time of year for them is early spring, when their raucous calls are impossible to miss. At other times you may have to spend some time in this area, waiting for a call or hoping to see one moving about the scrubby underbrush. Immediately east of the dumpsters is a dirt crossroad called either Root Patch or Flora Bottom Road, depending on whom you ask.

Past the dumpsters to the east, Cemetery Road goes out to Nannygoat Beach. Along the way is a large shallow pond split by the road. Check for waders or shorebirds all year. Of course, biting insects love shallow ponds, and so do alligators. There are plenty of other birds to keep you busy, such as arriving songbirds in the spring like Northern Parulas, White-eyed Vireos, and Blue-gray Gnatcatchers. In fall look for migrant sparrows in the more open areas and other migrants (both spring and fall).

There are basically three beach access points: "South Beach," near the Reynolds Mansion and the south tip of the island; Nannygoat Beach on the middle and southeast coast; and Cabretta Beach on the northern coast (the farthest north portion of this island complex is actually Blackbeard Island, and is inaccessible except by boat). The South Beach is actually just the southern part of Nannygoat Beach. The south tip is pretty far to go unless you are staying at the mansion, but the birding around the mansion and the south tip can be very rewarding. The South Beach southern tip is the best natural roost site on Sapelo, and the road to the lighthouse can be very good for migrants. The mudflats east of the lighthouse road are great for shorebirds including Whimbrels. If you don't have arrangements to be driven to Cabretta Beach, you probably can't get there and back on a day bicycle trip (unless you are in good shape), so go to Nannygoat Beach instead.

You can get there two ways: East of the mansion, head for a small beach pavilion near the southern part of the beach, or go east from Cemetery Road near the northern part. On the northern end of the beach is a large sand spit called the Big Hole, which is also a good roost site. Bikes can't be ridden on the sandy beach, so plan on doing some walking and be sure to take along plenty of food and water. Though a scope is always useful on any beach, if you are bike riding you will have trouble carrying one unless you have a scope backpack. Keep in mind when planning a bicycle trip that most of the roads are soft sand and can be very difficult to ride on without expending some energy! Cabretta Beach probably has a slightly better track record for Long-billed Curlews in winter, but all the beaches are largely deserted and good for gulls, terns, and shorebirds in season. Check offshore for ducks and loons in winter. The scrub just in from the beach can be full of landbird migrants in spring or fall, although fall is the time to look for rarities.

If you are staying for more than one day, you obviously have more options and can plan accordingly. Both the mansion and the Weekender may be able to help with transportation around the island for an additional fee. It can be very hot here in summer, but during the rest of the year this can be a great place to kick back and do some island birding.

General information: If you have arrangements with someone on the island, and they put in a transportation request with DNR, the ferry cost is only $1. If you are going over on the DNR tour, the cost is $10 for adults and $6 for children. The Weekender offers a three-bedroom apartment or four individual rooms, and dinner for an additional fee if you set it up in advance. The apartment is $115 per night; other rooms are $48 for a one-night stay or $38 per night for multinight stays. The individual rooms share a kitchen but each has its own bath. The accommodations are rustic and the rooms are small, as you are out on a barrier island, but each room has its own air conditioner. Take all supplies with you, as there is only a small general store on the island. If you want to try the day trip approach, you can rent your bicycles from the Weekender or Lula's Kitchen, usually for about $10 per day. If these establishments are full, bikes will not be available. If available, you may be able to rent a vehicle at the Weekender. The accommodations at Lula's

Kitchen are trailers (with air conditioners), at $75 per night for a three-bedroom and $65 per night for a two-bedroom. Evening meals are available upon request for an additional fee. Rooms at the mansion are around $125 per person per night with a two-night minimum stay, meals included.

Sapelo Island has a history similar to that of the other barrier islands—early private ownership followed by current state ownership. The only community on the island is Hog Hammock, with fewer than 100 residents. Most of these are descendants of the slaves brought here in the early 1800s. The University of Georgia Marine Institute is also on Sapelo.

ADDITIONAL HELP

DeLorme map grid: page 63, B9.
For more information: Sapelo Island Visitor Center, (912) 437-3324; Georgia Department of Natural Resources; the Weekender, (912) 485-2277; Lula's Kitchen, (912) 485-2270; Reynolds Mansion, (912) 485-2299; Darien Welcome Center, (912) 437-6684; McIntosh County Chamber of Commerce, (912) 437-4192.

48 Altamaha Waterfowl Management Area

County: McIntosh.
Habitats: Mixed pine/hardwood forest, floodplain hardwood forest, freshwater marsh shrubland, weedy fields, diked ponds.
Key Birds: Mottled Duck, Least Bittern, Glossy Ibis, Black-necked Stilt, Bald Eagle, rails, American Bittern, Painted Bunting, Wood Stork, Northern Harrier, swallows, sparrows, ducks.
Best times to bird: All year.

The birding: The Altamaha Waterfowl Management Area is one of the best overall sites in Georgia, worth a visit in any season. The birdable areas are broken up into three sections. The first is the series of sometimes-flooded former rice fields on the east side of US Highway 17. Second is the part of the WMA north of the Champney River, on the west side of US 17. This area has several ponds and fields and a forested dike area good for passerine migrants. Both these areas are part of Butler Island. The third is the area south of the Champney, west of US 17, called Champney Island, where there are sometimes-flooded fields and a large impoundment with an observation tower. This area usually has water even when the fields are dry and is always worth checking. Hunting is allowed, and if you are coming in the fall, check with DNR about hunting dates.

Directions: This area can be birded in many ways, and different seasons call for different techniques. We will start from the north for simplicity, but you can start anywhere. From Interstate 95, take Exit 49 (old 10), which is Georgia Highway 251. Turn east, toward Darien. In 1.1 miles you will reach US Highway 17, turn right. Proceed through the town of Darien, observing the speed limit. Scan the wires in town for Eurasian

48 Altamaha Waterfowl Management Area

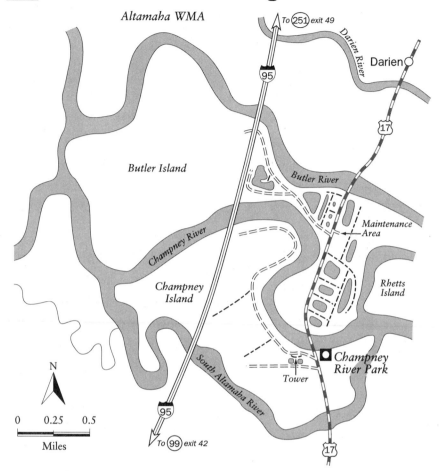

Altamaha WMA

To (251) exit 49

Darien River

95

Darien

17

Butler Island

Butler River

Maintenance Area

Champney River

Champney Island

Rhetts Island

South Altamaha River

95

To (99) exit 42

Tower

Champney River Park

17

N

0   0.25   0.5

Miles

Collared-Doves. Continue south, first across the Darien River and then the Butler River. At 2.6 miles turn left into a dirt parking area next to a maintenance shed. From here you can bird the entire area east of US 17. It's a series of dikes surrounding numerous former rice fields. The dikes are either parallel to US 17 or perpendicular; all of the perpendicular ones come back out to US 17. The first dikes are just south of where you are now; walk south on US 17 to reach them. Some are mowed at all times, and the ones that aren't are generally impassable.

Keep in mind that this area has lots of snakes. While most are only watersnakes, always watch where you step. Sometimes the ponds are mostly dry, although there is always water in small ditches along the dike. In winter this is one of the only places in Georgia to reliably find American Bitterns. No one place is best, so just walk around the dikes and hope to flush one. A better way is to walk out to the outermost dike before dawn, as they sometimes may be seen flying around just as it gets light. Very rarely there may be Fulvous Whistling-Ducks flying overhead in fall.

These ponds are full of rails, even when mostly dry. There are King and Virginia Rails and lots of Soras, but you will hear them far more often than you will see them. In the adjacent brackish marsh look for King or Clapper Rails. If there is water in the ponds, there may be ducks, mostly teal and shovelers but usually a few other species, including scattered Mottled Ducks. This is one of the only places in Georgia to find Mottled Ducks, but they are usually hidden in the tall brush. You will see American Coots and a few Common Moorhens as well. Keep your eyes open for sparrows, mostly Song and Swamp, with a chance to see Lincoln's or White-crowned Sparrows, among others. Common Yellowthroats are everywhere, with Marsh Wrens and a few Sedge Wrens. A few Tree Swallows are here all winter, and always keep your eyes open for raptors, including Bald Eagles. There are almost always a few Cooper's Hawks and Northern Harriers around in winter. In spring look for migrant passerines and swallows, and shorebirds wherever you can find open water.

Things slow down in the summer, but there are breeding Painted Buntings and sometimes Black-necked Stilts. Fall is one of the best times to bird, as the brushy areas can have lots of migrants such as Palm and Yellow Warblers. Numerous sparrows come through in October, including White-crowned and very rarely a Clay-colored or even a Lark Sparrow. When this area has water, it can be full of ducks. If you are here as the ponds are being drawn down or filled, the habitat may be good for shorebirds and Glossy or White Ibises.

The next section of the Altamaha covered is the area west of US 17, north of the Champney River. Very slightly south of the entrance to the maintenance area on US 17 is a dirt road going west (across US 17). In just 0.1 mile down this road is a dike road to your right. This is an excellent area during spring and fall migration, but better in fall. As you go down the dike, the brush on the right-hand side can be full of warblers, vireos, flycatchers, and other migrants, so bird it carefully. This is another good place to check for Painted Buntings. There are several different trails through the patch of forest, so you can walk around until you find a feeding flock. This is a great place to look for waterthrushes. Check the weed-choked small ponds on the right for moorhens and sparrows. This dike road is 0.3 mile long, and at the end if you turn right you will come back out to US 17 at a dirt road just south of the second bridge from Darien. The road is very rutted for vehicles and you will probably see more birds by walking anyway. Early morning is best.

When finished, go back to the main dirt road you were just on away from US 17. From the dike where you turned right, continue for 0.3 mile, scanning the lake on your right, although usually there aren't any ducks here. Ospreys and Anhingas are regular at this lake. At 0.3 mile another dirt road cuts off to the left. This road is not recommended for cars, but trucks should be okay. This road continues down the backside of a cattail and hyacinth pond for 0.4 mile, and then turns right to a good place to view the west end of this pond. This pond is one of the best places to look for Least Bitterns in summer. The best technique is to spend some

Purple Gallinule. RICHARD CROOK PHOTO

time watching as much of the pond as you can see, and watch for them flying back and forth. Though they are not here every year, scan carefully for Purple Gallinules. There are always Common Moorhens and a few ducks in winter. Also in winter check for American Bitterns, and sparrows along the edges.

To get to the other side of this pond, or if you don't want to come down this less than well-maintained road, go back to the split. Continue on the main road for 0.2 mile, and park. On your left is a small open dirt area with a wooden boardwalk at the end. Walk all the way out on the boardwalk, and look to your right at the same pond described above for the same species. Also check this area for Bobolinks during migration. There isn't much of interest farther along this road, but if you continue 0.5 mile you will reach a gate under I-95. You can walk farther along this trail if you like, especially for sparrows in winter.

To get to the third section of the Altamaha WMA, return to US 17 and turn right. Cross the Champney River bridge in 0.8 mile and look for a small dirt road on your right in another 0.2 mile. There are signs here for the Ducks Unlimited Marsh project and a wildlife viewing area sign. Turn right and proceed 0.3 mile to an observation tower. This is worth doing in all seasons, as it may be the only open water. This is the other good spot to look for Mottled Ducks all year and Least Bitterns in summer. There will be swallows here, and maybe ducks in winter. This area also is full of rails. When water levels are low, this can be excellent for shorebirds, including Black-necked Stilts. Look for Glossy Ibises as well. The small box for leaflets at the base of the tower usually has a few squirrel tree frogs under the pamphlets.

After scoping your fill, you can continue farther along this road 0.5 mile to find a series of diked areas on your left, which may be wet. This area is full of sparrows in winter and buntings in summer. You can drive about 1.6 miles beyond the tower, but the road gets progressively worse and the habitat drier. Return to US 17, and go straight across to the Champney River Park. Scan the large trees in the distance directly away from the road to look for Bald Eagles, which frequently roost here. The area around this park also has rails. There are restrooms here (though they are rarely cleaned). One last place to check is to turn left (south) on US 17 for only 0.1 mile to the next road, identified only by a sign that says "Massman." Turn right, and in migration, bird carefully through the forest for passerine migrants in the first 0.3 mile. You can continue another 0.5 mile and scan the area on your right to view the same area visible from the tower. You will have to walk across a small field to see over the tall brush on the edges of the impoundment (another area to look for Bobolinks during migration).

This is the last part of this wonderful area to bird, and you can either exit north the way you came or go south. To exit south, turn right on US 17. You will cross the South Altamaha River in 0.6 mile, and 1.7 miles beyond the river is GA 99 (also called Business Loop 95). Turn right, and you will reach I-95 in 1.2 miles at Exit 42 (old 9). You can also continue south on US 17 toward Brunswick in about 12 miles.

General information: This is the only WMA in this book that is a waterfowl management area. This area is just south of the town of Darien, which has many gas stations, restaurants, and other businesses. There are also hotels at virtually every exit along Interstate 95.

ADDITIONAL HELP

DeLorme map grid: page 63, C7.
For more information: Georgia Department of Natural Resources; Darien Welcome Center, (912) 437-6684; McIntosh County Chamber of Commerce, (912) 437-4192; Brunswick–Golden Isles CVB, (800) 933-2627.

49 St. Simons Island

County: Glynn.
Habitats: Maritime mixed pine/hardwood forest, coastal shrub, grassy field, salt marsh, tidal flat, beach, ocean, pond.
Key birds: Reddish Egret, Marbled Godwit, Red Knot, Gray Kingbird, Eurasian Collared-Dove, other shorebirds, gulls, terns.
Best times to bird: All year.

The birding: St. Simons Island is another barrier island, somewhat developed, but with some good beach and marsh habitat to bird in any season. This may be the

49 St. Simons Island
50 Andrews Island
51 Jekyll Island

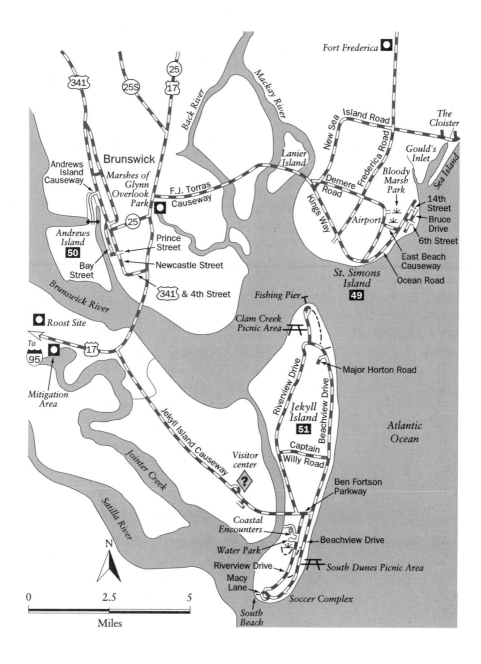

Fort Frederica

The Cloister

Island Road

New Sea

Frederica Road

Gould's Inlet

Sea Island

Mackay River

Back River

25

25S

17

341

Brunswick

Lanier Island

Bloody Marsh Park

Demere Road

Andrews Island Causeway

Marshes of Glynn Overlook Park

F.J. Torras Causeway

Kings Way

Airport

14th Street

Bruce Drive

6th Street

25

Andrews Island

50

Prince Street

Newcastle Street

Bay Street

341 & 4th Street

East Beach Causeway

Ocean Road

St. Simons Island

49

Brunswick River

Fishing Pier

Clam Creek Picnic Area

Roost Site

To 95

17

Major Horton Road

Mitigation Area

Riverview Drive

Beachview Drive

Jekyll Island

51

Atlantic Ocean

Jekyll Island Causeway

Jointer Creek

Visitor center

?

Captain Willy Road

Ben Fortson Parkway

Satilla River

Coastal Encounters

Beachview Drive

N

Water Park

Riverview Drive

South Dunes Picnic Area

Macy Lane

Soccer Complex

0   2.5   5

South Beach

Miles

best beach roost site, and it is the best place to look for Reddish Egrets. Most of the birding areas are in the southern part of St. Simons; nearby are numerous restaurants, hotels, and other services. There is also a small park worth checking before you enter the causeway.

Directions: From the interstate, exit Interstate 95 at Exit 38 (old 8) and follow Georgia Highway 25 Spur east for 4.3 miles to US Highway 17. This road is also called the Golden Isles Parkway. At US 17, turn right (south) for 1.6 miles to the F. J. Torras causeway on your left. If you are coming north on US 17, this causeway is 4.1 miles north of the Jekyll Island causeway, and can be birded in conjunction with that area. Just 0.6 mile south of the causeway is the Marshes of Glynn Overlook Park on your right. This small park has a short boardwalk out at the water, good for Marsh Wrens and waders. This is also one of the best spots to see a Clapper Rail at low tide. Other species to look for at low tide are Willet, Black-bellied Plover, either Greater or Lesser Yellowlegs, and any of the peeps.

Turn right again on US 17 and head toward the causeway. As you enter the causeway, there is a small building on the south side that has lots of pamphlets and other information concerning lodging, restaurants, and so forth. On the causeway, pay the $0.35 toll and drive 4 miles to St. Simons Island, scanning the vast marsh as you drive by. There are few pullouts along this road. In summer you may see Wood Storks lazily circling over the marsh, and a few terns. This is a good place to see Northern Harriers in winter.

Once you get to the island, stay straight on what is now Demere Road (don't follow the fork to the right). Pass Frederica Road and the airport, and pull into the small Bloody Marsh Monument Park on your left, 2.1 miles after the causeway ends; it's especially worth checking during migration. Continue on Demere for another 0.5 mile and turn left on East Beach Causeway. After 0.6 mile, turn left on Ocean Road. Drive 0.7 mile, scanning Bloody Marsh to your left for shorebirds or waders, including White Ibises. This is a good spot to check for the always-difficult Whimbrel during April or May. Then turn right on Fourteenth Street for 0.1 mile to Bruce Drive, turn left into the dead-end lot, and park. This is one of the best beaches in Georgia for birds, and you will want to scan here awhile. A scope is a virtual necessity because for most of the birds, you are viewing the south tip of Sea Island across water.

The bay on your left as you look out is Gould's Inlet. This is the most accessible place in Georgia for Reddish Egrets at all tides but high. Watch for their active feeding behavior here spring through fall, though there are fewer in spring. The exposed mudflat on the left of the inlet should be checked for shorebirds and terns, including Whimbrels, Marbled Godwits, and American Oystercatchers. In winter watch for diving ducks such as Buffleheads and Red-breasted Mergansers off the rocks in front of you. Mink are sometimes seen foraging among these rocks.

Aerial view of Gould's Inlet.

The beach to the right of Gould's Inlet is Sea Island, another great roosting spot for shorebirds, gulls, terns, Black Skimmers, and Brown Pelicans. This beach is worth scanning near the tide line for plovers, including Piping in winter and Wilson's in summer. Red Knots should be looked for mid-April through May. If you can scan over the beach, you can often see Northern Gannets in winter. Continue to scan to the right—you are now looking at Saint Simons—although this beach may have more people than birds. At very low tides there are wide expanses of exposed tidal flat, and if there aren't many people there may be hundreds of terns and shorebirds. Also watch whatever landbirds are around, as sometimes migrants work along the shore. You can spend as much time as you want here and still probably miss a few of the birds present; this is a spot to bird very methodically.

If you do not find Reddish Egrets, you have another shot nearby. Drive up Bruce Drive 0.5 mile to Sixth Street and turn left. Park anywhere you can without blocking someone's driveway—which may require parking next to some vegetation. At the end of this short street is a path only a couple hundred yards long through a small field to the beach. Look for swallows or Purple Martins over the field and passerines in the bushes, especially during migration. When you get to the beach, look to your left for a small pond above the tide line. Reddish Egrets may be found here (if you are lucky!) or out on the beach in front of you, but only at low tides and when there aren't many beach-goers. If the latter is the case, you may also find shorebirds. If you don't find a Reddish Egret here, your best hope is to kill a couple of hours back at Gould's Inlet.

When finished, return to Ocean Road and East Beach causeway. You now have several choices. You can leave the island the way you came, or take Demere to Frederica, right to Sea Island, and right to the Cloister for Gray Kingbirds. Another way to either leave St. Simons or go to the Cloister is a little longer but has more birding possibilities. Continue on Ocean (which is magically now a boulevard), through the business section and stay on the road as it becomes Kings Way. Look for Eurasian Collared-Doves anywhere along this stretch on the wires or in tall trees. After 2.2 miles, note the airport on your right at Frederica Road. The airport property may be worth scanning since it is the only open field habitat on this end of the island. Continue on Kings Way another 1.2 miles to New Sea Island Road, and turn right. The golf course pond on your right often has a few ducks during winter, such as Buffleheads or Lesser Scaups. In 0.3 mile you will be back to Demere Road, and a left turn will take you off the island.

To get to the Cloister, which is a resort hotel complex, go straight for 4.4 miles on Sea Island Road. At 2.7 miles you will recross Frederica Road. Fort Frederica is 2.2 miles to the left, but it's more interesting from a historical standpoint than as a birding spot. If you stay on Sea Island Road, in 0.6 mile you can scan the marsh on both sides for waders or shorebirds. Once you reach the Cloister in another 1.1 miles, turn left and drive around the complex, listening for Gray Kingbirds. They are usually in the tops of the small trees around the grounds, but they are not numerous. Once you have driven around the complex, return via Sea Island Road to exit the island.

General information: Saint Simons Island has many more restaurants and stores than Jekyll Island, and it might be a good choice for those who need to balance their own needs with those of a nonbirding companion. There are also numerous festivals and other events, mostly in summer, which may cause some congestion. Fort Frederica is an interesting historical site with a visitor center and many exhibits.

ADDITIONAL HELP

DeLorme map grid: page 63, E-8, F-8.
For more information: Brunswick–Golden Isles CVB, (800) 933-2627; Fort Frederica National Monument, (912) 638-3639.

50 Andrews Island

See map on page 197

County: Glynn.
Habitats: Spoil site, salt marsh, tidal flat, coastal shrubland.
Key birds: American Avocet, night-herons, salt marsh sparrows, waders, shorebirds.
Best times to bird: August through May.

The American Avocet roosting beach along the causeway.

The birding: The dredge spoil-site itself is off-limits, but the causeway to Andrews Island is good for waders and shorebirds and can easily be accessed by car. This site is very close to both Jekyll Island and St. Simons Island and can be combined with either or both of them. Caution: This is the most mosquito- and biting fly–infested spot on the Georgia coast, and it can be quite warm here, so take both the repellent of your choice and water.

Directions: From Interstate 95, exit at Exit 36 (old 7), which is US Highway 341. Drive south toward the coast 4.2 miles to the dirt causeway road (Homer L. Wilson Way) and turn right. This turn can be very tricky, so here are some hints. Watch the mileage markers on US 341. Your turn is immediately past marker 20. Also, just before that, the city of Brunswick sewage treatment plant is on the right side of US 341. Therefore, when you see the sewage plant, look for the marker, and then turn right. From US 17, take Georgia Highway 341 North. This road is 1.3 miles south of GA 25, or 2.2 miles north of the Jekyll Island causeway. Follow the signs for US 341, which unfortunately turns numerous times. First turning off US 17, it is signed as Fourth Avenue. Turn right after 0.7 mile onto Newcastle Street. Drive 0.5 mile, turn left on Prince Street, and drive 0.1 mile. Turn right, and in 0.7 mile you will pass GA 25. These side streets will keep you clear of traffic and take you by some good overhead wires for Eurasian Collared-Doves. Continue 1 mile to the causeway road and turn left. You are getting close when you see a convenience store on the right. Your turn is just past the store, and if you see the City of Brunswick Sewage Treatment plant on your left you have just missed the turn. Once you find the causeway, drive slowly down the dirt road.

Loggerhead Shrikes are frequent around the beginning of the causeway. At the first and only bend in the road, stop and pish for Seaside Sparrows and Nelson's and Saltmarsh Sharp-tailed Sparrows. High tide is best, and you will commonly see Marsh Wrens at the same time. The salt marsh all along this causeway can be good for these species. Also look for both Black-crowned and Yellow-crowned Night-Herons along the entire causeway, especially on the right at lower tides. If the tide is high, you may find them in some of the scrubby trees along the causeway.

Other waders or shorebirds may be seen, especially on the left past the marsh, where there is a small mud beach. This area gets as many American Avocets as any other spot along the coast, but you will be lucky to find them. This is also a good spot for Red-breasted Mergansers. On the right side, check the large open area for ducks at high tide or shorebirds at low tide. In 0.9 mile you will come to a locked gate. There are usually a few Eurasian Collared-Doves here, and in migration there can be warblers and other migrants throughout the coastal scrub.

Beyond the gate lies Andrews Island proper. This is the most reliable spot in the state for Common Ground-Doves, but unless you are blindly lucky and see them from the gate, you are out of luck. The spoil site is being expanded and is completely off-limits, but at some time it may be opened to birders. In case you missed the warning earlier, this is a hot, miserable place where your fluid loss from perspiration may be exceeded only by that from biting insects.

Willets and Common Nighthawks both nest and may be seen along the causeway. Least and Gull-billed Terns nest nearby, and may be found feeding here. During spring and especially fall migration, a few warblers occur in the brush along the causeway, mostly Prairie, Yellow, and (later) Palm and Yellow-rumped. During swallow migration, late summer to fall, you may find swallows here of several species. One other morsel to tempt you: When there are lots of birds inside the spoil site (especially in fall), there can be lots of hawks as well, particularly falcons and accipiters. This is a pretty reliable spot for Cooper's Hawks in winter.

General information: This spoil site is owned by the Georgia Ports Authority and leased to the U.S. Army Corps of Engineers; there are usually a couple of field trips per year by birding groups that are allowed to drive in.

ADDITIONAL HELP

DeLorme map grid: page 63, F7.
For more information: Brunswick–Golden Isles CVB, (800) 933-2627.

County: Glynn.
Habitats: Maritime mixed pine/hardwood forest, coastal shrubland, brackish marsh, salt marsh, tidal flat, beach, ocean.
Key birds: Roseate Spoonbill, Gray Kingbird, scoters, shorebirds, gulls, terns, passerine migrants.
Best times to bird: All year.

The birding: This is one of the best birding spots in Georgia, worth visiting any time of year. The number of species that has been seen here is staggering, and includes rarities from almost every family. The best parts of the island to bird vary with the seasons and tides, so note the specific information about each site. There are two spots to check along US Highway 17 before you actually go to Jekyll: a wader roost spot and a tidal flat created as a mitigation area for nearby construction, which is good for shorebirds at low tide. The causeway to Jekyll Island is more than 6 miles long, and goes through lots of good salt marsh with roosting areas at all tides. The island is a classic Georgia barrier island, with some forest and beach areas, and with scope access to nearby ocean and sound. There is quite a bit of development on this island, but its location makes it wonderful for migrants as well as interesting permanent residents. Plan on spending several hours to bird this great spot, and take a scope if you have one.

Directions: The causeway to Jekyll Island is located on US Highway 17 southeast of the city of Brunswick. From the south, exit Interstate 95 at Exit 29 (old 6) and follow US 17 east (right) for 5.4 miles to the causeway on your right. From the north, exit I-95 at Exit 38 (old 8) and follow Georgia Highway 25 Spur east (left) for 4.3 miles to US 17. This road is also called the Golden Isles Parkway. At US 17, turn right for 5.7 miles to the causeway on your left. From this starting point, you can either proceed toward the island or check the roost spot and mitigation area first.

To check the two latter areas, follow US 17 south (this will require backtracking, if you came from Exit 29) 2.3 miles from the causeway, and pull completely off the road on your right. The last large clump of vegetation across the marsh in front of you is currently a roost site for many species of waders, among them herons, egrets, ibises, and Roseate Spoonbills. You should see an industrial plant just to the right of this hammock if you are positioned correctly. Because the roost trees are not close, a scope is almost always required here. Roosting birds are best found at high tide or late in the day.

Carefully check for traffic, and then perform a U turn on US 17 to head back toward the causeway. In only 0.9 mile, you will be at the south end of the mitigation site, which extends about 0.3 mile on your right. This spot is better at low tide, and best in the middle of an incoming tide, when many species of shorebirds feed. Plovers (especially Wilson's), sandpipers, godwits, and dowitchers may all be found at times. Migration is best, of course. Look for Whimbrels in April, May,

August, and September. Marsh Wrens and salt marsh sparrows like Seaside Sparrows and Nelson's and Saltmarsh Sharp-tailed Sparrows frequent the marsh and some pishing or squeaking may encourage them to sit on the top of some marsh grass. You are likely to hear Clapper Rails, but just as unlikely to see them. Always look for hawks, because they know the shorebirds are here. Scan the tidal creeks and bays for ducks in winter, or gulls and terns year-round. When finished, drive 1.1 miles back to the causeway.

Start down the causeway toward Jekyll Island. Depending on the tide, there may be waders and shorebirds feeding or roosting anywhere along the causeway. Although most of the larger shorebirds will be Willets, look for both Marbled Godwits and the hard-to-find Whimbrels among them. The best time for Whimbrels is from April 1 to May 20. The salt marsh all along the causeway can be excellent for Marsh Wrens and all three saltmarsh sparrows (Seaside, Saltmarsh Sharp-tailed, and Nelson's Sharp-tailed, listed in decreasing order of abundance). The last two sparrows are here only in winter, and are more reclusive, but if you look and pish in areas of salt marsh with larger bushes nearby you can increase your chances of seeing one. A small bridge 1.4 miles down the causeway is an excellent spot to look for all these species; also look on the island or far side of the bridge.

Check for hawks all along here as well. Ospreys and Red-tailed Hawks are fairly common on the poles along the road, and around dusk you can sometimes see Great Horned Owls on those same poles. Northern Harriers may be seen hunting over the salt marsh in winter, and American Kestrels and Belted Kingfishers frequently sit on the wires. Breeding Willets will sit on these same wires from April to June. Accipiters may be seen in low numbers all year. The brush along the road is crawling with Yellow-rumped Warblers in winter and can hold any small migrants during migration. During late fall thousands of Tree Swallows feed around the wax myrtles along the causeway, and many fly so low that cars become a problem for them. In another 2.8 miles, pull into the visitor center on your left, and park. Walk around the right side of the building to view a large tidal flat, good at any tide but high (when it is submerged). There are restrooms here, and sometimes various Jekyll businesses have discount coupons for visitors available inside the visitor center.

Pull back onto the causeway, and continue toward Jekyll. In 0.5 mile is a short dirt road on the right that leads to a locked gate. The shrubby area before the gate is worth checking for migrants, occasionally including both Louisiana and Northern Waterthrushes. The salt marsh to the right of the road around the scrub is another good spot for salt marsh sparrows. Continue on the causeway toward Jekyll, scanning both sides until you cross the Intercoastal Waterway in 1.2 miles. There is a $3 "parking" fee to enter the island. From here, you can either continue straight ahead on Ben Fortson Parkway to a T intersection at Beachview Drive 0.2 mile ahead to cover the larger north end of Jekyll, or turn right on Riverview Drive immediately past the pay station to cover the south end. Both are excellent choices and are covered separately below.

The part of Jekyll Island south of Ben Fortson Parkway is much smaller than the north end, but has most of the best sites on Jekyll for year-round birding. After turning south onto Riverview Drive, turn right in 0.6 mile to a boat ramp behind the pond in front of you at the Coastal Encounters building. Check the feeder at the building as you drive past. This pond is usually empty, but the marsh you pass should be scanned for sparrows or rails. At the boat ramp, scan the Intercoastal Waterway in front of you, including the far shore and the shoreline to either side of you. Check the bushes for migrants. Go back to Riverview Drive, and turn right again for 0.1 mile to the water park, and turn into the lot. Your object is to scan the marsh to the left of the water park, so drive over to that corner. This marsh is best at middle to lower tides, and can have a variety of shorebirds, Clapper Rails, and rarely Gull-billed Terns. Avoid dead low tide, as the birds will be too far out to see. If that is the case, however, you can walk all the way around this marsh on the dirt road another 0.1 mile down Riverview Drive. This can be a very hot, buggy walk, and most birders avoid it.

The best spot on Jekyll and one of the best on the entire coast is the South Beach of the island. To get there, continue on Riverview Drive 1.8 miles to Macy Lane, and turn right. As you are driving, note that the woods along the road can be quite good for passerines during migration. Stop anywhere that looks or sounds good and you may be rewarded with a flock moving through. Note that there are trails on your left that go all the way through the center of the island to the beach side, and they can be good for migrants also (not to mention mosquitoes). Whip-poor-wills winter on the barrier islands, and this is a pretty good spot for finding them. If you are here at dusk, you may be rewarded with seeing one hunting along the road.

There is a recycling drop-off along here, and the large tower you pass near Macy Lane is a frequent perch at dusk for Great Horned Owls. After turning on Macy, drive straight ahead to where it turns left, and park on the grass to your right. There is a trail through the scrub in front of you; follow it while checking out whatever birds are lurking in the bushes. This area can have lots of migrants in both spring and fall, so proceed slowly. The trail makes a couple of short turns and then follows a primitive wooden walkway out to the beach. This trail may be wet near the beach, so wear appropriate footwear. If it is too wet here, you can also access the beach at the Soccer Complex discussed below. Also, stick to the trail, because you are passing through very sensitive habitat that is becoming rare in Georgia.

Due to coastal development, the largest pool of water is one of the last remaining examples of maritime wet grassland. You may find birds anywhere on the way out to the beach, so be alert for movement or "chip" notes. This spot may have a few Sedge Wrens in winter, best found by listening for their wet "chips." The trail ultimately puts you on the beach just north of the south tip of Jekyll, a great roost site for Brown Pelicans, gulls, terns, shorebirds, and other species. There may be birds spread out all along the beach, but the largest concentration will be to your right. While most of them will be out on the actual tip, some of the smaller shorebirds or plovers may be up the beach along the edge of the dunes. It may be worth walking around the south tip to check the beach to the right. Although American Avocets are unusual out here, if present they are often around this corner. The island off in the distance from the tip is Cumberland; scan the water off the beach for ducks or anything else resting on the water.

Dolphins are frequently seen, and if you feel lucky you can scan the gull flocks following the shrimp boats in winter for a rare Parasitic or other jaeger. When there are lots of birds, this is a great place to compare species and really study them. Many rarities have been found, probably more than at any other single Georgia location, so always look carefully.

Return to your vehicle the same way you came. Drive back out to the main road, which changes into Beachview Drive, and turn right. In 0.5 mile you will find the new Jekyll Island Soccer Complex on your right. There is another beach access here, but it is farther up from the main roost site at the south tip. To try it, turn in to the soccer fields and drive straight ahead to the boardwalk that leads out to the beach. This new complex is heavily treated to maintain the precious grass, but could attract grass-loving species during migration until they figure out how biologically barren it is. In another 0.9 mile, note the South Dunes Picnic Area on your right, which has beach access but not a very birdy stretch of beach. This park is, however, another good place to check for migrants in season. Continue another 1.1 miles and you will be back at the starting point. During this stretch you will see trails into the scrub on your left that connect to the trails near the water park.

To bird the north end of the island, continue north on Beachview Drive from Ben Fortson Parkway. Note the convention center on your right, which is one of the few locations in Georgia to find Gray Kingbirds in summer. Look for them anywhere around the buildings or in trees; they're usually calling loudly and persistently. If you don't find any here, scan the powerlines along Beachview Road, in either direction. Note the small shopping center across the street, which has restaurants and convenience stores. Continue north on Beachview; you can pull into any of the parking lots for beach or ocean views along the way if you see something worth checking out. After you pass numerous hotels and residences, in 3.5 miles from the start you will come to Major Horton Road on the left. There is a small pond 0.1 mile in (stay to the left) that occasionally has a duck or two. Across from this road is Villas by the Sea, which has good beach access to the north end. Continue on Beachview for 0.2 mile and park in the pullout to the right. During migration you may find small passerines working the woods, but in winter this is the place to look for scoters and other sea ducks. Follow the short path to the beach, and scan for anything on the water. The flock of sea ducks is usually out here or to your right, and at lower tides you can walk along the beach to search for them. Black Scoters are the most common, but all three scoters, Black, Surf, and White-winged, are found annually. Both Greater and Lesser Scaups are usually seen, mostly Lesser, and frequently there are Redheads mixed in. Long-tailed Duck is rare here but worth looking for, along with just about anything else.

Back on Beachview, continue another 0.2 mile to a trail to the right. This trail goes down to the ocean, and then turns left to cut through some great salt marsh until it reaches the very north tip of Jekyll. If you have time, it is a wonderful walk in any season and is about a mile long. There are lots of Clapper Rails all year, and some salt marsh sparrows in winter. Another option is to scan the ocean again, but you are scanning most of the same area as the last spot.

Continue along Beachview Drive for 0.5 mile, and turn right into the Clam Creek Picnic Area. Migrants may be in these woods, but are more likely out at the end. In 0.7 mile the road loops around, and you have a couple options. In winter park at the end and walk out on the fishing pier to scan for sea ducks. During migration walk out the small wooden bridge to the north tip of the island, a great spot for migrants that has had several super rarities over the years. Note the trail going off to the right, which is the same trail mentioned at the beginning of this paragraph. While you can bird the rest of the north end as well, you have hit most of the better spots and it is probably easier to return to the Ben Fortson Parkway the way you came.

General information: There are hotels and restaurants all along the ocean side of Jekyll, but the only gas is on the short stretch of Ben Fortson Parkway. Winter is usually pretty slow out here, but during spring break and various festivals held on Jekyll, finding space or accommodations can get difficult. Back out on Interstate 95 there are lots of motels and restaurants at all of the nearby exits, especially Exit 36 (old 7), or toward Brunswick and Saint Simons north on US Highway 17.

ADDITIONAL HELP

DeLorme map grid: page 63, G-7, G-8.
For more information: Jekyll Island CVB, (800) 841-6586; Brunswick–Golden Isles CVB, (800) 933-2627.

52 Cumberland Island

County: Camden.
Habitats: Maritime mixed pine/hardwood forest, coastal shrubland, freshwater marsh shrubland, weedy field, brackish marsh, salt marsh, tidal flat, beach, pond, ocean.
Key birds: American White Pelican, Common Ground-Dove, Painted Bunting, shorebirds, gulls, terns, salt marsh sparrows.
Best times to bird: September through May.

The birding: Cumberland Island is Georgia's largest barrier island, and a national seashore since 1972. There are a few remaining areas of private land, but most of it is national park. This is also one of the least-birded islands, and it's good in all seasons but summer (mostly because it is so hot). This is a great place to bird in fall, not only for neotropical migrants such as warblers and tanagers but also for sparrows later in

52 Cumberland Island

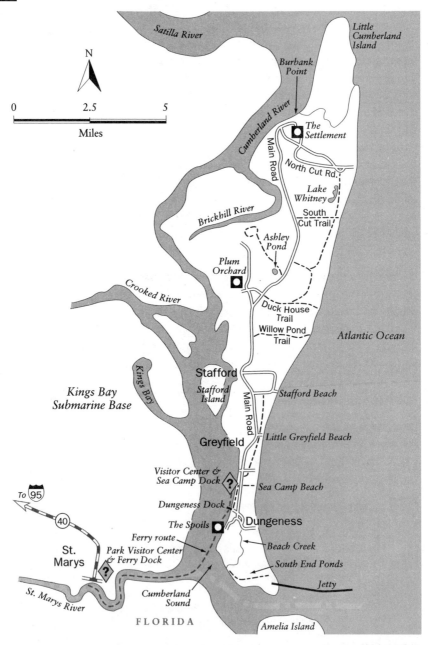

October. This island is great for raptors in fall, including Cooper's and Sharp-shinned Hawks and all three falcons: Peregrine, Merlin, and American Kestrel. A Peregrine usually spends the winter around the south end. Shorebirds migrate through along the beaches, and winter brings more gulls and offshore loons and ducks.

Spring brings lots of landbird migrants, mostly species that winter in the West Indies such as Northern Parula, Black-throated Blue, and Prairie Warblers, American Redstarts, White-eyed Vireos, and Blue-gray Gnatcatchers. Yellow-throated Warbler is a permanent resident, especially conspicuous in spring, and Painted Buntings may be found anywhere in appropriate scrub habitat. The south tip has hosted quite a few rarities over the years, and the island species list is more than 330.

You can walk anywhere you need to for birding, but because the island is about 18 miles long, you won't cover much of it in a day trip. Access is not a problem if you make reservations; you can plan either day trips or extended stays. There are several primitive campgrounds and one that's developed; reservations are strongly advised. One week is the maximum stay. There are no services on the island save water and restrooms. There is also a hotel on the island, the Greyfield Inn. This former Carnegie mansion provides lavish service, and the rates are not low.

Directions: Access is through the town of St. Marys. Take Interstate 95 to Exit 3 (old 2), which is Georgia Highway 40. Go east toward the coast for 9 miles to St. Marys. At 8.4 miles GA 40 ends; just continue on Osborne Street (the same road) to the end. After you turn right you will find the National Park Service building on your left. Park in the designated lot (not in front of the building), and hide any valuables because you will be gone for a minimum of several hours. While waiting for the ferry, check the edge of the river for waders or swallows and the trees around the dock for Eurasian Collared-Doves.

The boat ride takes about 45 minutes, following the St. Marys River (the border between Florida and Georgia) to Cumberland Sound. For the past several years there has been a flock of American White Pelicans wintering on St. Marys River. They are usually found about halfway through the trip. If you keep a state list, keep in mind that until you make the big swing left up the Cumberland Sound, everything on the right side of the boat (where the pelicans frequently roost) is in Florida. You may see some ducks in winter from the ferry, usually Red-breasted Mergansers, Lesser Scaups, or Buffleheads. There will be a few waders and shorebirds on the various sandbars or shellmounds you pass, but many will be too far away to identify.

Once you get to Cumberland Island, you have two choices of docks and strategies. The first stop is Dungeness, and the second is Sea Camp (all campers need to go to the Sea Camp dock to check in). For a winter day trip, your best bet is to get off at Dungeness and walk out to the beach past the ruins that give this dock its name. This walk is just under 1.5 miles through open sandy scrub, the last 0.5 mile worth checking in winter for sparrows and all year for Common Ground-Doves.

When you get to the beach, turn right to go to the south tip. This is the best area for roosting gulls, terns, and shorebirds. There is also a great shorebird mudflat inland just around the tip, worth checking in any season. This area is called South

Black-necked Stilt.

End Ponds on the map, but what you really want is just south of the "ponds," the South End Flats. The tip of the island is about 2 miles from where you hit the beach near Dungeness, and you can get to the flats by walking all the way around the south tip. Check the rock jetty near the south tip for Purple Sandpipers, but they are pretty rare, and you are likely to find only Ruddy Turnstones feeding on the rocks. The jetty area is always worth investigating for resting gulls, terns, and other beach species.

Along the beach is the best spot on the island for Reddish Egrets, and there is usually a pair or two of American Oystercatchers in the area. Look for Red Knots in migration among the dozens of other shorebirds and Piping Plovers in winter. Just north of the jetty is a trail in from the beach that also takes you to the flats. When the trail splits, follow the left split to the flats, which is great for all shorebirds including Whimbrels. Be careful on this trail, as this grass is the favored habitat of the diamondback rattlesnakes living here. Check areas above the tide line for sparrows, and offshore for ducks or loons. In fall anywhere along the coast can be good for raptors, including falcons, and this beach is one of the best. Rarely, jaegers (mostly Parasitic) are seen from shore in very late fall or winter.

If you don't want to go all the way to the tip, there are some very good areas right near the Dungeness ruins. Turn right at the ruins to follow a trail back out to the western (inland) shore of the island to an area called the Spoils, which is fairly reliable for Common Ground-Doves. Here you will find brackish marsh along Beach Creek and an inland salt marsh full of the three salt marsh sparrows: Seaside, and Saltmarsh and Nelson's Sharp-tailed. They occur in that ranking, from most to least. There are a variety of waders and shorebirds and a visible heron roost across the creek. During spring and fall the scrubby edges around the large trees can be very good for migrants. A pair of Great Horned Owls nests here annually, and a couple of Whip-poor-wills make this their wintering area.

The other option is to go to Sea Camp dock. You can take the short trail out to the beach (past the campground), which is 0.6 mile, and then cruise north or south. Birds do not congregate in this area as much as near the south tip. You can also walk north up Main Road to stay in the maritime forest during migration, taking various side trails out to the beach to check for landbirds along the edges; better in spring or fall migration. You can go as far as Stafford Beach, which has a large field along Main Road that's sometimes good for sparrows or other migrants. This field starts about 3.5 miles from Sea Camp. There are lots of Wild

Turkeys in this area, and you may find Cattle Egrets in summer. The wilderness area is just north of here.

If camping, you can obviously explore more of the island, depending on how much walking you are willing to do. Just north of Stafford is Ashley Pond, good for Wood Ducks and Anhingas, and for migrants in season. If you can get to the north end of the island, check the south end of Lake Whitney from the South Cut Trail and head over to Burbank Point for some great shorebirding. Make sure you get an island map and ask the National Park Service about other good birding spots. A bird list at the Sea Camp dock has recent sightings, but it is not always current. There are island bird checklists available there as well. Good birding opportunities are almost anywhere on this island; who knows what you might find! If you go in summer, it is usually VERY hot, but the birding can still be worthwhile. The island is full of Painted Buntings in the scrubby areas around the ruins and along the upper beach, and all of the other barrier island breeding species are here as well. You also get a different set of beach birds, including terns such as Least and Sandwich, and Wilson's Plovers. Be very careful about fluids in summer: You can get dehydrated or overheated quickly, without normal precautions.

General information: Reservations are required for campers, and strongly recommended even for just ferry riders. Reservations can only be made Monday through Friday from 10 A.M. to 2 P.M. at (912) 882-4335, up to 11 months in advance. The ferry runs daily March 1 through September 30, from October 1 through February 28, with two round trips leaving St. Marys at 9 and 11:45 A.M., arriving back at St. Marys at 11 and 5:40 P.M. Wednesday through Saturday there is an additional trip from Cumberland, leaving at 2:45 and arriving in St. Marys at 3:30 P.M. If you are planning a day trip in winter, be aware that there is frequently morning fog along the Georgia coast, which can set the ferry schedule back several hours until it burns off. The cost of the ferry is $10.17 for adults (figure that one out), less for seniors and children. You cannot take pets or bicycles on the ferry. There is also a day-use fee of $4, or you can get an annual day-use permit for $20. Backcountry camping is $2 per person per day, and Sea Camp is $4. There are restrooms and water at the following locations: both docks, the Dungeness ruins, and the Sea Camp campsite. A private company called Lang Seafood offers chartered trips over and back, and will take you, your camping gear, and a bicycle. Prices start at $65 per round trip and go higher for camping gear, bicycles, and extra people. Camping and day-use fees are still required through the National Park Service.

ADDITIONAL HELP

DeLorme map grid: page 71, B7, C6, C7, D6, D7.
For more information: Cumberland Island National Seashore, (912) 882-4335; St. Marys CVB, (800) 868-8687; Lang Seafood, (912) 882-4452.

5. *Status and Distribution Charts*

These bar graphs are a revised version of the ones I first created in 1995. Some have been highly modified, and some are the same. To the best of my ability to do so, they reflect an accurate picture of status and distribution for the species shown. The bar graphs should give you a more precise idea of what birds you can expect to see, and when to see them in each of Georgia's four regions. They follow the order of the Seventh Edition of the Check-list of North American Birds published by the American Ornithologists' Union in 1998. The following definitions correspond to the lines in the graphs:

Common Should find more than ten individuals per day in the appropriate habitat. In the case of flocking species such as gulls or blackbirds, you may see many more than this. This category also covers abundant species such as Yellow-rumped Warblers in winter.

Fairly Common Should find three to ten individuals per day in the appropriate habitat.

Uncommon Should find only one or two individuals per day in the appropriate habitat.

Rare Not likely to find one in any given day, but there should be a few individuals present in some portion of the appropriate habitat.

Casual May not even be reported every year. This is a somewhat variable designation, covering not only species seen annually but those that probably occur but are reported even less than once a year.

NOTES

1. These bar graphs are a prediction of what should be present on any given day. They can give you an idea of what to expect and what to look for, but they are not a listing of how many recorded sightings there are. In some cases, such as the Northern Saw-whet Owl, the bar graph shows what I feel the true status is, even though there are few records.

2. The term "appropriate habitat" may be very specific, depending on species. Some have exact requirements and are rarely found elsewhere. For instance, Loggerhead Shrikes are found in open areas and Louisiana Waterthrushes are always near fresh water. Knowing a species' habitat requirements is important, but keep in mind that during migration some species may be found in what is for them marginal habitat. A similar habitat-specific situation exists for those species found around water. Some of these species, when found inland, require very large bodies of water and are found on only the largest of lakes. Examples include Common Loons and Horned Grebes. Conversely, some species are very adaptable and may be found in a wide range of habitats.

3. Even when present in equal numbers, some species are much easier to find than others. For example, Turkey Vultures and Canada Geese are easy to see. Other species, such as Virginia Rail and LeConte's Sparrow, are very secretive. Naturally, observers with more experience will be more likely to find these difficult species.

Brown-headed Nuthatch. PAUL JOHNSON ILLUSTRATION.

4. Birds normally found near the edges of a particular region will occur in patterns similar to the adjoining region, because in many cases the boundaries are for humans and not birds.

5. Those species with an "I" next to their name are considered irregular from year to year. In some years, they may be common, whereas in other years they may be absent. The abundance shown is considered the average over all years.

6. Weather can play a tremendous role in the ability to find birds. On very windy or rainy days, many species are less likely to be seen. Weather can affect migration significantly. Prevailing wind from the wrong direction can virtually halt migration as migrants wait for more favorable conditions, and rainy weather may ground those birds already on the move. A visit over several days is more likely to produce average numbers such as those listed.

7. Note that many species listed in the Coast region are found only on the immediate coast, such as some gulls and most shorebirds.

8. In the Mountain region, some species, such as Killdeer, are found only in the lower elevations, whereas others, such as Common Ravens, are found only at the higher elevations. The bar shown represents an average over the entire area.

9. Some breeding species, such as Chuck-will's-widow and Great Crested Flycatcher, no longer vocalize after midsummer and become much more difficult to locate. This is indicated in the bar graphs as a lower likelihood of finding them, but does not necessarily signify fewer numbers.

10. Some species, such as Red-cockaded Woodpecker and Gray Kingbird, occur only in very localized areas. While these species may be more likely in very specific areas such as those mentioned in the text, the bar graphs for these birds also represent an average over the entire area.

Status and distribution

Bird Species	Region	Month of Occurrence J F M A M J J A S O N D
GAVIIDAE: LOONS		
☐ Red-throated Loon	Coast	
	Coastal Plain/Piedmont	
☐ Common Loon	Coast	
	Coastal Plain	
	Piedmont	
	Mountain	
PODICIPEDIDAE: GREBES		
☐ Pied-billed Grebe	Coast/Coastal Plain	
	Piedmont	
	Mountain	
☐ Horned Grebe	Coast	
	Coastal Plain	
	Piedmont/Mountain	
☐ Eared Grebe	Coast/Piedmont/Mountain	
PROCELLARIIDAE: SHEARWATERS and PETRELS		
☐ Black-capped Petrel*	Pelagic	
☐ Cory's Shearwater	Pelagic	
☐ Greater Shearwater*	Pelagic	
☐ Sooty Shearwater*	Pelagic	
☐ Manx Shearwater*	Pelagic	
☐ Audubon's Shearwater	Pelagic	
HYDROBATIDAE: STORM-PETRELS		
☐ Wilson's Storm-Petrel	Pelagic	
☐ Leach's Storm-Petrel*	Pelagic	
☐ Band-rumped Storm-Petrel*	Pelagic	
SULIDAE: GANNETS		
☐ Northern Gannet	Pelagic	
	Coast	
PELECANIDAE: PELICANS		
☐ American White Pelican	Coast	
	Coastal Plain	
☐ Brown Pelican	Coast	
PHALACROCORACIDAE: CORMORANTS		
☐ Double-crested Cormorant	Coast	
	Coastal Plain	
	Piedmont	
	Mountain	

See definitions and notes on page 212

Bird Species	Region	Month of Occurrence J F M A M J J A S O N D

ANHINGIDAE: DARTERS

☐ Anhinga — Coast / Coastal Plain / Piedmont

FREGATIDAE: FRIGATEBIRDS

☐ Magnificent Frigatebird — Coast

ARDEIDAE: BITTERNS *and* HERONS

☐ American Bittern — Coast / Coastal Plain / Piedmont / Mountain

☐ Least Bittern — Coast / Coastal Plain / Piedmont

☐ Great Blue Heron — Coast / Coastal Plain / Piedmont / Mountain

☐ Great Egret — Coast / Coastal Plain / Piedmont / Mountain

☐ Snowy Egret — Coast / Coastal Plain / Piedmont

☐ Little Blue Heron — Coast / Coastal Plain / Piedmont

☐ Tricolored Heron — Coast / Coastal Plain / Piedmont

☐ Reddish Egret — Coast

☐ Cattle Egret — Coast / Coastal Plain / Piedmont / Mountain

☐ Green Heron — Coast / Coastal Plain/Piedmont / Mountain

☐ Black-crowned Night-Heron — Coast / Coastal Plain / Piedmont

☐ Yellow-crowned Night-Heron — Coast / Coastal Plain / Piedmont / Mountain

▬▬ Common ── Uncommon ▬▬ Casual
▬▬ Fairly common ▒▒ Rare

Bird Species	Region	J F M A M J J A S O N D
THRESKIORNITHIDAE: IBISES and SPOONBILLS		
☐ White Ibis	Coast	
	Coastal Plain	
	Piedmont	
☐ Glossy Ibis	Coast	
☐ Roseate Spoonbill	Coast	
CICONIIDAE: STORKS		
☐ Wood Stork	Coast	
	Coastal Plain	
	Piedmont	
CATHARTIDAE: AMERICAN VULTURES		
☐ Black Vulture	Coast/Coastal Plain	
	Piedmont	
	Mountain	
☐ Turkey Vulture	Statewide	
ANATIDAE: SWANS, GEESE, and DUCKS		
☐ Fulvous Whistling-Duck*	Coast	
☐ Greater White-fronted Goose	Coast/Coastal Plain/Piedmont	
☐ Snow Goose	Coast	
	Coastal Plain/Piedmont/Mountain	
☐ Ross's Goose*	Coastal Plain/Piedmont/Mountain	
☐ Canada Goose	Coast	
	Coastal Plain	
	Piedmont/Mountain	
☐ Tundra Swan	Statewide	
☐ Wood Duck	Coast/Coastal Plain	
	Piedmont	
	Mountain	
☐ Gadwall	Coast/Coastal Plain	
	Piedmont	
	Mountain	
☐ American Wigeon	Coast	
	Coastal Plain	
	Piedmont	
	Mountain	
☐ American Black Duck	Coast/Coastal Plain	
	Piedmont	
	Mountain	
☐ Mallard	Coast/Piedmont/Mountain	
	Coastal Plain	
☐ Mottled Duck	Coast	

See definitions and notes on page 212

Bird Species	Region	Month of Occurrence J F M A M J J A S O N D
☐ Blue-winged Teal	Coast Coastal Plain Piedmont Mountain	
☐ Northern Shoveler	Coast Coastal Plain Piedmont Mountain	
☐ Northern Pintail	Coast Coastal Plain Piedmont Mountain	
☐ Green-winged Teal	Coast Coastal Plain Piedmont Mountain	
☐ Canvasback	Coast Coastal Plain Piedmont Mountain	
☐ Redhead	Coast/Coastal Plain Piedmont Mountain	
☐ Ring-necked Duck	Coast Coastal Plain/Piedmont Mountain	
☐ Greater Scaup	Coast Coastal Plain Piedmont Mountain	
☐ Lesser Scaup	Coast Coastal Plain Piedmont Mountain	
☐ Surf Scoter	Coast Coastal Plain/Piedmont	
☐ White-winged Scoter	Coast Coastal Plain/Piedmont	
☐ Black Scoter	Coast	
☐ Long-tailed Duck (Oldsquaw)	Coast	
☐ Bufflehead	Coast/Coastal Plain Piedmont Mountain	
☐ Common Goldeneye	Coast/Coastal Plain Piedmont/Mountain	

Common   Uncommon   Casual

Fairly common   Rare

Bird Species	Region	Month of Occurrence
		J F M A M J J A S O N D
☐ Hooded Merganser	Coast/Coastal Plain	
	Piedmont	
	Mountain	
☐ Red-breasted Merganser	Coast	
	Coastal Plain/Piedmont/Mountain	
☐ Ruddy Duck	Coast	
	Coastal Plain/Mountain	
	Piedmont	

ACCIPITRIDAE: KITES, HAWKS, EAGLES, *and* ALLIES

Bird Species	Region	Month of Occurrence
☐ Osprey	Coast	
	Coastal Plain	
	Piedmont	
	Mountain	
☐ Swallow-tailed Kite	Coast	
	Coastal Plain	
	Piedmont	
☐ Mississippi Kite	Coast	
	Coastal Plain	
	Piedmont	
☐ Bald Eagle	Coast	
	Coastal Plain/Piedmont	
	Mountain	
☐ Northern Harrier	Coast/Coastal Plain	
	Piedmont/Mountain	
☐ Sharp-shinned Hawk	Coast	
	Coastal Plain	
	Piedmont/Mountain	
☐ Cooper's Hawk	Coast	
	Coastal Plain	
	Piedmont/Mountain	
☐ Red-shouldered Hawk	Coast/Coastal Plain/Piedmont	
	Mountain	
☐ Broad-winged Hawk	Coast	
	Coastal Plain	
	Piedmont	
	Mountain	
☐ Red-tailed Hawk	Coast	
	Coastal Plain/Piedmont	
	Mountain	
☐ Rough-legged Hawk*	Mountain	
☐ Golden Eagle	Coast/Coastal Plain/Piedmont	
	Mountain	

See definitions and notes on page 212

218

Bird Species	Region	Month of Occurrence J F M A M J J A S O N D
FALCONIDAE: FALCONS		
☐ American Kestrel	Coast	
	Coastal Plain	
	Piedmont	
	Mountain	
☐ Merlin	Coast	
	Coastal Plain	
	Piedmont	
	Mountain	
☐ Peregrine Falcon	Coast	
	Coastal Plain	
	Piedmont	
	Mountain	
CRACIDAE: CHACHALACAS		
☐ Plain Chachalaca	Sapelo Island Only	
PHASIANIDAE: GROUSE and TURKEY		
☐ Ruffed Grouse	Mountain	
☐ Wild Turkey	Coast/Coastal Plain	
	Piedmont/Mountain	
ODONTOPHORIDAE: NEW WORLD QUAIL		
☐ Northern Bobwhite	Coast/Coastal Plain/Piedmont	
	Mountain	
RALLIDAE: RAILS, GALLINULES, and COOTS		
☐ Yellow Rail*	Coast	
☐ Black Rail	Coast	
	Coastal Plain/Piedmont	
☐ Clapper Rail	Coast	
☐ King Rail	Coast	
	Coastal Plain	
	Piedmont	
☐ Virginia Rail	Coast	
	Coastal Plain	
	Piedmont	
	Mountain	
☐ Sora	Coast	
	Coastal Plain	
	Piedmont	
	Mountain	
☐ Purple Gallinule	Coast/Coastal Plain	
☐ Common Moorhen	Coast	
	Coastal Plain	
	Piedmont	

■ Common   — Uncommon   Casual

■ Fairly common   Rare

Bird Species	Region	J F M A M J J A S O N D
☐ American Coot	Coast/Coastal Plain	
	Piedmont	
	Mountain	

GRUIDAE: CRANES

☐ Sandhill Crane	Okefenokee	
	Coast	
	Coastal Plain	
	Piedmont/Mountain	

CHARADRIIDAE: PLOVERS

☐ Black-bellied Plover	Coast	
	Coastal Plain	
	Piedmont	
☐ American Golden-Plover	Coast/Piedmont	
	Coastal Plain	
☐ Wilson's Plover	Coast	
☐ Semipalmated Plover	Coast	
	Coastal Plain	
	Piedmont	
☐ Piping Plover	Coast	
☐ Killdeer	Coast	
	Coastal Plain/Piedmont	
	Mountain	

HAEMATOPODIDAE: OYSTERCATCHERS

☐ American Oystercatcher	Coast	

RECURVIROSTRIDAE: STILTS *and* AVOCETS

☐ Black-necked Stilt	Coast	
☐ American Avocet	Coast	

SCOLOPACIDAE: SANDPIPERS, PHALAROPES, *and* ALLIES

☐ Greater Yellowlegs	Coast	
	Coastal Plain	
	Piedmont	
	Mountain	
☐ Lesser Yellowlegs	Coast	
	Coastal Plain	
	Piedmont	
	Mountain	
☐ Solitary Sandpiper	Coast	
	Coastal Plain/Piedmont	
	Mountain	
☐ Willet	Coast	
	Coastal Plain/Piedmont	

See definitions and notes on page 212

Month of Occurrence

Bird Species	Region	J F M A M J J A S O N D
☐ Spotted Sandpiper	Coast	
	Coastal Plain	
	Piedmont	
	Mountain	
☐ Upland Sandpiper	Coast	
	Coastal Plain	
	Piedmont	
	Mountain	
☐ Whimbrel	Coast	
☐ Long-billed Curlew	Coast	
☐ Marbled Godwit	Coast	
☐ Ruddy Turnstone	Coast	
	Coastal Plain	
☐ Red Knot	Coast	
☐ Sanderling	Coast	
	Coastal Plain/Piedmont	
☐ Semipalmated Sandpiper	Coast	
	Coastal Plain	
	Piedmont	
	Mountain	
☐ Western Sandpiper	Coast	
	Coastal Plain	
	Piedmont	
	Mountain	
☐ Least Sandpiper	Coast	
	Coastal Plain	
	Piedmont	
	Mountain	
☐ White-rumped Sandpiper	Coast	
	Coastal Plain	
	Piedmont	
☐ Baird's Sandpiper	Coast	
	Coastal Plain	
	Piedmont	
☐ Pectoral Sandpiper	Coast	
	Coastal Plain/Piedmont	
	Mountain	
☐ Purple Sandpiper	Coast	
☐ Dunlin	Coast	
	Coastal Plain	
	Piedmont	
☐ Stilt Sandpiper	Coast	
	Coastal Plain	
	Piedmont	

■ Common ——— Uncommon ▨ Casual
■ Fairly common ▨ Rare

221

Bird Species	Region	Month of Occurrence J F M A M J J A S O N D
☐ Buff-breasted Sandpiper	Coast	
	Coastal Plain	
	Piedmont	
☐ Short-billed Dowitcher	Coast	
	Coastal Plain	
	Piedmont	
☐ Long-billed Dowitcher	Coast	
	Coastal Plain/Piedmont	
☐ Common Snipe	Coast/Coastal Plain	
	Piedmont	
	Mountain	
☐ American Woodcock	Coast	
	Coastal Plain/Piedmont	
	Mountain	
☐ Wilson's Phalarope	Coast	
	Coastal Plain/Piedmont	
☐ Red-necked Phalarope	Pelagic	
	Coast	
	Coastal Plain/Piedmont	
☐ Red Phalarope	Pelagic	

LARIDAE: SKUAS, GULLS, TERNS, and SKIMMERS

Bird Species	Region	Month of Occurrence
☐ Pomarine Jaeger	Pelagic	
☐ Parasitic Jaeger	Pelagic	
	Coast	
☐ Laughing Gull	Coast	
☐ Franklin's Gull*	Coast	
	Coastal Plain	
☐ Bonaparte's Gull	Coast	
	Coastal Plain	
	Piedmont	
	Mountain	
☐ Ring-billed Gull	Coast	
	Coastal Plain	
	Piedmont	
	Mountain	
☐ Herring Gull	Coast	
	Coastal Plain	
	Piedmont	
☐ Lesser Black-backed Gull	Coast	
☐ Glaucous Gull	Coast	
☐ Great Black-backed Gull	Coast	
☐ Black-legged Kittiwake*	Pelagic	
☐ Gull-billed Tern	Coast	

See definitions and notes on page 212

Bird Species	Region	Month of Occurrence J F M A M J J A S O N D
☐ Caspian Tern	Coast	
	Coastal Plain	
☐ Royal Tern	Coast	
☐ Sandwich Tern	Pelagic	
	Coast	
☐ Common Tern	Pelagic	
	Coast	
	Coastal Plain/Piedmont	
☐ Forster's Tern	Coast	
	Coastal Plain	
	Piedmont	
☐ Least Tern	Coast	
☐ Bridled Tern	Pelagic	
☐ Sooty Tern	Pelagic	
☐ Black Tern	Pelagic/Coast	
	Coastal Plain	
	Piedmont	
	Mountain	
☐ Black Skimmer	Coast	

COLUMBIDAE: PIGEONS *and* DOVES

☐ Rock Dove	Coast/Coastal Plain/Piedmont	
	Mountain	
☐ Eurasian Collared-Dove	Coast/Coastal Plain	
	Piedmont/Mountain	
☐ Mourning Dove	Statewide	
☐ Common Ground-Dove	Coast/Coastal Plain	

CUCULIDAE: CUCKOOS

☐ Black-billed Cuckoo	Coast	
	Coastal Plain	
	Piedmont	
	Mountain	
☐ Yellow-billed Cuckoo	Coast	
	Coastal Plain	
	Piedmont	
	Mountain	

TYTONIDAE: BARN OWLS

☐ Barn Owl	Coast/Coastal Plain/Piedmont	
	Mountain	

STRIGIDAE: TYPICAL OWLS

☐ Eastern Screech-Owl	Statewide	
☐ Great Horned Owl	Coast	
	Coastal Plain/Piedmont/Mountain	

■■■ Common ——— Uncommon ▬▬▬ Casual
▬▬▬ Fairly common ░░░ Rare

Bird Species	Region	Month of Occurrence J F M A M J J A S O N D
☐ Barred Owl	Coast/Coastal Plain Piedmont/Mountain	
☐ Long-eared Owl*	Coastal Plain/Piedmont/Mountain	
☐ Short-eared Owl	Coast/Coastal Plain Piedmont	
☐ Northern Saw-whet Owl*	Coast/Piedmont/Mountain	

CAPRIMULGIDAE: GOATSUCKERS

Bird Species	Region	Month of Occurrence
☐ Common Nighthawk	Coast Coastal Plain/Piedmont Mountain	
☐ Chuck-will's-widow	Coast Coastal Plain/Piedmont Mountain	
☐ Whip-poor-will	Coast Coastal Plain Piedmont/Mountain	

APODIDAE: SWIFTS

Bird Species	Region	Month of Occurrence
☐ Chimney Swift	Coast Coastal Plain/Piedmont Mountain	

TROCHILIDAE: HUMMINGBIRDS

Bird Species	Region	Month of Occurrence
☐ Ruby-throated Hummingbird	Coast Coastal Plain Piedmont Mountain	
☐ Rufous Hummingbird	Statewide	

ALCEDINIDAE: KINGFISHERS

Bird Species	Region	Month of Occurrence
☐ Belted Kingfisher	Coast Coastal Plain/Piedmont Mountain	

PICIDAE: WOODPECKERS

Bird Species	Region	Month of Occurrence
☐ Red-headed Woodpecker	Coast/Coastal Plain/Piedmont Mountain	
☐ Red-bellied Woodpecker	Coast/Coastal Plain/Piedmont Mountain	
☐ Yellow-bellied Sapsucker	Coast Coastal Plain Piedmont Mountain	
☐ Downy Woodpecker	Statewide	
☐ Hairy Woodpecker	Coast/Coastal Plain Piedmont/Mountain	

See definitions and notes on page 212

Bird Species	Region	Month of Occurrence J F M A M J J A S O N D
☐ Red-cockaded Woodpecker	Coast Coastal Plain	
☐ Northern Flicker	Coast Coastal Plain/Piedmont/Mountain	
☐ Pileated Woodpecker	Coast/Mountain Coastal Plain/Piedmont	

TYRANNIDAE: TYRANT FLYCATCHERS

☐ Olive-sided Flycatcher	Coastal Plain Piedmont/Mountain	
☐ Eastern Wood-Pewee	Coast Coastal Plain Piedmont/Mountain	
☐ Yellow-bellied Flycatcher	Coastal Plain/Piedmont/Mountain	
☐ Acadian Flycatcher	Coast/Coastal Plain Piedmont Mountain	
☐ Willow Flycatcher	Coast Coastal Plain Piedmont/Mountain	
☐ Least Flycatcher	Coast Coastal Plain Piedmont Mountain	
☐ Eastern Phoebe	Coast Coastal Plain Piedmont Mountain	
☐ Great Crested Flycatcher	Coast Coastal Plain Piedmont/Mountain	
☐ Western Kingbird	Coast	
☐ Eastern Kingbird	Coast/Coastal Plain Piedmont/Mountain	
☐ Gray Kingbird	Coast	

LANIIDAE: SHRIKES

☐ Loggerhead Shrike	Coast/Coastal Plain Piedmont Mountain	

VIREONIDAE: VIREOS

☐ White-eyed Vireo	Coast Coastal Plain Piedmont Mountain	

■■■ Common   ——— Uncommon   ▨▨▨ Casual
■■■ Fairly common   ▨▨▨ Rare

225

Bird Species	Region	Month of Occurrence J F M A M J J A S O N D
☐ Yellow-throated Vireo	Coast Coastal Plain Piedmont/Mountain	
☐ Blue-headed Vireo	Coast Coastal Plain Piedmont Mountain	
☐ Warbling Vireo	Piedmont/Mountain	
☐ Philadelphia Vireo	Coast Coastal Plain Piedmont/Mountain	
☐ Red-eyed Vireo	Coast Coastal Plain Piedmont Mountain	

CORVIDAE: JAYS and CROWS

Bird Species	Region	
☐ Blue Jay	Statewide	
☐ American Crow	Statewide	
☐ Fish Crow	Coast Coastal Plain Piedmont	
☐ Common Raven	Mountain	

ALAUDIDAE: LARKS

Bird Species	Region	
☐ Horned Lark	Coastal Plain Piedmont/Mountain	

HIRUNDINIDAE: SWALLOWS

Bird Species	Region	
☐ Purple Martin	Coast Coastal Plain Piedmont Mountain	
☐ Tree Swallow	Coast Coastal Plain Piedmont/Mountain	
☐ Northern Rough-winged Swallow	Coast Coastal Plain Piedmont Mountain	
☐ Bank Swallow	Coast Coastal Plain Piedmont/Mountain	
☐ Cliff Swallow	Coast/Coastal Plain Piedmont/Mountain	
☐ Barn Swallow	Coast Coastal Plain/Piedmont Mountain	

See definitions and notes on page 212

Bird Species	Region	Month of Occurrence J F M A M J J A S O N D
PARIDAE: TITMICE		
☐ Carolina Chickadee	Statewide	
☐ Tufted Titmouse	Statewide	
SITTIDAE: NUTHATCHES		
☐ Red-breasted Nuthatch I	Coast/Piedmont	
	Mountain	
☐ White-breasted Nuthatch	Coast	
	Coastal Plain	
	Piedmont/Mountain	
☐ Brown-headed Nuthatch	Coast	
	Coastal Plain/Piedmont	
	Mountain	
CERTIIDAE: CREEPERS		
☐ Brown Creeper	Coast/Coastal Plain	
	Piedmont	
	Mountain	
TROGLODYTIDAE: WRENS		
☐ Carolina Wren	Statewide	
☐ House Wren	Coast	
	Coastal Plain	
	Piedmont/Mountain	
☐ Winter Wren	Coast	
	Coastal Plain	
	Piedmont	
	Mountain	
☐ Sedge Wren	Coast/Coastal Plain	
	Piedmont	
	Mountain	
☐ Marsh Wren	Coast	
	Coastal Plain	
	Piedmont	
	Mountain	
REGULIDAE: KINGLETS		
☐ Golden-crowned Kinglet	Coast/Coastal Plain	
	Piedmont	
	Mountain	
☐ Ruby-crowned Kinglet	Coast	
	Coastal Plain	
	Piedmont	
	Mountain	

Common   Uncommon   Casual
Fairly common   Rare

227

Bird Species	Region	Month of Occurrence J F M A M J J A S O N D

SYLVIIDAE: GNATCATCHER

☐ Blue-gray Gnatcatcher	Coast	
	Coastal Plain	
	Piedmont	
	Mountain	

TURDIDAE: THRUSHES

☐ Eastern Bluebird	Statewide	
☐ Veery	Coast/Coastal Plain	
	Piedmont	
	Mountain	
☐ Gray-cheeked Thrush	Coast	
	Coastal Plain	
	Piedmont/Mountain	
☐ Swainson's Thrush	Coast/Coastal Plain	
	Piedmont/Mountain	
☐ Hermit Thrush	Coast/Coastal Plain/Piedmont	
	Mountain	
☐ Wood Thrush	Coast	
	Coastal Plain/Piedmont	
	Mountain	
☐ American Robin	Coast	
	Coastal Plain	
	Piedmont	
	Mountain	

MIMIDAE: MOCKINGBIRDS *and* THRASHERS

☐ Gray Catbird	Coast	
	Coastal Plain	
	Piedmont	
	Mountain	
☐ Northern Mockingbird	Coast/Coastal Plain/Piedmont	
	Mountain	
☐ Brown Thrasher	Statewide	

STURNIDAE: STARLINGS

☐ European Starling	Statewide	

MOTACILLIDAE: PIPITS

☐ American Pipit	Coast	
	Coastal Plain	
	Piedmont	
	Mountain	

BOMBYCILLIDAE: WAXWINGS

☐ Cedar Waxwing	Coast/Coastal Plain	
	Piedmont	
	Mountain	

See definitions and notes on page 212

Bird Species	Region	Month of Occurrence J F M A M J J A S O N D

PARULIDAE: WOOD-WARBLERS

☐ Blue-winged Warbler — Coast / Coastal Plain / Piedmont / Mountain

☐ Golden-winged Warbler — Coast / Coastal Plain / Piedmont / Mountain

☐ Tennessee Warbler — Coast / Coastal Plain / Piedmont/Mountain

☐ Orange-crowned Warbler — Coast / Coastal Plain / Piedmont/Mountain

☐ Nashville Warbler — Coast / Coastal Plain / Piedmont/Mountain

☐ Northern Parula — Coast / Coastal Plain / Piedmont/Mountain

☐ Yellow Warbler — Coast / Coastal Plain / Piedmont / Mountain

☐ Chestnut-sided Warbler — Coast/Coastal Plain / Piedmont / Mountain

☐ Magnolia Warbler — Coast / Coastal Plain / Piedmont/Mountain

☐ Cape May Warbler — Coast / Coastal Plain / Piedmont / Mountain

☐ Black-throated Blue Warbler — Coast / Coastal Plain / Piedmont / Mountain

☐ Yellow-rumped Warbler — Coast / Coastal Plain / Piedmont / Mountain

☐ Black-throated Green Warbler — Coast / Coastal Plain / Piedmont / Mountain

▬▬▬ Common
▬▬▬ Fairly common
——— Uncommon
░░░ Rare
░░░ Casual

229

Month of Occurrence

Bird Species	Region	J F M A M J J A S O N D
☐ Blackburnian Warbler	Coast/Coastal Plain	
	Piedmont	
	Mountain	
☐ Yellow-throated Warbler	Coast	
	Coastal Plain	
	Piedmont	
	Mountain	
☐ Pine Warbler	Coast/Coastal Plain/Piedmont	
	Mountain	
☐ Prairie Warbler	Coast	
	Coastal Plain	
	Piedmont	
	Mountain	
☐ Palm Warbler	Coast	
	Coastal Plain	
	Piedmont	
	Mountain	
☐ Bay-breasted Warbler	Coast	
	Coastal Plain	
	Piedmont/Mountain	
☐ Blackpoll Warbler	Coast	
	Coastal Plain	
	Piedmont/Mountain	
☐ Cerulean Warbler	Coastal Plain	
	Piedmont	
	Mountain	
☐ Black-and-white Warbler	Coast	
	Coastal Plain	
	Piedmont	
	Mountain	
☐ American Redstart	Coast	
	Coastal Plain	
	Piedmont	
	Mountain	
☐ Prothonotary Warbler	Coast	
	Coastal Plain	
	Piedmont	
	Mountain	
☐ Worm-eating Warbler	Coast	
	Coastal Plain	
	Piedmont	
	Mountain	
☐ Swainson's Warbler	Coast	
	Coastal Plain	
	Piedmont	
	Mountain	

See definitions and notes on page 212

Bird Species	Region	Month of Occurrence J F M A M J J A S O N D
☐ Ovenbird	Coast	
	Coastal Plain	
	Piedmont	
	Mountain	
☐ Northern Waterthrush	Coast	
	Coastal Plain	
	Piedmont/Mountain	
☐ Louisiana Waterthrush	Coast	
	Coastal Plain/Piedmont	
	Mountain	
☐ Kentucky Warbler	Coast	
	Coastal Plain	
	Piedmont	
	Mountain	
☐ Connecticut Warbler	Coast	
	Coastal Plain	
	Piedmont	
	Mountain	
☐ Mourning Warbler	Coast/Coastal Plain/Piedmont	
	Mountain	
☐ Common Yellowthroat	Coast	
	Coastal Plain	
	Piedmont	
	Mountain	
☐ Hooded Warbler	Coast	
	Coastal Plain	
	Piedmont	
	Mountain	
☐ Wilson's Warbler	Coast	
	Coastal Plain	
	Piedmont/Mountain	
☐ Canada Warbler	Coast	
	Coastal Plain	
	Piedmont	
	Mountain	
☐ Yellow-breasted Chat	Coast	
	Coastal Plain	
	Piedmont	
	Mountain	

THRAUPIDAE: TANAGERS

Bird Species	Region	Month of Occurrence
☐ Summer Tanager	Coast/Coastal Plain	
	Piedmont	
	Mountain	
☐ Scarlet Tanager	Coast	
	Coastal Plain	
	Piedmont	
	Mountain	

▮ Common   — Uncommon   ▨ Casual
▬ Fairly common   ▨ Rare

231

Bird Species	Region	Month of Occurrence J F M A M J J A S O N D

EMBERIZIDAE: TOWHEES, SPARROWS, and ALLIES

Bird Species	Region
☐ Eastern Towhee	Statewide
☐ Bachman's Sparrow	Coast
	Coastal Plain
	Piedmont
☐ Chipping Sparrow	Coast
	Coastal Plain
	Piedmont
	Mountain
☐ Clay-colored Sparrow	Coast
☐ Field Sparrow	Coast
	Coastal Plain
	Piedmont
	Mountain
☐ Vesper Sparrow	Coast
	Coastal Plain/Piedmont
	Mountain
☐ Lark Sparrow	Coast
☐ Savannah Sparrow	Coast/Coastal Plain
	Piedmont/Mountain
☐ Grasshopper Sparrow	Coast
	Coastal Plain
	Piedmont
	Mountain
☐ Henslow's Sparrow	Coast/Coastal Plain
	Piedmont
☐ LeConte's Sparrow	Coast/Piedmont
	Coastal Plain
☐ Nelson's Sharp-tailed Sparrow	Coast
☐ Saltmarsh Sharp-tailed Sparrow	Coast
☐ Seaside Sparrow	Coast
☐ Fox Sparrow	Coast
	Coastal Plain/Mountain
	Piedmont
☐ Song Sparrow	Coast
	Coastal Plain
	Piedmont
	Mountain
☐ Lincoln's Sparrow	Coast/Coastal Plain
	Piedmont
☐ Swamp Sparrow	Coast/Coastal Plain
	Piedmont
	Mountain
☐ White-throated Sparrow	Statewide

See definitions and notes on page 212

Bird Species	Region	Month of Occurrence J F M A M J J A S O N D
☐ White-crowned Sparrow	Coast Coastal Plain/Mountain Piedmont	
☐ Dark-eyed Junco	Coast Coastal Plain Piedmont Mountain	
☐ Lapland Longspur*	Coast/Piedmont/Mountain	

CARDINALIDAE: CARDINALS, GROSBEAKS, and ALLIES

☐ Northern Cardinal	Statewide	
☐ Rose-breasted Grosbeak	Coast Coastal Plain Piedmont Mountain	
☐ Blue Grosbeak	Coast Coastal Plain Piedmont Mountain	
☐ Indigo Bunting	Coast Coastal Plain Piedmont Mountain	
☐ Painted Bunting	Coast Coastal Plain	
☐ Dickcissel I	Coast Coastal Plain/Piedmont	

ICTERIDAE: BLACKBIRDS and ORIOLES

☐ Bobolink	Coast Coastal Plain Piedmont Mountain	
☐ Red-winged Blackbird	Coast/Coastal Plain/Piedmont Mountain	
☐ Eastern Meadowlark	Coast Coastal Plain/Piedmont/Mountain	
☐ Yellow-headed Blackbird	Statewide	
☐ Rusty Blackbird	Coast/Mountain Coastal Plain Piedmont	
☐ Brewer's Blackbird	Coastal Plain Piedmont	
☐ Common Grackle	Coast/Coastal Plain/Piedmont Mountain	
☐ Boat-tailed Grackle	Coast Coastal Plain	

▬ Common	— Uncommon	▦ Casual
▬ Fairly common	▦ Rare	

Bird Species	Region	Month of Occurrence J F M A M J J A S O N D
☐ Shiny Cowbird*	Coast	
☐ Brown-headed Cowbird	Coast/Piedmont	
	Coastal Plain	
	Mountain	
☐ Orchard Oriole	Coast/Coastal Plain	
	Piedmont	
	Mountain	
☐ Baltimore Oriole	Coast	
	Coastal Plain	
	Piedmont	
	Mountain	

FRINGILLIDAE: FINCHES

Bird Species	Region	
☐ Purple Finch I	Coast/Coastal Plain	
	Piedmont/Mountain	
☐ House Finch	Coast	
	Coastal Plain/Piedmont	
	Mountain	

See definitions and notes on page 212

Bird Species	Region	Month of Occurrence J F M A M J J A S O N D
☐ Red Crossbill I	Mountain	
☐ Pine Siskin I	Coast Coastal Plain Piedmont Mountain	
☐ American Goldfinch	Coast Coastal Plain Piedmont Mountain	
☐ Evening Grosbeak	Coast/Coastal Plain Piedmont Mountain	

PASSERIDAE: OLD WORLD SPARROWS

☐ House Sparrow	Statewide	

Common · Uncommon · Casual
Fairly common · Rare

6. Species to Look For

With the great diversity of habitats available in Georgia, more than 300 species of birds are annual in the state. The following section gives suggestions for finding some of them, and should be used in conjunction with the bar graphs. Some species are found in very different parts of the state at differing times of the year, and some are found only sporadically. This list does not include the very rare or the common species, although suggestions for a few of the rare but somewhat regular species are given. As a general rule, species found widely throughout the state or in large numbers are not included, for example, Downy Woodpecker, Carolina Chickadee, and Northern Cardinal. If you are unsure why a species is not listed here, check the bar graphs for the answer. This section also uses the same terms and the same definitions as the bar graphs. The term Fall Line refers to the line between the Piedmont and Coastal Plain. The letters RBA at the end of a species description indicates that this species will usually be mentioned on the Rare Bird Alert when located. This list follows the order of the Seventh Edition of the *Check-list of North American Birds* published by the American Ornithologists' Union in 1998.

Red-throated Loon. Uncommon to rare in winter on the Coast, more likely along the northern section of the Coast. Best found by scanning offshore with a scope; the best location is Tybee Island, Site 44. Also rare inland during migration, where the most likely spots are the lakes along the western border of Georgia such as West Point (Site 11) and Lake Walter F. George (Site 29). RBA.

Common Loon. Uncommon along the Coast and uncommon inland in winter. Reliable at large inland lakes in winter, such as Lake Lanier (Site 18) and West Point Lake (Site 11).

Horned Grebe. Fairly common off the Coast in winter, and uncommon at large inland lakes. Usually found in same lakes as Common Loon.

Eared Grebe. Casual to rare in the Mountain, Piedmont, and Coast. Lake Lanier (Site 18) is a good bet, and they are rarely found offshore or at E. L. Huie (Site 15). RBA.

Northern Gannet. Can be seen in good numbers along the Coast in winter by scanning with a scope, more on the north end of the Coast. May be very close to shore during periods of strong easterly winds. Tybee Island (Site 44) is the most reliable spot.

American White Pelican. Sporadic migrant and winter resident along the Coast and very rare inland. For the last several years a flock has wintered on the St. Marys River, and can be seen from the Cumberland Island Ferry (Site 52). Sometimes they are seen only on the Florida side of the river along this route. RBA.

Anhinga. Fairly common along the Coast and in the Coastal Plain, with more in summer. Found in quiet freshwater ponds and marshes and frequently seen soaring during midday. Found at many sites, including Merry Brothers (Site 26), Bradley Unit of Eufaula NWR (Site 29), Grand Bay WMA (Site 33), Okefenokee NWR (Site 36), East Georgia Turf Farm (Site 39), Savannah Airport Ponds (Site 42), Youman's Pond (Site 45), and Harris Neck NWR (Site 46).

Northern Gannet.

Magnificent Frigatebird. Casual visitor along the Coast, with sightings most often from Jekyll Island, (Site 51). Of course this is where most of the birders are as well. RBA, but usually ephemeral.

American Bittern. Uncommon in winter along the Coast, and uncommon in migration in the Coastal Plain. True status obscured by this species' well-known secretiveness. Your best shot is in winter at the Altamaha WMA (Site 48), or at Grand Bay WMA (Site 33) at the Bombing Range. Sometimes reported from Harris Neck NWR (Site 46) or the Laurens County Loop (Site 35), but always as a matter of luck. RBA.

Least Bittern. Uncommon breeder, mostly along the Coast. The best spot is Altamaha WMA (Site 48), followed by Eufaula NWR Bradley Unit (Site 29). RBA.

Little Blue Heron. Common along Coast all year, and common in Coastal Plain in summer. Uncommon summer wanderer to Piedmont. Found at all Coast sites.

Tricolored Heron. Common on the Coast in summer, fairly common in winter. Usually found near salt water. Any island causeway, especially Jekyll (Site 51), or other shallow feeding areas. Rare in Coastal Plain in late summer and fall.

Reddish Egret. Rare along the Coast in summer and early fall, found exclusively in salt water. The most reliable spot is Gould's Inlet on Saint Simons Island (Site 49), but can be found on any barrier island with the salt flats preferred for feeding. A very active feeder, often running around with wings raised. Other spots to check are the flats south of the jetty on Cumberland Island (Site 52), and Sapelo Island (Site 47). RBA.

Cattle Egret. Common in summer along Coast and in Coastal Plain, usually in agricultural land. Prefers grassy and plowed fields. Frequently seen in grassy median and shoulders along Interstate 16 in summer.

Black-crowned Night-Heron. Resident along the Coast, common in summer and uncommon in winter. Youman's Pond (Site 45) and Andrews Island causeway (Site 50) are the most reliable. Also found sometimes at Merry Brothers (Site 26).

Yellow-crowned Night-Heron. Usually found in the same places as Black-crowned, but in smaller numbers. Nests on the Savannah River along the Augusta Levee (Site 28).

Glossy Ibis. Usually uncommon along the Coast in summer and casual to rare in winter, but irregular. The most reliable spot is the Savannah Airport Ponds (Site 42), but only if there is water in this shallow area. These ponds dry up in periods of low rainfall. The Altamaha WMA (Site 48) can be very good, but when the grass in the ponds is high the birds may be hidden. RBA.

Roseate Spoonbill. Usually found only south of Jekyll Island (Site 51), either along the Jekyll causeway, along US Highway 17 south of the causeway, or at the roost site listed. RBA.

Wood Stork. Common breeder on the Coast, fairly common breeder in Coastal Plain and along Coast in fall. Usually a few will be seen soaring at just about any coastal spot, but largest numbers at Harris Neck NWR (Site 46). Also reliable at Youman's Pond (Site 45) or along Jekyll Island causeway (Site 51). Found annually in late summer or fall at Dyar Pasture (Site 24).

Black Vulture. Common permanent resident below the Fall Line, easy to see soaring on any given day (if it isn't raining). Almost always a few clustered around the entrance to Harris Neck NWR (Site 46). Becomes more difficult to find the farther upstate you go. Can be identified at long range by quick flaps of short wings, which don't seem to help.

Turkey Vulture. Common throughout the state at all seasons. Sometimes seen in flocks during migration.

Wood Stork.

Fulvous Whistling-Duck. Casual along the Coast, especially in fall. Usually transient when seen. Your best hope is Altamaha WMA in the impoundments east of US 17 or from the tower west of US 17 (Site 48), but this is a long shot. RBA.

Greater White-fronted Goose. Casual throughout the state in fall and winter, usually one or two birds in with Canada Geese or by themselves. The only spot approaching reliable is the Bradley Unit of the Eufaula NWR (Site 29), but they may be out on the river and difficult to find. RBA.

Snow Goose. Rare in fall along Coast, and casual throughout the state in fall and winter. Generally found in singles or pairs, but sometimes in small flocks. No one location seems reliable, although they are reported at least annually from E. L. Huie (Site 15) and Eufaula NWR (Site 29). Can be maddeningly irregular at times. May also be found with Canada Geese at farm ponds. RBA.

Ross's Goose. Casual throughout the state, with only about 10 records so far but almost all in recent years. Mostly found with flocks of Snow Geese (in itself a rare event) or in singles at farm ponds with Canada or domestic geese. RBA.

American Black Duck. Uncommon to rare in fall and winter. Usually only singles or small groups. E. L. Huie (Site 15) or Blanton Creek WMA (Site 11) is about the most consistent. RBA.

Mottled Duck. Rare on Coast all year. Seems to be increasing along the Coast, possibly from expanding introduced population in South Carolina. Usually a few birds at Altamaha WMA (Site 48), but often hidden in vegetation. When it has water, Onslow Island (Site 41) is good for this species. RBA.

Northern Pintail. Rare to uncommon throughout state except absent from the Mountain region. No one spot is reliable, although most often reported from E. L. Huie (Site 15) and Merry Brothers Ponds (Site 26). Lake Horton (Site 16) has had this duck several times in the past few years. RBA.

Gadwall. Fairly common to uncommon throughout Georgia except absent from Mountain. Usually found in small, sheltered ponds. Regular spots include B. F. Grant WMA and Rum Creek WMA (Site 22), Garden Lakes (Site 2), Merry Brothers Ponds (Site 26), and E. L. Huie (Site 15).

American Wigeon. Fairly common below the Fall Line in winter, but scattered. Altamaha WMA (Site 48) is good when there is water. Inland try Garden Lakes (Site 2), Merry Brothers (Site 26), and Lake Seminole WMA (Site 30).

Canvasback. Uncommon to rare throughout the state, absent from mountains. Common and easily seen at Lake Seminole WMA (Site 30), by far the most reliable spot in Georgia. RBA.

Redhead. Almost as difficult to find as Canvasback throughout the state. Uncommon along the Coast, usually just offshore with scoters or scaup rafts, such as those along the north end of Jekyll Island (Site 51). Scattered small flocks in the Coastal Plain, including a fairly reliable one at the GA 300 Pond (Site 31). RBA.

Greater Scaup. Uncommon along the Coast, usually in large rafts of Lesser Scaup or scoters. The north end of Jekyll Island is probably best (Site 51). Rare inland, usually with Lesser Scaup. Most often reported at E. L. Huie (Site 15).

Long-tailed Duck (Oldsquaw). Casual along the Coast, and semiannual inland. Most often found in near-shore rafts of scaup and scoters, especially the large flock typically at the north end of Jekyll Island (Site 51). RBA.

Black Scoter. Numbers vary from year to year along the Coast in winter, but usually fairly common to common. May be seen at any coastal spot, but largest numbers usually found on the north end of Jekyll Island (Site 51).

Surf Scoter. Rare on Coast in winter. May be seen anywhere along the Coast, but most likely (you guessed it) in the duck rafts along the north end of Jekyll Island (Site 51). Casual inland during migration, most likely in the Chattahoochee River lakes along the Alabama border (West Point Lake, Site 11, and Lake Walter F. George, Site 29). RBA.

White-winged Scoter. Similar status as Surf Scoter, but more rare both on the Coast and inland. Check same locations as Surf Scoter. RBA.

Common Goldeneye. Rare in Piedmont and Mountain regions in winter, casual below the Fall Line. The most difficult of the annual ducks in Georgia. Not exactly reliable anywhere; your best shot is in fall or winter at West Point Dam (Site 11) or Sweetwater Creek State Park (Site 12). Sometimes spotted during the winter at Lake Lanier (Site 18) or E. L. Huie (Site 15), but often inconsistent. RBA.

Swallow-tailed Kite. Uncommon breeder in the largest river swamps, mostly near the Coast. Can be lucked into on any given day and during migration, but hard to pin down. The largest population is probably along the Altamaha River, and the most reliable site for actually finding one is the Altamaha River Overlook (Site 38). Usually mentioned on RBA.

White-winged Scoter.

Mississippi Kite. Uncommon breeder in Coastal Plain and Coast but much more widespread than Swallow-tailed Kite. Can be seen at the Altamaha River Overlook (Site 38), Big Hammock WMA (Site 37), and at the Savannah-Ogeechee Canal (Site 43). Farthest inland sites are Savannah Lock and Dam (Site 27) and Ocmulgee National Monument (Site 21).

Bald Eagle. Rare permanent resident in most of state, with slightly higher numbers in winter, especially along Coast. Numbers increasing in Georgia; as of 1999 there were 49 nests in the state. Almost guaranteed at Lake Seminole WMA (Site 30). Can also be found at many of the larger lakes inland, including Carter's Lake (Site 4), Lake Oconee and Lake Juliette (Site 22), and Lake Walter F. George (Site 29). In winter often seen below West Point Dam (Site 11). Also frequently seen near Altamaha WMA (Site 48).

Northern Harrier. Fairly common winter resident below the Fall Line. Look for large weedy fields; if you see a concentration of these hawks, you might wait until dusk to see if there are any Short-eared Owls. Harriers are fairly widespread, but one good location is the Cobb Owl Fields (Site 31). Fairly reliable over coastal marshes also.

Sharp-shinned Hawk. Fairly common winter resident and migrant throughout the state, especially on the Coast in fall, where it is common. Any barrier island is good, especially Jekyll Island (Site 51) and Cumberland Island (Site 52). Rare breeder throughout the state, and any nesting information should be reported to the RBA.

Cooper's Hawk. Uncommon permanent resident, but uncommon to rare as a breeder. Fairly common as a migrant above the Fall Line. Can also be found the easiest along the Coast in fall, although in fewer numbers than Sharp-shinned. Same locations as Sharp-shinned Hawk.

Red-shouldered Hawk. Fairly common permanent resident but easy to find since it calls persistently, a series of strident *"keer, keer, keer"* calls. Slightly fewer numbers in Mountain. Most often found around water, especially floodplain hardwood forest and cypress-tupelo swamp.

Broad-winged Hawk. Fairly common breeder in mountains, uncommon breeder in Piedmont, and rare and local breeder in Coastal Plain. Can be found at any Mountain site, and at Ocmulgee National Monument (Site 21). Most often seen in migration along Mountain ridges or at Kennesaw Mountain (Site 13). May be confused with Red-shouldered Hawk, but note wider tail bands and call of Broad-winged, a high thin whistle.

Rough-legged Hawk. Less than annual above Fall Line in winter. Any open area with lots of fields and pastures is possible, like Crockford–Pigeon Mountain WMA area (Site 1). RBA.

Golden Eagle. Rare permanent resident at Crockford–Pigeon Mountain WMA (Site 1), where this species was reintroduced during the 1980s. Casual migrant throughout state in fall and winter. RBA.

American Kestrel. Common and conspicuous winter resident, easily seen along roadsides on wires and poles. Casual breeder throughout state. The Florida subspecies *F. s. paulus* is most often seen near Statesboro where an aggressive nest box program monitors breeding success, or near Augusta. Recent studies suggest that this is the only subspecies that breeds in Georgia, and that all the northern birds leave in spring.

Merlin. Uncommon to rare as a spring or fall migrant and winter resident. Best seen along the Coast in fall at any beach location. All beach sites are good, especially Jekyll Island (Site 51) or Cumberland Island (Site 52).

Peregrine Falcon. Casual migrant and winter resident throughout the state, and fairly common fall migrant along beaches. Same locations as Merlin, especially following cold front passage. Casual breeder in Piedmont, where a hacked pair has nested in downtown Atlanta for the past several years.

Plain Chachalaca. Introduced on Sapelo Island in the 1920s, and now a secretive uncommon resident there (Site 47). Easy to find when calling, but remarkably stealthy for such a large bird.

Ruffed Grouse. Rare breeder in the Mountain region. Present in higher numbers than actual sightings would indicate, but most likely encountered at Brasstown Bald (Site 8) or Rabun Bald (Site 9). May also be seen in many of the Mountain WMAs, including Cohutta WMA (Site 5). Listen for the "drumming" of males in spring.

Wild Turkey. Increasing throughout the state, and frequently seen in large fields and pastures. Piedmont NWR (Site 19) and Beaverdam WMA (Site 34) are reliable spots.

Northern Bobwhite. Decreasing throughout the state for reasons not fully understood, but suspicions include habitat loss and land use changes. Still can be found in agricultural areas with weedy fields and hedgerows.

Black Rail. Casual breeder in eastern Piedmont and possible permanent resident on Coast. The only known inland site is on private land, but studies in South Carolina indicate it could be a rare breeder in wet shortgrass pastures or marshes in the eastern Piedmont. When present, the signature *"kikikerr"* call is given for long periods of time. Reported sporadically from the Coast, usually at Altamaha WMA (Site 48), at any time of year. RBA.

Clapper Rail. Common permanent resident in salt marshes on Coast. Can be difficult to see, but easily heard, especially at dawn and dusk. Check salt marshes at lower tide levels when the birds may be found feeding in the open. A good location is the Marshes of Glynn Park (Site 49), or try the water park marsh on Riverview on Jekyll Island (Site 51) or the Andrews Island causeway (Site 50).

King Rail. Uncommon breeder and permanent resident in Coastal Plain and in fresh water along Coast, and rare breeder in Piedmont. Much more often heard than seen. The highest number of them are wintering birds at Altamaha WMA (Site 48), but they are very difficult to see. Places you might see them in summer include the Bradley Unit of Eufaula NWR (Site 29), Grand Bay WMA (Site 33), the boardwalk at the Suwanee Recreation Area in the Okefenokee (Site 36), or Harris Neck NWR (Site 46).

Virginia Rail. Uncommon winter resident on Coast where it is more often heard than seen. The largest numbers are at Altamaha WMA (Site 48). Rare breeder in the Piedmont, and should be looked for in freshwater marshes with cattails or needlerushes (such as juncus) with shallow edges. Anyplace you find Sora in migration could have Virginia Rail in summer, as they favor the same habitat.

Sora. Uncommon in winter and fairly common in migration on Coast, mostly in shallow marshes such as flooded rice fields and at Altamaha WMA (Site 48). Easily heard and the least shy of all the freshwater rails. Quietly observing an area where they have been heard can provide good looks if you have the patience. Uncommon migrant in Coastal Plain and Piedmont, where it should be looked for in the same marshes as Virginia Rail.

Purple Gallinule. Rare breeder along Coast and in southern Coastal Plain. Most reliable spots are Carter's Pond near Grand Bay WMA (Site 33), Silver Lake in Lake Seminole WMA (Site 30), and the Bradley Unit of Eufaula NWR (Site 29). Not as reliable but worth checking are Altamaha WMA (Site 48) and ponds at Harris Neck NWR (Site 46). RBA.

Common Moorhen. Common breeder below the Fall Line. Found at all the spots for Purple Gallinule, and many others.

Sandhill Crane. The nonmigratory Florida race is an uncommon breeder at Okefenokee NWR (Site 36), where their numbers are increased in winter by migratory northern Sandhills. Uncommon winter resident in Coastal Plain. Large numbers are always found in winter at Grand Bay WMA (Site 33), and in recent years a flock has been wintering in the fields along Cobb Cheek Road (Site 31). Frequently seen in migration in the western Piedmont in February to mid-March and again from November to early December, where they are usually first heard calling while flying overhead.

Black-bellied Plover. Common and conspicuous on all beaches during fall through spring, and a few in summer.

American Golden-Plover. Rare migrant, primarily in Coastal Plain spring and fall and in Piedmont in fall. The most likely place to find one is at a sod farm in fall. Try Ridge and Valley Sod Farms (Site 3), Perry Super Sod Farm (Site 32), and East Georgia Turf Farm (Site 39). RBA.

Wilson's Plover. Fairly common breeder above high tide line at all beach spots. Easy to find at Jekyll Island South Beach and at the mitigation site along US 17 (Site 51).

Piping Plover. Fairly common to uncommon winter resident along beaches. Prefers beaches without disturbances, such as Cumberland Island (Site 52) and Sapelo Island (Site 47), but can be found at Jekyll Island (Site 51) and Tybee Island (Site 44).

American Oystercatcher. Uncommon breeder along Coast. Sea Island across Gould's Inlet from Saint Simons Island (Site 49) and Tybee Island (Site 44) are best, but can be found at some time along any beach.

Black-necked Stilt. Uncommon breeder in shallow freshwater ponds along Coast. Found in ponds on barrier islands such as Cumberland Island (Site 52) and Sapelo Island (Site 47). Not as good but worth checking are Altamaha WMA (Site 48) and Onslow Island (Site 41). RBA.

American Avocet. Uncommon migrant and rare winter resident, primarily along Coast. Casual inland in migration. The two best spots are the causeway to Andrews Island (Site 50) and Onslow Island (Site 41) when it has water. Less often found at Jekyll Island South Beach (Site 51). RBA.

Typical freshwater migrant shorebirds, such as Greater and Lesser Yellowlegs, Solitary Sandpiper, Spotted Sandpiper, Pectoral Sandpiper, and all three small "peeps" (Semipalmated, Western, and Least Sandpipers): The best inland spot is E. L. Huie (Site 15), but any shallow pond or pool can hold a few birds during migration. Any sod farm can be good as well, especially if there is a small pond. Sod farms locations are Sites 3, 32, and 39. Arrowhead Wildlife Education Center

(Site 2) can be good but is inconsistent. Almost all the coastal sites have some freshwater areas used by shorebirds, and the three peeps and Spotted Sandpipers may be found on tidal flats as well. Particularly good spots include Onslow Island (Site 41) when it has water, Savannah Airport Ponds (Site 42), and Altamaha WMA (Site 48). Presence of these shorebirds is highly dependent on water levels, which may be transitory because of recent weather or water level management.

Upland Sandpiper. Uncommon to rare spring migrant and rare fall migrant, absent from Mountain. Check same locations as for American Golden-Plover. One other spot to check is Laurens County Loop in April (Site 35). Also rarely reported from Bush Field Airport in Augusta (Site 27). RBA.

Whimbrel. Common spring and fairly common fall migrant on Coast. Rare winter resident along Coast. Check St. Simons Island (Site 49), Jekyll Island (Site 51), and Cumberland Island (Site 52). RBA.

Long-billed Curlew. Casual to rare winter resident, but only on beaches without disturbance. Almost never seen from Jekyll or St. Simons Islands. Your best bet is Sapelo Island (Site 47), followed by Cumberland Island (Site 52). RBA.

Marbled Godwit. Uncommon along Coast fall through spring. Most reliable at Gould's Inlet, St. Simons Island (Site 49), followed by Jekyll Island South Beach or the mitigation site along US 17 (Site 51). RBA.

Red Knot. Common to fairly common spring and fall migrant at all beaches, and uncommon winter resident. Gould's Inlet area on St. Simons Island (Site 49) and Cumberland Island (Site 52) are the most reliable.

White-rumped Sandpiper. Uncommon spring migrant, absent from Mountain region, fairly common the last half of May near the Coast in fresh water. Casual at best in fall. Check any freshwater ponds near the Coast. If water levels are good for shorebirds, your best bets are Onslow Island (Site 41) and Altamaha WMA (Site 48). Seen annually during the last half of May at E. L. Huie (Site 15). RBA.

Baird's Sandpiper. The opposite of White-rumped, Baird's is virtually unknown in spring and rare in fall, primarily in the Piedmont. Your best shot (still a long one) is to try the inland sod farms, Sites 3 and 32. E. L. Huie (Site 15) is another place to look. RBA.

Purple Sandpiper. Casual along Coast in winter. Found only at rock jetties, which are also casual in Georgia. By far the most reliable spot is Tybee Island (Site 44). Also reported occasionally from Cumberland Island jetty (Site 52). RBA.

Stilt Sandpiper. Uncommon to rare during migration, except absent from Mountain, with a few more seen in fall. Coastal freshwater spots such as Altamaha WMA (Site 48) and Onslow Island (Site 41) are good in both seasons when the habitat is appropriate. Inland the best spot is E. L. Huie (Site 15), which is better in fall. In recent years, a number of these sandpipers have been wintering in the various spoil sites of the Savannah NWR. This represents the northernmost wintering area of this species, and is worth monitoring. The only one of these spoil sites located in Georgia is Onslow Island. RBA.

Buff-breasted Sandpiper. Rare fall migrant, with most records in September. Best spots are the sod farms, Sites 3, 32, and 39. Also found rarely at E. L. Huie (Site 15). RBA.

Long-billed Dowitcher. Rare to uncommon on the Coast in migration, casual in winter on the Coast and inland during fall. Always outnumbered by Short-billed Dowitchers except inland in winter, when both are casual but Long-billed is slightly more likely. These birds are almost always solo or in pairs. In spring, easy to identify by plumage. Adults in fall are almost unidentifiable except by call, a harsh *"keek"* in Long-billed and a whistled *"tu-tu-tu"* in Short-billed. Juveniles, which occur later in fall than adults, are easy to tell apart. Long-billed are very plain above, with tertial feathers having thin gray edges and rufous tips. Short-billed juveniles are brighter above, and the tertials have wide, reddish edges with lots of internal markings like tiger stripes and bars. On the Coast a good spot to check is the mitigation site along US 17 (Site 51) and both water-dependent shorebird sites (Onslow Island, Site 41, and Altamaha WMA, Site 48). Inland a fairly good location is E. L. Huie (Site 15). RBA.

Common Snipe. Common winter resident statewide except in Mountain region, where it is uncommon in winter at lower elevations. Found in freshwater marshes and wet fields and meadows, as well as more traditional shorebird sites. Good locations include E. L. Huie (Site 15), Arrowhead Wildlife Education Center (Site 2), the Bradley Unit of Eufaula NWR (Site 29), Onslow Island (Site 41), Savannah Airport Ponds (Site 42), Altamaha WMA (Site 48), and all three sod farms (Sites 3, 32, and 39).

American Woodcock. Uncommon permanent resident in Piedmont and Coastal Plain, with variable numbers in Mountain. Greater numbers in winter, but most of these birds leave by the end of February. Easiest to find when conducting courtship flight displays in February. One fairly consistent spot is the wet area on the river side of Willeo Road at the Chattahoochee Nature Center (Site 14). Areas with display flights will usually be on the RBA.

Wilson's Phalarope. Casual spring and fall migrant statewide, absent from Mountain region, rare in fall along Coast. When the habitat is right, Onslow Island is the most likely spot (Site 41). Semiannual at E. L. Huie (Site 15). RBA.

Parasitic Jaeger. Casual in fall and rare in winter from shore along the Coast. More numerous as an offshore migrant. The only way to find them unless you are lucky enough to find one on the beach (VERY lucky) is to scan the flocks of gulls that follow shrimp boats. This requires a good spotting scope and lots of patience. A cloudy day and onshore winds help. If you try this, be aware that the more robust Pomarine Jaeger is also possible, although significantly rarer from shore. The best place to try is Jekyll Island (Site 51), although a few have been spotted from Tybee Island (Site 44). RBA.

Franklin's Gull. Less than annual in fall. Most reports from Coast but perhaps more likely below Walter F. George Dam (Site 29). RBA.

Little Gull. Only a handful of records for the state. Your best hope of finding one is along the Coast or mixed in with a flock of Bonaparte's Gulls below a dam spillway inland. RBA.

Bonaparte's Gull. Fairly common along Coast in winter, uncommon in Coastal Plain and rare in Piedmont in winter. Away from Coast, usually found at large lakes above or below the dam. The most reliable inland site is West Point Dam (Site 11), followed by Lake Lanier (Site 18).

Ring-billed Gull. Common along Coast all year, nonbreeding. This is the common gull at inland lakes in winter, and is found at virtually all of them then in varying numbers.

Herring Gull. Common on Coast in winter, uncommon in summer (nonbreeding). The birds that linger into the summer may be so ratty they represent an ID challenge. Uncommon to rare at inland lakes in winter, more likely at larger lakes in the Piedmont such as Lake Lanier (Site 18) or West Point (Site 11). The more gulls found at a given lake, the more likely there will be a Herring Gull or two.

Lesser Black-backed Gull. Uncommon in winter along beaches, but numbers increasing slightly. Casual in summer, but as numbers increase, expect these records to increase also. RBA.

Great Black-backed Gull. Fairly common in winter along coastal beaches, with a few lingering into summer. Almost always outnumber Lesser Black-backed.

Black-legged Kittiwake. Rare migrant offshore in late fall and winter. Not to be expected, but several records from late fall along Chattahoochee River corridor, mostly below Walter F. George Dam (Site 29). RBA.

Gull-billed Tern. Fairly common to uncommon breeder on Coast. Good places to check include Altamaha WMA (Site 48) and Jekyll Island (Site 51), both at the mitigation site along US 17 and the water park on Riverview. Sometimes seen near Andrews Island (Site 50) and Onslow Island (Site 41).

Caspian Tern. Uncommon along Coast at roost sites all year except absent midsummer. Check Tybee Island (Site 44), Saint Simons Island (Site 49), Jekyll Island (Site 51), and Cumberland Island (Site 52). May be seen over any fresh or salt water near coast. Also casual inland during migration.

Sandwich Tern. Uncommon breeder in Georgia, found at all the beach coastal spots during summer, and fairly common in fall. Sometimes hard to see in among the larger Royal Terns, but you should always be able to find a couple at Tybee Island (Site 44), St. Simons Island (Site 49), Jekyll Island (Site 51), or Cumberland Island (Site 52).

Common Tern. Uncommon to rare on the Coast during spring and fall at the same spots as Sandwich Tern. More numerous offshore.

Forster's Tern. Common on all beaches except absent midsummer. In addition to the sites listed for Sandwich Tern, the bridge over to Fort Pulaski (Site 44) almost always has some sitting on the pilings. They usually allow a close approach for photographers. Rare in fall as an inland migrant. Reliable inland in fall at West Point Dam (Site 11).

Least Tern. Fairly common breeder in summer on Coast. Check the same beach spots as Sandwich Tern, or Onslow Island (Site 41). Frequently nests on flat rooftops.

Black Tern. Uncommon to common migrant in fall, mostly during August, and mostly along the beaches. More numerous offshore. Also a rare spring migrant during May across the state. Look for them at large inland lakes or along rivers, or at E. L. Huie (Site 15).

Black Skimmer. Common and conspicuous all year at all beach locations (Sites 44, 47, 49, 51, 52).

Eurasian Collared-Dove. A recent arrival in Georgia, this species is undergoing a rapid expansion in range. Permanent resident and easily found along the Coast in St. Marys (Site 52), near Andrews Island (Site 50), and on St. Simons (Site 49), and will increase in numbers and locations with time. Also spreading inland, mostly north roughly along I-75. Small colonies are established in many inland cities as far north as Rome.

Common Ground-Dove. Uncommon and local below the Fall Line. Frequently found in agricultural areas in the Coastal Plain. Specific places to look include Lower Poplar Street in Macon (Site 20), Beaverdam WMA (Site 34), Laurens County Loop (Site 35), East Georgia Turf Farm (Site 39), Onslow Island (Site 41), Andrews Island (Site 50), and Cumberland Island (Site 52).

Black-billed Cuckoo. Rare to casual migrant throughout state, mostly in spring. No one place is consistent, but Kennesaw Mountain (Site 13) and Cochran Shoals (Site 14) get as many as anywhere. Of course, these are also the two most heavily birded spots during migration. RBA.

Yellow-billed Cuckoo. Common breeder and migrant throughout state, larger numbers below Fall Line. Frequently quiet and surprisingly hard to detect during migration. Widespread and fairly easy to find when calling, good locations include Ocmulgee National Monument (Site 21), Beaverdam WMA (Site 34), and Big Hammock WMA (Site 37).

Barn Owl. Rare permanent resident throughout the state except absent from Mountain region. Currently no reliable sites. Keep your eyes open when driving around at night, especially near feed or seed stores or granaries where rodents are likely. If you are at a place that has abandoned silos, check them, as these are favorite roost sites, but do not go onto private property to do so.

Eastern Screech-Owl. Fairly common permanent resident throughout state, but can be hard to see. Easy to attract with an owl box in your yard. Sometimes respond to a whistled imitation of their call, and they're almost always closer than they sound.

Great Horned Owl. Fairly common to uncommon permanent resident throughout state. Most often seen at dusk, when they tend to perch high up on a snag or pole. Easiest to find along the Coast. Try Jekyll Island (Site 51) along the causeway or on wires for the large antenna on the southwest side of the island, or the Altamaha WMA (Site 48) on Osprey platforms. The Dungeness area on Cumberland Island (Site 52) is also reliable. Look for them also along any highway at dusk in the tops of trees.

Barred Owl. Fairly common permanent resident below Fall Line, uncommon above. Easily heard at Okefenokee Swamp (Site 36) and sometimes at Youman's Pond (Site 45). Frequently found near large river floodplain swamps, such as those at Sites 34, 37, 40, and 43. Sometimes call during the day on cloudy or rainy days.

Long-eared Owl. Casual at best anywhere in the state, absent from Coast. Almost certainly present somewhere in Georgia every winter, but very rarely seen or reported. Large dense pine stands near open fields for feeding areas are best, but that describes about half the state. They usually roost about 20 feet aboveground near the trunk. RBA.

Short-eared Owl. Rare below Fall Line in winter. The only currently reliable spot is the Cobb Owl Fields (Site 31). Prefer weedy fields with tall brush, or cotton fields, since these two areas are favored habitat for cotton rats. Any field with lots of Northern Harriers during daytime should be checked at dusk, because lots of Harriers also indicates abundant prey. Strongly crepuscular, active only at dusk and dawn. Casual above high tide line on beaches. RBA.

Northern Saw-whet Owl. Similar situation as Long-eared Owl, these tiny owls are almost surely in the state somewhere every year. Most likely in the Mountain region, or along upper Coast. A likely spot would be Burrell's Ford (Site 10) where some were found in the winter of 1999-2000. Breed not far away in western North Carolina and eastern Tennessee. Roost very low in small evergreens or vine tangles, and may be found by whitewash along the base of the trunk from repeated use of a favored perch. RBA.

Common Nighthawk. Fairly common to uncommon breeder, but most likely to be seen during fall migration (mostly September). At that time can sometimes be seen in large groups feeding in very brightly lit parking lots, ballparks, or near bright signs. The more light, the better.

Chuck-will's-widow. Common breeder except in Mountains. Easy to hear, but difficult to see. An exception is Pine Log WMA (Site 4), where you can drive in while the gate is still open in early May and see this species and Whip-poor-wills along the roads. Paulk's Pasture WMA (Site 40) is another location for this species along the roads after dark. Casual along Florida border in winter.

Whip-poor-will. Fairly common breeder above Fall Line. Easy to see along with Chuck-will's-widows at Pine Log WMA (Site 4). Whip-poor-wills present in large numbers at Burrell's Ford (Site 10) also. Casual winter resident on southern barrier islands, reported annually from Jekyll Island (Site 51) and Cumberland Island (Site 52). Difficult to find, but frequently gives the single-note *"whip"* call in winter, instead of regular song.

Chimney Swift. Common summer resident and breeder throughout state. Conspicuous as they chatter overhead. Can be seen at close range at artificial nesting structure at Arrowhead Wildlife Education Center (Site 2). Frequently gather in large groups at staging areas in fall, such as over Kennesaw Mountain (Site 13).

Ruby-throated Hummingbird. Common migrant and uncommon breeder throughout the state. Easy to attract with nectar-producing flowers or hummingbird feeders, especially in fall when large numbers are passing through. Many parks have hummingbird feeders as well.

Other **Hummingbirds.** Georgia now has records of seven species of western hummingbirds, all of which have been at feeders and will be on the RBA when present. Rufous is by far the most common, with about 20 to 30 reports per winter from September to March.

Red-headed Woodpecker. Uncommon permanent resident except in Mountains, where it is still uncommon, but found only in winter in the lowlands. Loves dead or dying timber in swampy areas and in clearcuts. Good locations include the Kennesaw Marsh (Site 13) and both Newman Wetlands Center and Lake Shamrock (Site 15).

Yellow-bellied Sapsucker. Fairly common winter resident. Not as noisy as most woodpeckers, but can be located by its quiet, whiny *"keer"* call. Look also for the neat rows of small holes that this woodpecker drills for both sap and the insects attracted to it. A good location is Kennesaw Mountain (Site 13), or anywhere along the Chattahoochee River (Site 14).

Hairy Woodpecker. Uncommon permanent resident in upland hardwood forest, mostly above the Fall Line. Best located by the sharp *"pik"* call. Found in all Mountain and Piedmont sites with forest.

Red-cockaded Woodpecker. This endangered woodpecker is a rare permanent resident found only in two public areas in Georgia: Piedmont NWR (Site 19) and Suwanee Canal Recreation Area (Site 36). The largest populations in Georgia are either on private land or on large army bases, and all are inaccessible.

Pileated Woodpecker. This large woodpecker is a fairly common permanent resident in the Mountains and along the Coast, and uncommon to fairly common in between. Areas of perfect habitatælarge tracts of mature treesæ may locally have higher numbers. Widespread, any location with this habitat will have a few of these magnificent woodpeckers. All reported sightings of "Ivory-billed Woodpeckers" in the past 30 years or so have been Pileated.

Olive-sided Flycatcher. Casual migrant in spring and fall except absent from Coast. Likes to perch on the very highest perch available. Good locations include all the migrant spots along rivers, especially the Chattahoochee (Sites 11, 14, 29, and 30), Kennesaw Mountain (Site 13), and Newman Wetlands Center (Site 15). RBA.

Yellow-bellied Flycatcher. Casual to rare but regular fall migrant throughout state. Can be found at same spots as Olive-sided, but best location by far is Ocmulgee National Monument (Site 21), where in recent years it has been almost reliable. RBA.

Acadian Flycatcher. Common to uncommon breeding summer resident and migrant, more common toward Coast, where it can't be missed in floodplain hardwood forest. Listen for the strident *"pee-stup"* call, with a sharp ending to the second syllable. Good locations include Grand Bay WMA (Site 33), Beaverdam WMA (Site 34), Okefenokee NWR (Site 36), Big Hammock WMA (Site 37), and the Savannah-Ogeechee Canal (Site 43).

Willow Flycatcher. Casual breeding summer resident north of the Fall Line and migrant throughout the state, mostly in fall. Only three known breeding areas, two on private property. The only public access location is along the Little Tennessee River south of Dillard (Site 9). A pair nested in 1998 and 1999 in the Ingles grocery store parking lot along US 76 in Blairsville, so that new spot may also be worth checking. In migration, check same areas as Olive-sided and realize that most will be silent and inseparable from the Alder Flycatcher, which is probably a casual fall migrant as well but almost never reported. Also found along the Coast in fall, and a good place to try is Altamaha WMA (Site 48). RBA.

Least Flycatcher. Casual breeder in northeast corner of the state, and casual migrant throughout, mostly in fall or late summer. A couple of breeding pairs are found each year in the Rabun Bald area (Site 9), either along Hale Ridge Road or in Sky Valley, but not usually in the exact location year to year. Check same locations as Olive-sided in migration, plus Coastal Plain sites including Altamaha WMA (Site 48). RBA.

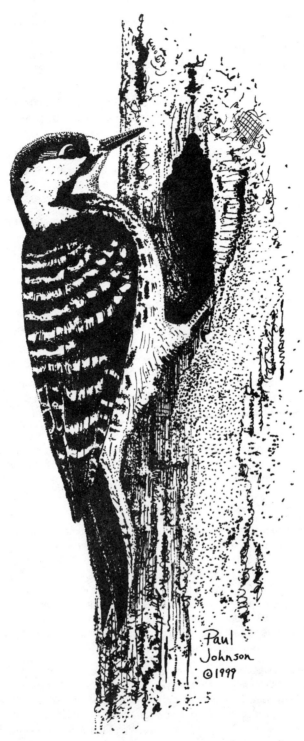

Red-cockaded Woodpecker. PAUL JOHNSON ILLUSTRATION

Western Kingbird. Casual in all seasons except absent in summer, with most records from Coast. The bulk of the records come from barrier islands in fall or winter. RBA.

Gray Kingbird. Rare breeder on Coast. Prefers large live oaks but found in a variety of situations. The two most reliable sites are the Convention Center on Jekyll Island (Site 51) and the Cloister on Sea Island (Site 49). Has also nested in the large trees in the middle of the shopping center on the west side of US 17 immediately south of the Torras causeway to St. Simons Island, and in the Village on St. Simons Island. Usually on RBA.

Loggerhead Shrike. Permanent resident throughout the state, more common closer to the Coast. Fairly common below Fall Line, frequently seen along fences and wires. Look around Lake Seminole (Site 30), Cobb Owl Fields (Site 31), Laurens County Loop (Site 35), and the East Georgia Turf Farm (Site 39). Also seen on the roads leading to Youman's Pond (Site 45) and Harris Neck NWR (Site 46). Difficult to find in Mountain region, but check along GA 157 in Cumberland Plateau Area (Site 1). Statewide numbers of shrikes formerly bolstered in winter by migratory subspecies *(Lanius ludovicianus migrans)* from the northeast, but this subspecies has undergone such a precipitous decline that few if any make it to Georgia in winter.

White-eyed Vireo. Common breeder and migrant throughout the state but fairly common in the Mountains. Uncommon in winter along the Coast and rare in the Coastal Plain. Very vocal.

Blue-headed Vireo. Split from Solitary Vireo. Found in Mountain region all year, rare in winter but fairly common in summer. Check Cloudland Canyon State Park (Site 1), Cohutta WMA (Site 5), Ivy Log Gap (Site 6), Neel's Gap and Sosebee Cove (Site 7), Brasstown Bald (Site 8), Rabun Bald (Site 9), and Burrell's Ford (Site 10). Distribution more localized in Piedmont, but some are found breeding as far south as Piedmont NWR (Site 19). Dawson Forest WMA (Site 17) is a good place to look. Below Fall Line, uncommon migrant and fairly common along the Coast in winter. Usually silent, but found in flocks of foraging chickadees, titmice, and kinglets.

Yellow-throated Vireo. Fairly common breeder and migrant throughout state. Listen for the slow and burry but still vireo-like song. Fairly widespread and not difficult to find; try Pine Log WMA (Site 4), Piedmont NWR (Site 19), Ocmulgee National Monument (Site 21), Watson Spring (Site 23), Beaverdam WMA (Site 34), Okefenokee NWR (Site 36), or Savannah-Ogeechee Canal (Site 43).

Warbling Vireo. Casual migrant spring and fall, north of the Fall Line. No one spot is consistent, but reported annually from Kennesaw Mountain (Site 13) or along the Chattahoochee River (Site 14). RBA.

Philadelphia Vireo. Casual migrant in spring above Fall Line, but rare to uncommon in fall anywhere in the state, mostly above the Fall Line. Your best shot is in mid-September to mid-October at a migrant spot in the Piedmont. The highest number of reports comes from Kennesaw Mountain (Site 13), but also reported along the Chattahoochee River (Site 14). RBA.

Red-eyed Vireo. Common breeder and migrant throughout the state in all regions. Very persistent singer, even in the heat of summer.

Fish Crow. Abundant and impossible to miss permanent resident on the Coast, and increasing throughout the rest of Georgia, except absent from Mountains so far. Formerly found in Piedmont only in summer, but now a few are found all year. More likely inland around lakes and along rivers.

Common Raven. Rare permanent resident of higher mountains. Most likely in spring or summer, as they disperse to points unknown in winter. Two best spots are Brasstown Bald (Site 8) and Rabun Bald (Site 9), but may be missed on any given day.

Horned Lark. Above the Fall Line a fairly common winter resident and rare breeder, mostly at sod farms and grassy pastures. Below the Fall Line a casual breeder and rare winter resident. Good spots include the Ridge and Valley Sod Farms (Site 3) and Perry Super Sod Farm (Site 32). More difficult but findable at the East Georgia Turf Farm (Site 39).

Purple Martin. Common breeder below Fall Line, conspicuous at nesting houses or gourds, usually near water. Arrives as early as the beginning of February in south Georgia. Uncommon breeder in Piedmont. Difficult to find anywhere in the state after early September.

Tree Swallow. Abundant migrant along Coast and fairly common all winter in southeast Georgia. Uncommon migrant throughout the rest of the state. Rare breeder above the Fall Line, including E. L. Huie (Site 15) the past several years and Carter's Lake (Site 4). Increasing as a breeding species, and should be looked for at new locations such as near lakes with either nest boxes or dead trees with cavities.

Bank Swallow. Rare spring migrant, and uncommon to rare fall migrant throughout the state. Check areas of ponds such as Arrowhead Wildlife Education Center (Site 2), E. L. Huie (Site 15), and Altamaha WMA (Site 48). Larger lakes can also be good, especially Lake Oconee at Dyar Pasture WMA (Site 24), those on the Laurens County Loop (Site 35), and Kennedy Pond (Site 39). Mid-July through August is best. Like all swallows, also found at all sod farms and along Coast in migration.

Cliff Swallow. Expanding rapidly to the southeast in Georgia. Uncommon to rare breeder in Georgia, but increasing. Good locations for breeding colonies include Etowah River (Site 3), any bridge over West Point Lake (Site 11), Ocmulgee River (Site 19), and Lake Oconee and Lake Jackson bridges (Site 22). Rare to uncommon migrant at same spots as Bank Swallows.

Red-breasted Nuthatch. Casual to rare irruptive over most of state, with numbers varying from about zero to 10 to 15 reports in different winters. In "invasion" years, may be found at migration spots like Kennesaw Mountain (Site 13) as early as September in fall and as late as early May in spring. A very few breed in the old-growth forest along Burrell's Ford Road (Site 10). If there are any in Georgia in winter, there should be a couple in the Virginia pines along Rocky Gap Road in Crockford–Pigeon Mountain WMA (Site 1). RBA.

White-breasted Nuthatch. Uncommon permanent resident above the Fall Line, found in any large area of upland hardwood forest. Rare to casual below the Fall Line, in sometimes-isolated colonies. One example is perhaps the farthest-south colony in Georgia at Paulk's Pasture WMA (Site 40).

Brown-headed Nuthatch. Common permanent resident in mature pines throughout Piedmont and Coastal Plain. Any site with pine forest has them, and the easiest way to find them is to listen for their squeaky-toy calls as they move through the tops of the trees. Found easily at just about any Piedmont or upper Coastal Plain site, especially at Newman Wetlands Center (Site 15) and Piedmont NWR (Site 19). Rare in Mountain region at lower elevations, and uncommon the closer you get to the Coast.

Brown Creeper. Uncommon winter resident above Fall Line and rare winter resident below. Not exactly reliable anywhere, but forest near the Kennesaw Marsh (Site 13) is almost so. Often found in floodplain hardwood forest along streams or rivers.

Winter Wren. Uncommon winter resident and migrant throughout except rare along Coast and in extreme southern Coastal Plain. Sometimes very shy in tangles and vines along stream bottoms and rivers, but very vocal, a sharp two-noted *"kip-kip."* Good locations include Kennesaw Mountain and Marsh (Site 13), and Chattahoochee River (Site 14). Breeds only in one location reliably, Brasstown Bald (Site 8), but sometimes found in summer on Rabun Bald (Site 9).

Sedge Wren. Uncommon migrant and winter resident along Coast and in Coastal Plain, found in wet grassy fields and powerline cuts. Spots to try are Bradley Unit of Eufaula NWR (Site 29), Grand Bay WMA (Site 33), Paulk's Pasture WMA (Site 40), and Altamaha WMA (Site 48). Rare migrant in Piedmont, and one small wintering population at the Kennesaw Marsh (Site 13).

Marsh Wren. Fairly common permanent resident along Coast in salt marsh, common in winter with birds from breeding areas farther north. The particular subspecies that breeds in Georgia is "Worthington's Marsh Wren," *Cistothorus palustris griseus.* This subspecies is found only from south coastal South Carolina to northern Florida, and is very gray instead of brown along the back and flanks, compared with other Marsh Wrens. It is so distinctive that Burleigh enthuses in *Georgia Birds* that "it is possible to recognize this subspecies without actually collecting it." Spots to check are any area of salt marsh such as near Fort Pulaski (Site 44), St. Simons Island (Site 49), the causeway to Andrews Island (Site 50), Jekyll Island (Site 51), and Cumberland Island (Site 52). Northern races of Marsh Wren are rare migrants inland in marshes and wet grassy fields.

Golden-crowned Kinglet. Generally a common winter resident above the Fall Line, but numbers vary somewhat from year to year. Usually found in large pines in loose flocks, frequently with chickadees and titmice. Rare to uncommon below the Fall Line in winter. A very few may breed in old-growth forest near Burrell's Ford (Site 10).

Ruby-crowned Kinglet. Common winter resident throughout state except fairly common in winter in Mountains. Can be found in almost all habitats except deep forest. A very curious bird, one of the most responsive species to pishing, or squeaking noises.

Blue-gray Gnatcatcher. Common breeder throughout state, and uncommon to rare in winter along Coast and into Coastal Plain. Usually found in scrub or brushy areas in winter.

Eastern Bluebird. Common permanent resident throughout the state. Easy to find on wires and fences along virtually all secondary roads except higher elevations of Mountains. Many parks and refuges have houses for them.

Veery. Uncommon migrant throughout the state in spring and fall. Uncommon to rare breeder in Mountains; check Neel's Gap and Sosebee Cove (Site 7), Brasstown Bald (Site 8), and Rabun Bald (Site 9). Recently detected in larger numbers than previously thought during nocturnal thrush counts at Kennesaw Mountain. Migrating thrushes give distinctive calls at night while flying and can often be identified by species by experienced listeners. Good nonbreeding locations include Kennesaw Mountain (Site 13), and most other migrant locations, especially those above the Fall Line.

Gray-cheeked Thrush. Rare to casual spring migrant and rare to uncommon migrant in fall throughout the state. **Bicknell's Thrush** is a former subspecies that has recently been accorded species status, and is probably a rare migrant along the Coast, although this is not certain. The vast majority of "Gray-cheeked" types in Georgia are Gray-cheeked and not Bicknell's. These two are not identifiable in the field without song. Planned studies to record nocturnal calls of migrants of both Gray-cheeked types may clear up actual status and routes of both types. Nocturnal counts at Kennesaw have shown Gray-cheeked, like Veery, passes through in larger numbers than previously thought. See other comments under Veery.

Swainson's Thrush. Uncommon to fairly common migrant throughout the state, more above the Fall Line. See additional comments under Veery.

Hermit Thrush. Common winter resident throughout state except in Mountains, where uncommon in winter. Found frequently in floodplain forest along rivers and streams. Good locations include Sweetwater Creek State Park (Site 12), Chattahoochee River (Site 14), and any area of hardwood forest, especially brushy areas along edges. Usually responds to pishing or squeaking with a low *"chuck"* call.

Wood Thrush. Common breeder and migrant except on Coast, where it is fairly common. Found in any area of hardwood or mixed forest. See comments under Veery.

Gray Catbird. Common breeder statewide except uncommon breeder on Coast. Fairly common in winter on Coast, and uncommon in Coastal Plain in winter. Unobtrusive except for mewing call, which it frequently gives.

American Pipit. Fairly common to uncommon winter resident, numbers variable from year to year. Found at sod farms (Sites 3, 32, and sometimes 39), grassy fields, and sometimes mudflats such as E. L. Huie (Site 15) or various drawn-down lakes or ponds. Also found in plowed agricultural fields, especially peanut.

Cedar Waxwing. Common winter resident throughout state, and rare breeder in Mountains. Found in flocks in winter, sometimes highly nomadic, but usually around some source of berries such as holly or wax myrtle. Sometimes found in huge numbers all along Coast.

Blue-winged Warbler. Uncommon to fairly common breeder in Mountains, and uncommon migrant above the Fall Line. Try Dawson Forest WMA (Site 17) for breeders, Pine Log WMA (Site 4) for migrants and possible breeders, and Kennesaw Mountain (Site 13) or Ocmulgee National Monument (Site 21) for migrants. Prefers second-growth fields and pastures for breeding, usually 6 to 11 years after clearing.

Golden-winged Warbler. Declining in southern part of range, including Georgia, at least partly due to competition and interbreeding with Blue-winged. Formerly an uncommon breeder in the Mountains but no nests have been found in the past couple of years here. Also prefers scrub and brush, like Blue-winged, but favors younger areas from one to three years after clearing. This habitat has become very rare due to fire suppression and lower rates of clearing at the right elevations, above 2,500 feet. Uncommon migrant above the Fall Line; try Kennesaw Mountain (Site 13) or Chattahoochee River (Site 14).

Tennessee Warbler. Uncommon spring migrant, mostly above the Fall Line, and uncommon to common in fall statewide. Common in fall in Piedmont and Mountains, often found in large numbers at migration sites like Kennesaw Mountain (Site 13) and along Chattahoochee River (Site 14).

Orange-crowned Warbler. Rare to fairly common winter resident and migrant. More common farther south and east in winter, and most easily found along Coast or Coastal Plain in weedy fields and shrubby areas. Fairly reliable during April and October at Kennesaw Mountain (Site 13), especially at the stairs to the saddle.

Nashville Warbler. Casual spring migrant above Fall Line, and rare in fall throughout state. Best spots are along Coast or Piedmont migration sites like Kennesaw Mountain (Site 13) or Chattahoochee River (Site 14). RBA.

Northern Parula. Common and widespread breeder below Fall Line; abundant along Coast and on all barrier islands in maritime mixed pine/hardwood forest. Fairly common migrant and uncommon breeder above Fall Line. Requires Spanish moss or usnea lichen (old man's beard) to build nests in.

Yellow Warbler. Uncommon breeder in Mountain region in lower elevations along rivers and other water areas. Look for them in the areas covered by the Ivy Log Gap (Site 6), Neel's Gap to Lake Winfield Scott (Site 7), and Rabun Bald (Site 9) sections. Fairly common to common migrant throughout state, especially in fall. Lower Poplar Street (Site 20) and East Georgia Turf Farm (Site 39) are good in both seasons. If you miss this warbler along the Coast (especially in coastal scrub) in August and early September, you aren't trying.

Chestnut-sided Warbler. Common breeder in Mountains in cut-over and second-growth areas. Look for them at Lake Conasauga (Site 5), Ivy Log Gap (Site 6), Neel's Gap (Site 7), Brasstown Bald (Site 8), and Rabun Bald (Site 9). Uncommon to rare migrant over whole state in spring, uncommon below Fall Line and common above in fall. Kennesaw Mountain is a good spot for migrants (Site 13).

Magnolia Warbler. Uncommon spring migrant above Fall Line, rare to casual below. Common fall migrant above Fall Line, especially along all rivers (try Chattahoochee, Site 14) and at Kennesaw Mountain (Site 13). Fairly common to uncommon fall migrant in Coastal Plain and along Coast.

Cape May Warbler. Fairly common spring migrant throughout state, peaking in early May. Rare to casual in fall away from the Coast, but fairly common along coast then. Try Coastal Scrub at Jekyll Island (Site 51) or on Cumberland Island (Site 52).

Black-throated Blue Warbler. Fairly common breeder at higher elevations in Mountain region. Look at Lake Conasauga SMA (Site 5), Brasstown Bald (Site 8), or Rabun Bald (Site 9). Fairly common to uncommon migrant in both seasons over entire state, but not really reliable anywhere except along Coast in fall.

Yellow-rumped Warbler. Common to abundant winter resident and migrant over entire state. Large numbers seen at Kennesaw Mountain in spring (Site 13), many molting into breeding plumage. If you miss this warbler in wax myrtle thickets along the coast in winter, get new ears and binoculars. By far the most common wintering warbler in Georgia.

Black-throated Green Warbler. Fairly common breeder in Mountain region, and may be found in local breeding areas as low as 1,100 feet. Usually in mature forest with at least some evergreen component. Check same sites as Chestnut-sided, plus Cloudland Canyon State Park (Site 1), but different habitat. Fairly common migrant above Fall Line in both seasons. Can be seen virtually every day between mid-July and mid-October at Kennesaw Mountain (Site 13).

Blackburnian Warbler. Uncommon breeder in Mountain region, found at Lake Conasauga SMA (Site 5), Ivy Log Gap (Site 6), and Neel's Gap (Site 7). Uncommon spring migrant in Piedmont, and fairly common in fall there. Difficult to find below Fall Line. Good Piedmont sites include Kennesaw Mountain (Site 13) and the Chattahoochee River (Site 14).

Yellow-throated Warbler. Breeds throughout state, uncommon in Mountains to common along Coast, where it is a permanent resident (uncommon in winter). Uncommon migrant throughout state. Two subspecies are found in Georgia. Away from the northwestern corner, the breeder is the nominate *Dendroica dominica dominica*, which prefers pines and cypress trees. Easily found on any barrier island or at Savannah Lock and Dam (Site 27) or Beaverdam WMA (Site 34). Possibly breeding in the northwestern corner of the state and passing through as a rare migrant above the Fall Line is *D. d. albilora*, the western subspecies that prefers sycamore trees. They are difficult to tell apart in the field.

Pine Warbler. Common permanent resident except in Mountains, where it is uncommon, in mature pines. Persistent singer, starting in late winter. Found all over the state; check same areas as Brown-headed Nuthatch.

Prairie Warbler. Common to fairly common breeder and migrant, most common in middle of state. Check young pine plantations and pine forest edges or overgrown clearcuts. Widespread; two good places to look for them are Johnson Mountain (Site 4) and Piedmont NWR (Site 19). Common migrant along the coast in coastal scrub in late summer and early fall.

Palm Warbler. Overall a common to fairly common migrant and winter resident. This is another warbler with two subspecies in Georgia, but more easily recognizable. The "Western" Palm Warbler, *Dendroica palmarum palmarum*, is a common migrant throughout the state and common winter resident along the Coast. This is the plainer subspecies, with yellow generally restricted to the throat and undertail coverts. The "Yellow" Palm Warbler, *D. p. hypochrysea*, is a rare to uncommon migrant, mostly away from the coast, and an uncommon to rare winter resident in the interior. The "Yellow" Palm tends to arrive later in fall and leave earlier in spring, and is always more yellow overall, including the entire breast and belly.

Bay-breasted Warbler. Uncommon spring migrant above the Fall Line, mostly in May. Uncommon to common fall migrant, higher numbers above the Fall Line. Later in fall also, with greatest numbers in late September and October. Two good spots are Kennesaw Mountain (Site 13) and the Chattahoochee River (Site 14).

Blackpoll Warbler. Fairly common to common spring migrant all over the state. Easy to find at any migrant spot, especially late April and early May. Casual fall migrant, mostly on Coast with a handful of interior records. The vast majority of the fall migrants of this species leave the Canadian Maritimes for an 80-hour plus, 2,500-mile, nonstop flight off the coast to their wintering grounds in South America, which explains why so few are seen in fall. Pretty impressive for a 10-gram bird.

Cerulean Warbler. Rare probable breeder along Ivy Log Gap Road (Site 6) and possibly at a couple of nearby locations such as Gum Log Gap. Nesting not confirmed, but suspected by singing and other breeding behaviors. Fairly common spring and fall migrant above the Fall Line, especially at Kennesaw Mountain (Site 13). Ceruleans are usually seen daily from late July through early September there.

Black-and-white Warbler. Fairly common to common migrant and breeder above Fall Line. Rare to uncommon below Fall Line in winter. Breeders found primarily in upland hardwood forest at almost any site in Mountains. Found at virtually every migration location throughout state.

American Redstart. Uncommon and local breeder above Fall Line, and rare in Coastal Plain. Most reliable spot is Lake Winfield Scott (Site 7). Away from Mountains, usually found near rivers and streams. Common migrant throughout state in both seasons in all habitats.

Prothonotary Warbler. Common breeder below Fall Line, uncommon along rivers above. Good locations include Ocmulgee National Monument (Site 21), Merry Brothers (Site 26), Augusta Levee (Site 28), Bradley Unit of Eufaula NWR (Site 29), Grand Bay WMA (Site 33), Beaverdam WMA (Site 34), Big Hammock WMA (Site 37), Savannah-Ogeechee Canal (Site 43), and of course Okefenokee NWR (Site 36), which is riddled with them.

Worm-eating Warbler. Fairly common breeder in Mountains, rare breeder in Piedmont, and uncommon to rare migrant throughout state. Highest numbers at Cloudland Canyon State Park (Site 1); also found at Cohutta WMA (Site 5), Ivy Log Gap (Site 6), and along Burrell's Ford (Site 10). Migrants are fairly quiet and frequently stay hidden in brush and vines, but often feed in clusters of dried leaves. Also give a very distinctive call, a fast *"zeet-zeet,"* almost always in a two-note series. Found regularly at Kennesaw Mountain (Site 13) in migration, and along all rivers such as Chattahoochee (Site 14), Ocmulgee (Site 21), Oconee (Site 34), and Altamaha (Site 37). Also found along coast in both seasons.

Swainson's Warbler. Uncommon breeder below Fall Line in floodplain hardwood forest, where it requires infrequently flooded areas with cane to feed and nest in. Places with the highest numbers include Beaverdam WMA (Site 34) and Big Hammock WMA (Site 37). Numerous other sites include areas with just a few pairs. Also an uncommon to rare breeder in the Blue Ridge section of the Mountain region, best found at Burrell's Ford (Site 10). Generally silent, shy, and infrequently detected during migration.

Ovenbird. Fairly common breeder above Fall Line, becoming scattered and local in south Piedmont. Loud and persistent singer, easy to find at all upland hardwood forest locations in Mountains. Fairly common to uncommon migrant throughout state, but easily overlooked as it silently walks around forest floor. Good locations for migrants are those with open forest understory and include Sweetwater Creek State Park (Site 12), Kennesaw Mountain (Site 13), Dawson Forest WMA (Site 17), Ocmulgee National Monument (Site 21), Watson Spring (Site 23), and South Dunes Picnic Area on Jekyll Island (Site 51).

Northern Waterthrush. Fairly common migrant in both seasons throughout the state. Later than Louisiana Waterthrush. Check wet areas in Chattahoochee River (Site 14), Newman Wetlands Center (Site 15), Dawson Forest WMA (Site 17), Lower Poplar Street (Site 20), Augusta Levee (Site 28), Beaverdam WMA (Site 34), Okefenokee NWR (Site 36), Harris Neck NWR (Site 46), and Altamaha WMA (Site 48).

Louisiana Waterthrush. Fairly common breeder along clear and flowing streams except absent from Coast and southwestern corner. Good locations include Cloudland Canyon State Park (Site 1), Pine Log WMA (Site 4), Burrell's Ford (Site 10), Chattahoochee River (Site 14), Newman Wetlands Center (Site 15), Dawson Forest WMA (Site 17), Piedmont NWR (Site 19), Watson Spring (Site 23), and Beaverdam WMA (Site 34). A very early migrant in spring arriving in mid-March, and also early in fall passing through starting in early July. Migrates earlier than Northern Waterthrush in both seasons, but can be found at many of the same locations.

Kentucky Warbler. Common to rare breeder throughout state except absent from southeast corner, most numerous in Coastal Plain and Piedmont. Good numbers at Pine Log WMA (Site 4), Chattahoochee River (Site 14), Piedmont NWR (Site 19), Ocmulgee National Monument (Site 21), Watson Spring (Site 23), Beaverdam WMA (Site 34), and Big Hammock WMA (Site 37). Fairly common to uncommon migrant throughout state, but secretive and prefers to stay hidden in brush.

Connecticut Warbler. Rare spring migrant only above Fall Line. Not reliable anywhere but reported almost annually from Kennesaw Mountain (Site 13) and along Chattahoochee River (Site 14). This skulker is rarely found unless singing. In fall, casual migrant primarily along Coast, but rarely seen unless caught in mistnets. Latest migrating warbler in both seasons. RBA.

Mourning Warbler. Casual in spring in Mountains, most likely in extreme northwest corner of state but rarely reported. Casual fall migrant everywhere except absent from Mountains; rarely reported in this season also. Like Connecticut, most reports are birds trapped for banding along coast. Less than annual in either season, the regular warbler you are least likely to find. Almost as late as Connecticut. RBA.

Common Yellowthroat. Common breeder and migrant throughout state except absent from upper elevations in Mountains, and common winter resident on Coast. Also winters in Coastal Plain and Piedmont but only fairly common to uncommon. Quickly responds to "pishing" or squeaking in brush or any wet habitat all year long.

Hooded Warbler. Common migrant and common to uncommon breeder, mostly in Coastal Plain or Mountains. Frequently located by loud *"chip,"* which is almost continuously given. Found in all the locations for Kentucky Warbler, and many others.

Wilson's Warbler. Rare migrant in fall above Fall Line, reported most often from Kennesaw Mountain (Site 13) and Chattahoochee River (Site 14). Casual in spring above Fall Line, and on Coast. Casual winter resident, primarily in Coastal Plain. RBA.

Canada Warbler. Rare breeder and uncommon migrant above Fall Line. Breeds only at highest elevations in Georgia, including Brasstown Bald (Site 8) and Rabun Bald (Site 9). Seen in migration at Kennesaw Mountain (Site 13), Chattahoochee River (Site 14), and Ocmulgee National Monument (Site 21).

Yellow-breasted Chat. Common breeder and uncommon migrant throughout state, with highest numbers in Piedmont and Coastal Plain. Often found in same habitat as Prairie Warbler, but the variety and uniqueness of the song (also given at night) will amaze you. Large numbers at Pine Log WMA (Site 4), Dawson Forest WMA (Site 17), Piedmont NWR (Site 19), Merry Brothers (Site 26), and Beaverdam WMA (Site 34). Silent and very secretive during migration, except in spring, when it sometimes sings.

Summer Tanager. Common breeder and migrant throughout state, except fairly common in Mountains. Found at all sites with a forest component, and at all migration spots. Good locations include Pine Log WMA (Site 4), Kennesaw Mountain (Site 13), Dawson Forest WMA (Site 17), Piedmont NWR (Site 19), Ocmulgee National Monument (Site 21), Augusta Levee (Site 28), Beaverdam WMA (Site 34), and Harris Neck NWR (Site 46).

Scarlet Tanager. Very similar breeding distribution as Ovenbird, and found in same locations. Fairly common to rare as a migrant, with fewer the closer you get to the Coast. Kennesaw Mountain is a good location for migrants (Site 13).

Bachman's Sparrow. Uncommon permanent resident in Coastal Plain and rare along Coast in mature open pine forest with thick brush or scrub understory. Found at both Red-cockaded Woodpecker locations, Piedmont NWR (Site 19) and Okefenokee NWR (Site 36), and at Lake Seminole WMA (Site 30) and Grand Bay WMA (Site 33). Virtually impossible to find when not singing. Unlike most sparrows, sings from a high, exposed perch. Also a rare breeder in Piedmont, but usually in partial clearcuts. One spot to check is Pine Log WMA (Site 4).

Chipping Sparrow. Common permanent resident in Piedmont, fairly common breeder in Mountains, and uncommon to common breeder and winter resident in Coastal Plain. Most easily found in or near pine forests in winter, in flocks along forest edges or roads through forest. Widespread.

Clay-colored Sparrow. Rare to casual late fall migrant along Coast. Not regular anywhere, but try any barrier island (Sites 44, 47, 49, 51, or 52) or the dikes east of US 17 at Altamaha WMA (Site 48). RBA.

Field Sparrow. Common breeder above Fall Line, fairly common breeder in Coastal Plain and common winter resident, and fairly common winter resident along Coast. Look for it anywhere you have Prairie Warblers, or Yellow-breasted Chats, i.e., clearcuts or young pine plantations.

Vesper Sparrow. Uncommon to fairly common winter resident, mostly below the Fall Line. Found around plowed fields and in thinly weeded fields. Check Lake Seminole WMA (Site 30), Beaverdam WMA (Site 34), Laurens County Loop (Site 35), Harris Neck NWR (Site 46), and East Georgia Turf Farm (Site 39).

Lark Sparrow. Casual late fall migrant along Coast; try same spots as for Clay-colored. RBA.

Savannah Sparrow. Common winter resident throughout state in all types of fields and bare dirt areas. More widespread than Vesper, but found in those spots easily. The larger, paler "Ipswich" race is rare on all barrier islands in winter.

Grasshopper Sparrow. Uncommon breeder in lower Mountain region and Piedmont, and rare breeder in Coastal Plain. Try fields near both sod farms in Site 3, Johnson Mountain (Site 4), fields along Ward Road (Site 23), fields near Lake Hartwell (Site 25), and Laurens County Loop (Site 35). Rare to uncommon in winter in grassy, fresh clearcuts along Coast, but very difficult to find.

Henslow's Sparrow. Rare winter resident below Fall Line, mostly in eastern section of state, but nightmarish to actually get a look at. Very secretive, and found only in wet grassy pine woodland. The only vestige of this habitat left is usually under large powerlines, so check under every powerline you find as long as it is PUBLIC LAND. The best technique is to have a line of searchers in boots walk slowly in a line and try to see every sparrow that flushes. See additional comments in Paulk's Pasture WMA (Site 40). RBA.

LeConte's Sparrow. Rare winter resident below Fall Line, but occurs in a wider range of habitats and is very slightly easier to find than Henslow's. The same technique is used for this sparrow. In addition to being found under powerlines, look in large weedy or grassy fields, especially those with brooms edge or panicum grass. In general, likes fields to be moist without as much standing water as Henslow's. One location with good numbers of this elusive sparrow is the Bradley Unit at Eufaula NWR (Site 29). RBA.

Nelson's Sharp-tailed Sparrow. All three salt marsh sparrows (this and the following two species) are found in similar habitat and the same locations. Uncommon winter resident in salt marsh along Coast, and casual inland migrant. Sometimes easier to find at high tide along marsh edges, and usually responsive to pishing or squeaking. Check proper habitat at Fort Pulaski (Site 44), Sapelo Island (Site 47), Andrews Island (Site 50), all around Jekyll Island (Site 51), and at Cumberland Island (Site 52).

Saltmarsh Sharp-tailed Sparrow. Fairly common winter resident along Coast. See comments under Nelson's Sharp-tailed Sparrow.

Seaside Sparrow. Common winter resident and fairly common breeding permanent resident. Numbers increase in winter from birds that breed farther north. See comments under Nelson's Sharp-tailed Sparrow.

Fox Sparrow. Uncommon winter resident in Piedmont, rare winter resident in Mountains and Coastal Plain. Generally likes weedy areas with a few saplings, and sometimes located by its call note, similar to Brown Thrasher's but softer. No one area reliable, but check any area with lots of sparrows, like the fields along Columns Drive and other parts of the Chattahoochee River (Site 14).

Lincoln's Sparrow. Rare fall migrant in Piedmont, and casual in fall and winter anywhere except absent from Mountains. No one spot reliable, but check weedy fields, sometimes wet, in areas with large numbers of sparrows. The two locations with several reports in recent years are the Kennesaw Marsh (Site 13), and the dikes east of US 17 at the Altamaha WMA (Site 48). RBA.

Swamp Sparrow. Common winter resident in marshes and wet weedy fields below Mountains. Very responsive to pishing at Kennesaw Marsh (Site 13), along Chattahoochee River (Site 14), Newman Wetlands Center (Site 15), in fields around all lakes (Sites 16, 18, 22, 25, 29, and 30), Lower Poplar Street (Site 20), Dyar Pasture WMA (Site 24), Merry Brothers (Site 26), Laurens County Loop (Site 35), Harris Neck NWR (Site 46), and at all sod farms (Sites 3, 32, and 39).

White-crowned Sparrow. Uncommon winter resident in Piedmont, rare winter resident in rest of state. No one site is reliable, but uncommon in late fall along Coast. Try any barrier island, or dikes east of US 17 at Altamaha WMA (Site 48).

Dark-eyed Junco. Common permanent resident in Mountains, and common winter resident in Piedmont. Found at any higher elevation site in Mountains; try Lake Conasauga (Site 5), Brasstown Bald (Site 8), and Rabun Bald (Site 9). Common and widespread at feeders and along forest edges in winter. Uncommon to rare winter resident below Fall Line.

Lapland Longspur. Casual winter resident above Fall Line or along Coast, but no reports in recent years. Formerly found several times on Cumberland Plateau (Site 1). RBA.

Snow Bunting. Much less frequent than annual winter visitor along Coast, usually beaches. RBA.

Rose-breasted Grosbeak. Uncommon breeder at higher elevations in Mountains, and fairly common to uncommon migrant throughout state (frequently at feeders, especially in spring). Breeding locations include Brasstown Bald (Site 8) and Rabun Bald (Site 9). Good migrant locations include Kennesaw Mountain (Site 13), Chattahoochee River (Site 14), and Lower Poplar Street (Site 20).

Blue Grosbeak. Common to fairly common breeder, especially in brushy or weedy fields in the Coastal Plain. Areas to search include Merry Brothers (Site 26), Lake Seminole WMA (Site 30), Grand Bay WMA (Site 33), Beaverdam WMA (Site 34), Laurens County Loop (Site 35), East Georgia Turf Farm (Site 39), Harris Neck NWR (Site 46), and Altamaha WMA (Site 48). Also can be seen at Piedmont NWR (Site 19).

Indigo Bunting. Common breeder and migrant throughout state except absent from barrier islands. Very loud, conspicuous, and persistent singer all day. Found in almost all habitats except continuous forest.

Painted Bunting. Common breeder along Coast in coastal scrub. Found on all islands, especially the less-developed ones. Also found at Altamaha WMA (Site 48). A few found inland in Coastal Plain along major rivers, and locally as far as Lower Poplar Street (Site 20). The highest numbers inland are at Merry Brothers (Site 26).

Dickcissel. Irruptive casual breeder and fall migrant, usually in Piedmont or Coastal Plain. No consistent locations. RBA.

Bobolink. Fairly common to common spring migrant except absent from Mountains, more along Coast. Check Lower Poplar Street (Site 20), Ocmulgee National Monument (Site 21), Laurens County Loop (Site 35), East Georgia Turf Farm (Site 39), Harris Neck NWR (Site 46), and (perhaps best) Altamaha WMA (Site 48). Uncommon in fall away from Coast and common along Coast, at same locations as spring. RBA.

Eastern Meadowlark. Common permanent resident except uncommon on Coast in summer. Found in grassy fields throughout, easier in spring and summer when singing.

Rusty Blackbird. Uncommon to rare winter resident in Piedmont and Coastal Plain, and rare elsewhere. Look for it in flocks of other blackbirds and grackles, or sometimes in small flocks by themselves near swampy forest or marsh. No one place really reliable, but several reports each winter from E. L. Huie ponds (Site 15) or near the Atlanta Motor Speedway (Site 16). RBA.

Brewer's Blackbird. Rare winter resident in Coastal Plain. Casual above Fall Line in winter, mostly in Piedmont. The only reliable location is the Laurens County Loop (Site 35).

Boat-tailed Grackle. Common permanent resident along Coast, impossible to miss. This is the pale-eyed Atlantic subspecies, *Quiscalus major torreyi*. The Gulf Coast brown-eyed subspecies *(Q. m. westoni)* is an uncommon permanent resident in lower Coastal Plain, near Valdosta and Thomasville. Look for it near Grand Bay WMA (Site 33).

Shiny Cowbird. Casual at any time of year, mostly along Coast. May be mixed in with flocks of Brown-headed Cowbirds. Species presence in the southeastern United States is increasing, so reports in Georgia will probably increase also. Only a handful of records so far; no particular location trend. RBA.

Orchard Oriole. Common breeder and migrant below Fall Line, fairly common breeder in Piedmont, and uncommon breeder in Mountains at lower elevations. Often found in same locations and habitat as Blue Grosbeak, especially those areas with a few small trees, so check the sites listed for that species. Early fall migrant, most are gone by mid-August.

Baltimore Oriole. Rare spring migrant across state, rare to uncommon fall migrant across state. Consistent locations are along all rivers (Sites 14, 21, 28, 29, 30, 34, and 37), Kennesaw Mountain (Site 13), and Lower Poplar Street (Site 20). Casual breeder in mountains, and one small but reliable colony of breeders at Central City Park in Macon (Site 20). Also casual to rare in winter in lower Coastal Plain, frequently around pecan orchards.

Purple Finch. Irregular in winter, mostly above Fall Line. Some winters they are almost common at feeders, and other winters there are no reports at all. Check feeders in good years among House Finches, especially in Mountain region. Try residences near Blackrock Mountain State Park (Site 9). If any have been around in the winter, frequently seen on Kennesaw Mountain in late April (Site 13). RBA.

Red Crossbill. Casual, irregular, and enigmatic permanent resident, mostly in Mountains. Most recent reports are from the Cohutta WMA (Site 5), but rarely found again in the same location. Also a very few reports from the northeastern section of Georgia, including Burrell's Ford (Site 10). In 1999 a pair was found in summer in Pine Log WMA (Site 4), in habitat very similar to an area in northern Alabama where breeding has occurred the past several years. RBA.

Pine Siskin. Irruptive winter resident usually found in pines or at feeders, and in varying numbers in different winters. Almost always a few at feeders near Blackrock Mountain State Park (Site 9), but they often wander between different feeders during the winter. RBA.

American Goldfinch. Common permanent resident above Fall Line, at feeders and in weedy fields, especially those with sunflowers or thistle. Common winter resident in Coastal Plain and rare breeder in same habitat. Uncommon in winter along Coast.

Evening Grosbeak. Casual to uncommon irruptive winter resident, usually reliable only at feeders once they show up. Numbers vary widely from one winter to the next, but usually at least a few someplace in the Mountains. The most-often reported non-feeder location is in Cohutta WMA near Lake Conasauga or Betty Gap (Site 5). RBA.

7. Official Georgia State List

This checklist follows the Seventh Edition of the Check-list of North American Birds (1998), published by the American Ornithologists' Union.

REGULAR SPECIES LIST
(393 Species)

Red-throated Loon
Common Loon
Pied-billed Grebe
Horned Grebe
Red-necked Grebe*
Eared Grebe
Western Grebe*
Black-capped Petrel*
Cory's Shearwater
Greater Shearwater*
Sooty Shearwater*
Manx Shearwater*
Audubon's Shearwater
Wilson's Storm-Petrel
Leach's Storm-Petrel*
Band-rumped Storm-Petrel*
White-tailed Tropicbird*
Red-billed Tropicbird*
Masked Booby*
Northern Gannet
American White Pelican
Brown Pelican
Double-crested Cormorant
Great Cormorant*
Anhinga
Magnificent Frigatebird
American Bittern
Least Bittern
Great Blue Heron
Great Egret
Snowy Egret
Little Blue Heron
Tricolored Heron
Reddish Egret
Cattle Egret
Green Heron
Black-crowned Night-Heron
Yellow-crowned Night-Heron
White Ibis
Glossy Ibis

Roseate Spoonbill
Wood Stork
Black Vulture
Turkey Vulture
Black-bellied Whistling-Duck*
Fulvous Whistling-Duck*
Greater White-fronted Goose
Snow Goose
Ross's Goose*
Canada Goose
Brant
Tundra Swan
Wood Duck
Gadwall
Eurasian Wigeon*
American Wigeon
American Black Duck
Mallard
Mottled Duck
Blue-winged Teal
Cinnamon Teal*
Northern Shoveler
Northern Pintail
Green-winged Teal
Canvasback
Redhead
Ring-necked Duck
Greater Scaup
Lesser Scaup
King Eider*
Common Eider*
Harlequin Duck*
Surf Scoter
White-winged Scoter
Black Scoter
Long-tailed Duck (Oldsquaw)
Bufflehead
Common Goldeneye
Hooded Merganser
Common Merganser*
Red-breasted Merganser

Masked Duck*
Ruddy Duck
Osprey
Swallow-tailed Kite
Mississippi Kite
Bald Eagle
Northern Harrier
Sharp-shinned Hawk
Cooper's Hawk
Northern Goshawk*
Red-shouldered Hawk
Broad-winged Hawk
Red-tailed Hawk
Rough-legged Hawk*
Golden Eagle
American Kestrel
Merlin
Peregrine Falcon
Plain Chachalaca
Ruffed Grouse
Wild Turkey
Northern Bobwhite
Yellow Rail*
Black Rail
Clapper Rail
King Rail
Virginia Rail
Sora
Purple Gallinule
Common Moorhen
American Coot
Limpkin*
Sandhill Crane
Whooping Crane*
Black-bellied Plover
American Golden-Plover
Snowy Plover*
Wilson's Plover
Semipalmated Plover
Piping Plover
Killdeer
American Oystercatcher
Black-necked Stilt

---

* Review species.

American Avocet
Greater Yellowlegs
Lesser Yellowlegs
Solitary Sandpiper
Willet
Spotted Sandpiper
Upland Sandpiper
Whimbrel
Long-billed Curlew
Marbled Godwit
Ruddy Turnstone
Red Knot
Sanderling
Semipalmated Sandpiper
Western Sandpiper
Least Sandpiper
White-rumped Sandpiper
Baird's Sandpiper
Pectoral Sandpiper
Purple Sandpiper
Dunlin
Stilt Sandpiper
Buff-breasted Sandpiper
Ruff*
Short-billed Dowitcher
Long-billed Dowitcher
Common Snipe
American Woodcock
Wilson's Phalarope
Red-necked Phalarope
Red Phalarope
South Polar Skua*
Pomarine Jaeger
Parasitic Jaeger
Laughing Gull
Franklin's Gull*
Little Gull*
Bonaparte's Gull
Ring-billed Gull
Herring Gull
Iceland Gull*
Lesser Black-backed Gull
Glaucous Gull
Great Black-backed Gull
Black-legged Kittiwake*
Sabine's Gull*
Gull-billed Tern
Caspian Tern

Royal Tern
Sandwich Tern
Common Tern
Arctic Tern*
Forster's Tern
Least Tern
Bridled Tern
Sooty Tern
Black Tern
Brown Noddy*
Black Skimmer
Dovekie*
Razorbill*
Rock Dove
Eurasian Collared-Dove
White-winged Dove*
Mourning Dove
Passenger Pigeon (Extinct)
Common Ground-Dove
Carolina Parakeet (Extinct)
Black-billed Cuckoo
Yellow-billed Cuckoo
Smooth-billed Ani*
Barn Owl
Eastern Screech-Owl
Great Horned Owl
Snowy Owl*
Burrowing Owl*
Barred Owl
Long-eared Owl*
Short-eared Owl
Northern Saw-whet Owl*
Common Nighthawk
Chuck-will's-widow
Whip-poor-will
Chimney Swift
Magnificent Hummingbird*
Ruby-throated Hummingbird
Black-chinned
    Hummingbird
Anna's Hummingbird*
Calliope Hummingbird*
Broad-tailed Hummingbird*
Rufous Hummingbird
Allen's Hummingbird*
Belted Kingfisher
Red-headed Woodpecker
Red-bellied Woodpecker

Yellow-bellied Sapsucker
Downy Woodpecker
Hairy Woodpecker
Red-cockaded Woodpecker
Northern Flicker
Pileated Woodpecker
Ivory-billed Woodpecker
    (Extinct)
Olive-sided Flycatcher
Eastern Wood-Pewee
Yellow-bellied Flycatcher
Acadian Flycatcher
Alder Flycatcher*
Willow Flycatcher
Least Flycatcher
Eastern Phoebe
Say's Phoebe*
Vermilion Flycatcher*
Great Crested Flycatcher
Western Kingbird
Eastern Kingbird
Gray Kingbird
Scissor-tailed Flycatcher
Loggerhead Shrike
White-eyed Vireo
Yellow-throated Vireo
Blue-headed Vireo
Warbling Vireo
Philadelphia Vireo
Red-eyed Vireo
Blue Jay
Florida Scrub-Jay*
American Crow
Fish Crow
Common Raven
Horned Lark
Purple Martin
Tree Swallow
Northern Rough-winged
    Swallow
Bank Swallow
Cliff Swallow
Barn Swallow
Carolina Chickadee
Tufted Titmouse
Red-breasted Nuthatch
White-breasted Nuthatch
Brown-headed Nuthatch

---

* Review species.

Brown Creeper
Carolina Wren
Bewick's Wren*
House Wren
Winter Wren
Sedge Wren
Marsh Wren
Golden-crowned Kinglet
Ruby-crowned Kinglet
Blue-gray Gnatcatcher
Northern Wheatear*
Eastern Bluebird
Veery
Gray-cheeked Thrush
Bicknell's Thrush*
Swainson's Thrush
Hermit Thrush
Wood Thrush
American Robin
Varied Thrush*
Gray Catbird
Northern Mockingbird
Brown Thrasher
European Starling
American Pipit
Sprague's Pipit*
Cedar Waxwing
Bachman's Warbler (Extinct)
Blue-winged Warbler
Golden-winged Warbler
Tennessee Warbler
Orange-crowned Warbler
Nashville Warbler
Northern Parula
Yellow Warbler
Chestnut-sided Warbler
Magnolia Warbler
Cape May Warbler
Black-throated Blue Warbler
Yellow-rumped Warbler
Black-throated Gray
    Warbler*
Black-throated Green
    Warbler
Townsend's Warbler*
Blackburnian Warbler
Yellow-throated Warbler
Pine Warbler
Kirtland's Warbler*
Prairie Warbler

Palm Warbler
Bay-breasted Warbler
Blackpoll Warbler
Cerulean Warbler
Black-and-white Warbler
American Redstart
Prothonotary Warbler
Worm-eating Warbler
Swainson's Warbler
Ovenbird
Northern Waterthrush
Louisiana Waterthrush
Kentucky Warbler
Connecticut Warbler
Mourning Warbler
MacGillivray's Warbler*
Common Yellowthroat
Hooded Warbler
Wilson's Warbler
Canada Warbler
Yellow-breasted Chat
Summer Tanager
Scarlet Tanager
Western Tanager*
Green-tailed Towhee*
Eastern Towhee
Bachman's Sparrow
American Tree Sparrow*
Chipping Sparrow
Clay-colored Sparrow
Field Sparrow
Vesper Sparrow
Lark Sparrow
Lark Bunting*
Savannah Sparrow
Grasshopper Sparrow
Henslow's Sparrow
LeConte's Sparrow
Nelson's Sharp-tailed
    Sparrow
Saltmarsh Sharp-tailed
    Sparrow
Seaside Sparrow
Fox Sparrow
Song Sparrow
Lincoln's Sparrow
Swamp Sparrow
White-throated Sparrow
Harris's Sparrow*
White-crowned Sparrow

Dark-eyed Junco
Lapland Longspur*
Snow Bunting*
Northern Cardinal
Rose-breasted Grosbeak
Black-headed Grosbeak*
Blue Grosbeak
Indigo Bunting
Painted Bunting
Dickcissel
Bobolink
Red-winged Blackbird
Eastern Meadowlark
Western Meadowlark*
Yellow-headed Blackbird
Rusty Blackbird
Brewer's Blackbird
Common Grackle
Boat-tailed Grackle
Shiny Cowbird*
Brown-headed Cowbird
Orchard Oriole
Baltimore Oriole
Bullock's Oriole*
Purple Finch
House Finch
Red Crossbill
Common Redpoll*
Pine Siskin
American Goldfinch
Evening Grosbeak
House Sparrow

PROVISIONAL SPECIES LIST
(11 Species)
Species accepted but not
enough evidence for Regular
List. All are review species.

Northern Fulmar
Brown Booby
Swainson's Hawk
Mountain Plover
Hudsonian Godwit
Long-tailed Jaeger
Roseate Tern
White-winged Tern
Bell's Vireo
Virginia's Warbler
Painted Redstart

Appendix A: *Addresses and Phone Numbers*

Georgia Department of Natural Resources. All wildlife management areas (WMAs) and state parks are administered by the Department of Natural Resources (DNR).

For the purposes of obtaining specific information concerning a particular WMA or area of the state, note that DNR is divided into seven wildlife resources divisions covering different areas of the state.

Northwest: 2592 Floyd Springs Road, Armuchee, GA 30105; (706) 295-6041.

Northeast: 2150 Dawsonville Highway, Gainesville, GA 30501; (770) 535-5700.

West Central: 1014 Martin Luther King Boulevard, Fort Valley, GA 31030; (912) 825-6354.

East Central: 142 Bob Kirk Road, NW, Thomson, GA 30824; (706) 595-4222.

Southwest: 2024 Newton Road, Albany, GA 31701; (912) 430-4254.

Southeast: 1773-A Bowen's Mill Highway, Fitzgerald, GA 31750; (912) 426-5267.

Coastal: One Conservation Way, Suite 310, Brunswick, GA 31520; (912) 262-3173.

There are also several excellent websites for DNR and specifically for WMAs. The general DNR website is http://www.georgianet.org/dnr/. For information on WMAs, try http://www.ganet.org/dnr/wild/game_mgmt/ga_wmas.html. The most useful site is http://www.ganet.org/dnr/wild/game_mgmt/ga_wmalist.html, which has all the dates for hunts, and links to download maps for WMAs.

For state parks, contact: Georgia State Parks and Historic Sites, 1352 Floyd Tower East, 205 Butler Street S.E., Atlanta, GA 30334. The number for general information is (404) 656-3530. For park reservations, call (800) 864-7275. Their website is http://www.gastateparks.org.

There are two national forests in Georgia, the Chattahoochee and Oconee, both administered by the USDA Forest Service. The forest supervisor for Georgia can be reached through the USDAFS, 508 Oak Street N.W., Gainesville, GA, 30501. Telephone (706) 536-0541.

For specific forests, contact:

Armuchee Ranger District, 806 E. Villanow Street, P.O. Box 465, LaFayette, GA 30728; (706) 638-1085.

Brasstown Ranger District, 1881 Highway 515, P.O. Box 9, Blairsville, GA 30514; (706) 745-6928.

Chattooga Ranger District, P.O. Box 196, Burton Road, Clarkesville, GA 30523; (706) 754-6221.

Cohutta Ranger District, 401 Old Ellijay Road, Chatsworth, GA 30705; (706) 695-6736.

Oconee Ranger District, 1199 Madison Road, Eatonton, GA 31024; (706) 485-7110.

Tallulah Ranger District, 825 Highway 441 South, P.O. Box 438, Clayton, GA 30525; (706) 782-3320.

Toccoa Ranger District, E. Main Street, Box 1839, Blue Ridge, GA 30513; (706) 632-3031.

For all other organizations or locations mentioned in the text:

Arrowhead Wildlife Education Center, 2592 Floyd Springs Road, Armuchee, GA 30105; (706) 295-6041.

Atlanta Audubon Society, Box 29189, Atlanta, GA 30359; (770) 955-4111. Website: www.atlantaaudubon.org.

Atlanta CVB, (800) 285-2682.

Atlanta Motor Speedway, (770) 946-4211.

Augusta Metropolitan CVB, (800) 726-0243.

Bainbridge–Decatur County Chamber of Commerce, (800) 243-4774.

Blackrock Mountain Park, P.O. Drawer A, Mountain City, GA 30562; (706) 746-2141.

Blairsville–Union County Chamber of Commerce, (706) 745-5789.

Brunswick–Golden Isles CVB, (800) 933-2627.

Carter's Lake Resource Manager's Office, P.O. Box 96, Oakman, GA 30732; (706) 334-2248.

Cartersville CVB, (800) 733-2280.

Chatsworth–Murray County Chamber of Commerce, (706) 695-6060.

Chattahoochee Nature Center, 9135 Willeo Road, Roswell, GA 30075; (770) 992-2055.

Chattahoochee River National Recreation Area, 1978 Island Ford Parkway, Atlanta, GA 30350; (770) 399-8070.

Clayton County Water Authority, 1600 Battle Creek Road, Morrow, GA 30260; (770) 603-5605.

Cloudland Canyon Park, Route 2, Box 150, Rising Fawn, GA 30738; (706) 657-4050.

Cobb County CVB, (800) 451-3480.

Cordele-Crisp Tourism Committee, (912) 273-5132.

Cumberland Island National Seashore, P.O. Box 806, St. Marys, GA 31558; (912) 882-4336.

Cumming-Forsyth Chamber of Commerce, (770) 887-6461.

Dade County Chamber of Commerce, (706) 657-4488.

Dalton–Whitfield County CVB, (800) 331-3258.

Darien Welcome Center, (912) 437-6684.

Dawson County Chamber of Commerce, (706) 265-6278.

Dublin–Laurens County Chamber of Commerce, (912) 272-5546.

Etowah Indian Mounds, 813 Indian Mounds Road, S.W., Cartersville, GA 30120; (770) 387-3747.

Eufaula NWR, 509 Old Highway 165, Eufaula, AL 36027; (334) 687-4065.

Florence Marina Park, Route 1, Box 36, Omaha, GA 31821; (912) 838-6870.

Forsythe–Monroe County Chamber of Commerce, (888) 642-4628.

Fort Frederica National Monument, Route 9, Box 286-C, St. Simons Island, GA 31522; (912) 638-3639.

Fort Pulaski National Monument, P.O. Box 30757, Savannah, GA 31410; (912) 786-5787.

George T. Bagby Park, Route 1, Box 201, Fort Gaines, GA 31751; (912) 768-2571.

Georgia Power Lake Information, (888) 472-5253.

Georgia Power Land Department Field Office (Lake Oconee), (706) 485-8704.

Greater Rome CVB, (800) 444-1834.

Greene County Chamber of Commerce, (800) 886-5253.

Harris Neck NWR, P.O. Box 8487, Savannah, GA 31412; (912) 652-4415.

Hart State Park, 330 Hart State Park Road, Hartwell, GA 30643; (706) 376-8756.

Hartwell Lake Natural Resource Management Center, (707) 376-4788.

Hinesville-Liberty County Chamber of Commerce, (912) 368-4445.

James H. "Sloppy" Floyd Park, Route 1, Box 291, Summerville, GA 30747; (706) 857-0826.

Jekyll Island CVB, (800) 841-6586.

J. Strom Thurmond Lake Resource Manager, Route 1, Box 12, Clarks Hill, SC 29821; (706) 722-3770.

Kennesaw Mountain National Battlefield Park, 905 Kennesaw Mountain Drive, Kennesaw, GA 30152; (770) 427-4686. Website: www.nps.gov/kemo.

Lake Hartwell Project Manager, P.O. Box 278, Hartwell, GA 30643; (706) 376-4788.

Lake Jackson Land Management Office, 180 Dam Road, Jackson, GA 30233; (770) 775-4753.

Lake Lanier Visitor Center, P.O. Box 567, Buford, GA 30515; (770) 945-9531.

Lake Oconee/Sinclair Land Management Office, 125 Wallace Dam Road, Eatonton, GA 31024; (706) 485-8704.

Lake Seminole Resource Manager, P.O. Box 96, Chattahoochee, FL; (912) 662-2001.

Lane Packing Company, (800) 277-3224.

Lang Seafood, (912) 882-4452.

Laura S. Walker State Park, 5653 Laura Walker Road, Waycross, GA, 31503; (912) 287-4900.

Len Berg's, (912) 742-9255.

Lula's Kitchen, (912) 485-2270.

Macon–Bibb County CVB, (800) 768-3401.

McIntosh County Chamber of Commerce, (912) 437-4192.

Milledgeville–Baldwin County CVB, (800) 653-1804.

Mistletoe State Park, 3723 Mistletoe Road, Appling, GA 30802; (706) 541-0321.

Newman Wetlands Center, 2755 Freeman Road, Hampton, GA 30228; (770) 603-5606.

Ocmulgee National Monument, 1207 Emery Highway, Macon, GA 31201; (912) 752-8257.

Okefenokee Chamber of Commerce (Folkston), (912) 496-2536.

Okefenokee NWR, Route 2, Box 3330, Folkston, GA 31537; (912) 496-3331.

Okefenokee Swamp Park, (912) 283-0583.

Perry Area CVB, (912) 988-8000.

Piedmont NWR, Route 1, Box 670, Round Oak, GA 31038; (912) 986-5441.

Providence Canyon Conservation Park, Route 1, Box 158, Lumpkin, GA 31815; (912) 838-6202.

Rabun County CVB, (706) 782-4812.

Reynolds Mansion, (912) 485-2299.

St. Marys CVB, (800) 868-8687.

Sapelo Island Estuarine Reserve/Reynolds Mansion, P.O. Box 15, Sapelo Island, GA 31327; (912) 485-2251.

Sapelo Island Visitors Center, Route 1, Box 1500, Darien, GA 31305; (912) 437-3224.

Savannah CVB, (912) 944-0456.

Savannah NWR, P.O. Box 8487, Savannah, GA 31412; (912) 652-4415.

Savannah and Ogeechee Canal, 681 Fort Argyle Road, Savannah, GA 31419; (912) 748-8068.

Seminole State Park, Route 2, Donalsonville, GA 31745; (912) 861-3137.

Statesboro–Bulloch Chamber of Commerce, (912) 764-6111.

Stephen C. Foster State Park, Route 1, Box 131, Fargo, GA 31631; (912) 637-5274.

Suwanee Canal Recreation Area Concessionaire, (800) SWAMP-96.

Sweetwater Creek Conservation Park, P.O. Box 816, Lithia Springs, GA 30057; (770) 732-5871.

Towns County Chamber of Commerce, (706) 896-4966.

U.S. Army Corps of Engineers, Savannah District, Box 889, Savannah, GA 31402; (912) 652-5997.

U.S. Fish & Wildlife, Coastal Refuges, (912) 652-4415.

Valdosta–Lowndes County CVB, (800) 569-8689.

Vogel State Park, 7485 Vogel State Park Road, Blairsville, GA 30512; (706) 745-2628.

Walasi-Yi Center, (706) 745-6095.

Walton Game Management Office, (770) 918-6416.

Waycross–Ware County CVB, (912) 283-3742.

Wayne County (Jesup) Tourism Board, (912) 427-2028.

Weekender, The, (912) 485-2277.

West Point Lake Resource Manager, 500 Resource Management Drive, West Point, GA 31833; (706) 645-2937.

Appendix B: References

American Ornithologists' Union. 1998. *Check-list of North American Birds* (7th ed.). American Ornithologists' Union, Lawrence, Kans.

Benyus, J. M. 1989. *The Field Guide to Wildlife Habitats of the Eastern United States*. Simon & Schuster, New York, N.Y.

Brown, F. and N. Jones (eds.). 1991. *The Georgia Conservancy's Guide to the North Georgia Mountains*. The Georgia Conservancy, Atlanta, Ga.

Burleigh, T. D. 1958. *Georgia Birds*. University of Oklahoma Press, Norman, Okla.

Dunn, J. L. (chief consultant). 1999. *National Geographic Society Field Guide to the Birds of North America*.(3rd ed.). National Geographic Society, Washington, D.C.

Dunn, J. and K. Garrett. 1997. *A Field Guide to Warblers of North America*. Houghton-Miflin, New York, N.Y.

Godfrey, M. A. 1997. *Field Guide to the Piedmont*. The University of North Carolina Press, Chapel Hill, N.C.

Hamel, P. B. 1992. *Land Manager's Guide to the Birds of the South*. The Nature Conservancy, Chapel Hill, N.C.

Haney, J. C., P. Brisse, D.R. Jacobson, M. W. Oberle, and J. M. Paget. 1986. *Annotated Checklist of Georgia Birds*. Georgia Ornithological Society Occasional Publication No. 10.

Hodler, T. W. and H. A. Schretter. 1986. *The Atlas of Georgia*. The University of Georgia, Athens, Ga.

Imhof, T. A. 1976. *Alabama Birds*. University of Alabama Press, University, Ala.

Johnson, P. 1997. *An Annotated Checklist of Birds of Middle Georgia*. [Self-published].

McNair, D. B., and W. Post. 1993. *Supplement to Status and Distribution of South Carolina Birds*. Charleston Museum Ornithological Contribution No. 8.

Post, W., and S. A. Gauthreaux, Jr. 1989. *Status and Distribution of South Carolina Birds*. Contributions from the Charleston Museum, No. 18.

Robertson, W. B., Jr. and G. E. Woolfenden. 1992. *Florida Bird Species: An Annotated List*. Florida Ornithological Society Special Publication No. 6.

Robinson, J. C. 1990. *An Annotated Checklist of the Birds of Tennessee*. University of Tennessee Press, Knoxville, Tenn.

Root, T. 1988. *Atlas of Wintering North American Birds*. University of Chicago Press, Chicago, Ill.

Schoettle, T. 1997. *A Guide to a Georgia barrier island*. Watermarks Publishing, St. Simons Island, Ga.

Stevenson, H. M. and B. H. Anderson. 1994. *The Birdlife of Florida*. University Press of Florida, Gainesville, Fla.

Appendix C: Georgia Ornithological Society

The Georgia Ornithological Society (GOS) is the statewide organization serving people who have an interest in the study, protection, and preservation of birds and their habitat. Founded in 1936, its members include professional biologists/ornithologists, active amateur birders, and many individuals who simply have an interest in birds.

GOS facilitates weekend meetings twice a year, usually spring and fall, in various locations around the state. These meetings include field trips and programs, and are an opportunity for association and good fellowship with others interested in birds.

GOS members receive two quarterly publications:

THE ORIOLE   The GOS journal is devoted to research and information about birds in the state.

GOShawk   The GOS newsletter provides birding news, news of meetings, and member activities.

GOS also publishes books called Occasional Publications including the *Annotated Checklist of Georgia Birds*. The currently available edition is dated from 1986, but a revision is in progress. Complete information about GOS can be found at the GOS website. The URL is http://www.gos.org. This website also has links to many of the local birding clubs in Georgia. The mailing address for GOS is P.O. Box 5825, Valdosta, GA 31603.

Appendix D: Rare Bird Alerts

There are two rare bird alert telephone links in the state, both sponsored by the Georgia Ornithological Society:

Statewide: (770) 493-8862

South Georgia: (912) 244-9190

Appendix E: Endangered, Threatened, and Species of Concern

This is the most current list of all federally and state-listed birds that occur in Georgia, with applicable notes for each species. Endangered species are denoted with an (E), and threatened species by a (T). State categories generally follow the federal ones; birds that are not federally listed but are state-listed will have a (GA) after the name. Georgia also has an additional category of Rare. A Rare species is one "that may not be endangered or threatened but should be protected because of its scarcity," and these species are denoted by an (R). See the "Species to Look For" section of this book for details on most of these species.

Wood Stork (E)

Swallow-tailed Kite (R) (GA)

Bald Eagle (T) This species has been recovering dramatically and has been proposed for delisting in July 2000.

Wilson's Plover (R) (GA)

Piping Plover (T)

American Oystercatcher (R) (GA)

Gull-billed Tern (T) (GA)

Roseate Tern (T) On state Provisional List only, has not been reported in Georgia since 1979.

Least Tern (R) (GA) Breeding populations in the interior of North America are federally endangered.

Red-cockaded Woodpecker (E)

Common Raven (R) (GA)

Bewick's Wren (R) (GA) This one could actually be Vanished (V), because the Appalachian subspecies of this wren has just about vanished in the past 10 to 15 years, and there have been no recent sightings in GA.

Kirtland's Warbler (R) (GA)

Bachman's Sparrow (R) (GA)

The U.S. Fish & Wildlife Service has a web page devoted to the current status of all federally listed species, including a state-by-state list. The URL is: http://www.fws.gov/r9endspp/endspp.html.

Index

Page numbers in bold italic refer to the bar graphs; those in bold refer to maps; and those in italic refer to photographs.

About the Author

Giff began birding in 1975 when his outdoor interests evolved from fishing. His many other outdoor activities include bird photography and dragonfly identification. Many of his photographs have been published in various periodicals and books. Upon graduating from the United States Naval Academy, he spent seven years as a U.S. Navy pilot before joining Delta Airlines in 1988.

Since moving to Atlanta in 1991, he has been actively involved with birding and birding organizations in Georgia. He is a member of the Atlanta Audubon Society and has served on its board of directors. He has belonged to the Georgia Ornithological Society (GOS) since he moved to Georgia, and he is currently on the GOS Checklist and Records Committee, as well as the South Carolina Record Committee of the Carolina Bird Club.

The seasonal and geographic occurrence of Georgia birds is one of his favorite topics. Giff participates in the Georgia Breeding Bird Atlas Project and has done Breeding Bird Surveys for many years. In 1994, he created the first bar graph charts for the GOS publication, *Birder's Guide to Georgia,* detailing in graphic form where and when birds can be seen in Georgia. (These charts are revised and updated in this book.) Giff was the first person to recognize and document the importance of Kennesaw Mountain as Georgia's best overall location for observing neotropical migrants. He has organized many years of Kennesaw Mountain observations by many individuals for the Partners in Flight Program.

Giff has demonstrated that he can apply all of his substantial scientific knowledge of Georgia birds to birding endeavors. He holds the record for the Georgia Big Year, the number of bird species seen in a single year in Georgia, with 316 species seen in 1998. Similarly, he is a member of the team that holds the all-time Georgia Big Day, the number of species seen in a single day, a record of 183 species seen on April 24, 1996. He has also been the team captain of the birders who currently hold the monthly record for Georgia Monthly Big Days for every other month of the year.